Vernacular Buildings of Whitchurch & Area

and their Occupants

Vernacular Buildings of Whitchurch & Area

and their Occupants

by
Madge Moran

With best wishes,

Madge Moran

Logaston Press

LOGASTON PRESS
Little Logaston, Logaston,
Woonton, Almeley, Herefordshire HR3 6QH

First published by Logaston Press 1999
Copyright © M. Moran 1999

ISBN 1 873827 16 4

Set in Baskerville & Times by Logaston Press
and printed in Great Britain by
Hillman Printers (Frome) Ltd

This book is dedicated to the memory of
Geoffrey Grenville Jones Owen,
who loved Whitchurch

Contents

Preface

This book is the result of work done by members of a research class based in Whitchurch and sponsored by the Department of Adult and Continuing Education, Keele University. The class first came together in September 1989 when the syllabus consisted of a straight-forward series of 22 weekly lectures intended to introduce the subject of Vernacular Architecture in Shropshire. For the follow-up in 1990/1 it was decided to attempt a modest schedule of recording buildings in the town. This was seen as a logical development, and, because nothing like it had been done in Whitchurch, as something of a pioneering effort. By 1991/2 it was clear that one important element was either missing entirely or was being obtained from secondary sources. This was the documentary evidence, and it was then that Dr. Philip Morgan undertook one of the winter terms teaching the skills of reading and interpreting original documents such as wills and inventories relating to Whitchurch. These had already been extracted from the Lichfield Joint Record office by Sylvia Watts, a Ph.D. student at Wolverhampton University, and transcribed and presented by her to the Local Studies Library in Shrewsbury in two volumes. The pattern of one term's practical work with myself, and one with a different tutor, latterly Paul Anderton, M.A., was repeated thereafter. The class meets for two hours on Tuesday mornings and has to include 'learning' time. The measured drawings, are, therefore, the results of 'homework'.

With a class of this nature, skills and indeed levels of interest vary enormously, as does the age range and physical fitness. But the loyalty of the members and their enthusiasm for the project has never wavered, and for me it has been a great pleasure to guide their efforts and to see their skills develop and result in a publication of which they can be proud. No-one, including myself, has had any professional training in architecture, but we count this as a 'plus' rather than a 'minus' as we tackle the problems from an historical approach and base our methodology on that outlined by the Royal Commission on Historical Monuments. Thus our records are acceptable for inclusion in the national archive and we have the satisfaction of producing a book which we hope will not only be a useful work of reference, but also of considerable interest to a wide readership.

Madge Moran
August 1999

Acknowledgements

We have first to thank the owners who kindly allowed us into their homes and premises to measure, draw, and when possible to study the deeds. We were welcomed without reserve and often supplied with refreshment. We hope that they feel that this book justifies the hours of disruption they have suffered. Next we thank the Owen Family Trust for sponsorship and support. In addition to funding most of the dendrochronology the Trust came to our rescue when publication seemed impossible. We thank Dan Miles for his expertise in dendrochronology. Timbers in north Shropshire are notoriously difficult to date, but Dan persisted where others, we feel sure, would have admitted defeat. The Department of Adult and Continuing Studies at Keele University provided us with a base and continues to sponsor the classes.

For permission to publish extracts from documents held in private and public collections we thank the Bodleian Library (cover illustration); Lichfield Joint Record Office (Amelia Corser's will. See 17 Green End); Mr. A. Heber-Percy (extracts from Mary Heber's correspondence. See Dodington House) and Richard Hughes (Ash Wood archives).

While it is sometimes considered invidious to single out names for special mention, I am sure that the class would want the work of Jean North and Pat Gates to be acknowledged. Pat's meticulous drawings of elevations, details and three-dimensionals are a joy in themselves, and her patience and skill in assembling the Great Chamber ceiling at Alkington Hall left us all breathless as did her copying of the wall-paintings at the old Raven Inn. Jean's skill in taking our (sometimes) rough drawings and putting them into the final presentation form has taken a load from my shoulders. She undertook much of the basic measuring and drawing and directed the work of the various teams. She also presented the remarkable isometric drawing of Ridgwardine Manor and traced both the introduction to the manorial court roll shown on p.2 and Pat's drawing of the Alkington ceiling. Judith Hoyle only joined the class in 1993, but swiftly proved her capabilities by undertaking most of the basic work at Alkington Hall, returning several times with her team to check measurements. She also masterminded the Park Farm survey at Alkington, and here the good-natured rivalry between the two owners regarding who had the older or more interesting house caused much amusement.

We acknowledge with thanks the work of Elizabeth Marshall in labelling our drawings so neatly and effectively. Elizabeth is not a member of the class but offered to help us in this way. Two houses we recorded belong to members of the class; no. 8, Dodington to Jack Thornton, although he was with us for only a short time, and Ash Wood to Richard Hughes. Richard's family have farmed at Ash Wood since at least 1515, and probably earlier than that. He has also helped the work of the class in many ways, including supplying us all with new clip-boards and paper at the outset! Mary Perry made the notes left by her late father, Mr. G.G.J. Owen, available to us and has supplied the class with much local knowledge. Mr. Owen was a gentleman in advance of his time in appreciating the importance of vernacular buildings and in deploring the wholesale destruction of superficially 'unfit' cottages. He could distinguish cruck construction from box-framing and was a notable bibliophile, a trait inherited by his daughter. It is with pleasure that we dedicate this book to his memory. Joan Barton undertook most of the historical research and we would like to acknowledge the help obtained from the Shropshire Records and Research Centre (formerly the Local Studies library and the County Record Office) in Shrewsbury, the Caldicott library in Whitchurch, and the staff of the Victoria County History in Shrewsbury. Finally, members who feel perhaps that their role has been been that of an Indian rather than that of a Chief may reflect that in the field of vernacular recording 'they also serve who only hold a tape ...' (with apologies to Milton).

The list below comprises the class as it was in December 1998 in the last term of practical work before this book was compiled. Most have been members from the start. We hope to continue the class and newcomers are always welcomed.

Joan Barton
Patricia Gates
Judith Hoyle
Richard Hughes
Grace Jenkins
Barbara Latham
Stanley North
Jean North
Joyce Pautard
Roger Pearce
Mary Perry
June Potter
Kathleen Priddy
Michael Scott

Pat Gates undertook to make a photographic record of the houses and this is contained in several volumes. It is available for study. Pat may be contacted through the Dept. of Adult and Continuing Education at Keele University. I am also indebted to my son William Moran for more of the photographs used in this book.

The illustrations of the coloured wall paintings at 17 Watergate reproduced on the rear of the cover are also the work of Pat Gates.

Foreword

Over the last forty years the study of vernacular houses—their forms, their functions, and their history—has been largely transformed. Much of that has been brought about by men and women with no professional ties to architecture, but with a great interest in the buildings of their county or region and with the motivation to cope with the often arduous field-work, the painstaking documentary research and the accurate and detailed draughtmanship that the furtherance of the subject demands.

In 1990 Mrs. Madge Moran, on behalf of Keele University Extra-Mural Department, began an annual series of lectures on vernacular architecture to classes in Whitchurch. Under her guidance members of those classes have used their talents and their acquired knowledge to investigate the domestic architecture of the town. On the face of it there was little of interest to work upon, but—and this will probably be true of other towns—once undaunted and knowledgeable people began to study the houses carefully many surprises cropped up, and Whitchurch, which looked as though it had been wholly re-built in the 18th and 19th centuries, was found to have a large number of early and significant buildings, often originally timber-framed.

It is not to be supposed that the present volume will greatly alter the general view of domestic architecture, but it will be a useful contribution to our stock of knowledge. More than that, it gives rise to three encouraging conclusions: that however un-promising a subject for study the buildings of an English country town may seem to be they will provide far more interest and information than anyone had suspected; that there will not only be many houses worth investigating,but, once the interest has been aroused, many people capable of investigating them; and that however uninterested in a book of this sort a large publishing house or a university press may be, there are local publishers ready to step into the breach and bring the work to fruition.

Eric Mercer O.B.E., M.A., F.S.A.
(retd. deputy-secretary R.C.H.M.)

Introduction

First impressions of Whitchurch are of a run-of-the-mill market town with nothing much to offer either to the tourist or the architectural enthusiast. This is no Lavenham, Broadway or, (nearer home) Ludlow, and, unlike its grand northern neighbour, Chester, the Roman occupation of the site has left no visible remains above ground apart from a few stones on the corner of Yardington, and even they were re-laid recently to mark a boundary. A reasonable question would be 'Why bother with Whitchurch?' The classic answer is, of course, 'Because it's there', but this needs elaborating. We began our investigations with no great hopes of making startling discoveries, but we were conscious that nothing had been done to record the buildings in the area and felt that we were in a position to make a useful contribution towards a definitive study. Specialised vernacular studies of given areas are becoming increasingly popular and are meat and drink to the architectural historian. We hope that our work fills a gap in the records and will be seen as a small but useful work of reference—it is not intended to be a comprehensive account of the development of Whitchurch and its surroundings.

Our choice of what to record was arbitrary at first. Much depended on local knowledge and personal contacts and so it came as some surprise, before long, to realise that our recordings were charting almost the whole gamut of vernacular architecture as applied to Shropshire, from a base-cruck ('The Old Eagles') to a classical 18th-century town house (The Mansion House). We thought it legitimate to take in some of the hinterland, and so for a rural base-cruck we went to Oldfields in Moreton Say parish, a house that had been recorded before the group was formed, and for a full-cruck-framed manor house we chose Manor Cottage, Prees—which has a surprising history. There was even one surviving full-cruck truss within the town (6/8 Dodington) and upper crucks were in evidence at 25 Dodington and at the 'Horse and Jockey'. The late medieval period also manifested itself in no less than three solar crosswings in the High Street: 21/23 High St. ('Walker's'), no. 60 High Street and The High Street Garage. Sadly, in all three examples the hall range had been either rebuilt or demolished. We lacked an example of crown-post roof construction, but found archaeological evidence at Grove Farm in Ash Parva for a crown-post truss of the type typical of Shropshire.

It is noticeable that many of our records are of buildings in Dodington. When the Domesday Survey was compiled Dodington was recorded as a separate manor from Whitchurch and, though now an integral part of the town, it has always been regarded as being an area of special importance. Its buildings are comparatively well preserved, although the mutilation of the Mansion House in the 1950s/60s was deplorable. Where site plans of houses in Dodington are included in the surveys they are taken from the 1880

OS map and show a marked leaning towards the west. This is possibly because they follow the line of the plough as it made the wide S-bend on the early open fields. The burgage plots may simply have been superimposed on these.

Plans range from the simple croglofft cottage at 38 Watergate to the complicated development at Dodington House, but we did not find an intact fully-developed three-unit medieval plan of hall-with-cross-passage, service end and solar end, although the survival of three solar units in the High Street suggests that they existed. The rural examples at Ash Wood, Manor Cottage Prees and Oldfields have parts missing or drastically altered, but they are the nearest we found. No examples of spere trusses were noted, and we were left with the impression that such status symbols were lacking in north Shropshire even though they are standard features in many of the houses in the south of the county. The two transitional houses, Barkhill House and Ellesmere House have identical plans and show the stage that planning had reached by the end of the 17th century, with an entrance hall giving access to all the rooms. Lobby-entry plans were not numerous, although some were noted in passing in Prees, and at Ridgwardine Manor a unilateral type of lobby entry is still in use, although its presence posed many problems of interpretation. The best example is at The Ditches Hall in Wem, a house that was recorded before the class came into being. Ash Wood had a lobby-entry at one time, but this was the result of adaptation and is known to have existed only from an early photograph in the owner's possession.

As in Shrewsbury and Ludlow, few buildings from the first half of the 16th century can be immediately identified, but 23 and 25 Dodington seemed to indicate a rebuilding programme beginning in mid-century, and perhaps it is significant that our two dendrochronologically dated cruck-built houses, Ash Wood and Manor Cottage, are from this time. The crosswing at Grove Farm supplied a good example of how timber-framing had developed in the countryside by the late 16th or the early years of the 17th century, and here, as at Providence Grove, we noted a Cheshire influence stylistically. We were able to show a reasonably complete example of a mid-17th century town house of modest proportions in The Olde House, Dodington, and an example of a similar date but from lower down the social scale in 38 Watergate. The latter contained a croglofft, a feature more familiar in traditional Welsh houses, but the way in which 'lofts' appear in inventories suggests that they were perhaps a common feature in Whitchurch houses.

Where timber-framing is concerned, Whitchurch is no different from many other areas in its use of relatively expensive close-studding for the elevations which are seen by the public and the less expensive square-framing for those which are not. In the local dialect this is 'Queen Anne at the front and Mary Anne at the back'. An exception is the house we recorded near Market Drayton, Ridgwardine Manor. Here close-studding apparently occurred on all the elevations. Brace patterns are less easily summarised. Braces are functional but seldom decorative, the most ambitious we saw being of the S-form. Often we thought that the carpenters responsible for the framing regarded bracing as an area where economies could be made, wind-bracing sometimes being omitted altogether. Externally there are examples of both up and down braces, but generally speaking brace patterns cannot be regarded as contributing to the essential character of this part of Shropshire. On the other hand, it is clear that the infilling of the panels was done with great care, wattle and daub work taking various forms.

17th-century encroachment in the High Street was discovered in the block that contains The Fish Shop and the Spinning Wheel Café, as well as in 60 High Street (recently 'Something Else', now 'Tolchards') on the opposite side of the road. Keen observers will note an echo of the northern end of Broad Street in Ludlow in the way in which both streets have a block of timber-framed houses on the eastern side as the summit of a low hill is approached. In each case the summit is crowned with the parish church. But whereas in Ludlow the medieval rectory remains in use, the present rectory in Whitchurch is modern. However, the 18th-century rectory was not destroyed, and it is hoped to record that building in a future session. An extensive archive exists, and it will be interesting to compare the documentary evidence with the standing building.

Ellesmere House and Barkhill House provided excellent examples of the transitional phase between timber-framing and fully brick construction. For the early or mid-18th century we chose 17 Green End, and here we may have identified a hitherto unknown work of the Shrewsbury architect, Thomas Farnolls Pritchard. The apogee of the Georgian period came with the Mansion House and parts of Dodington House. Ash Wood provided a good example of how a working farmhouse could change and be adapted to suit different conditions, and was particularly valuable because we were able to obtain firm dendrochronological dating for the cruck range and for the insertion of a ceiling with a soffit-moulded spine-beam into the single-bay open hall. Because there is an unbroken history of occupancy by one family, we could trace the documentary history from 1515 and learn the provenance of most of the furniture and other contents. The links between Ash Wood and Grove Farm are interesting and raised much discussion, and when we were able to see and handle inherited artifacts history really began to live for us. When, towards the end of the third session, we were given the opportunity to record Alkington Hall there was much debate concerning its suitability for inclusion in what was seen as a volume of largely vernacular buildings. Though at present a working farm, this was a gentry house in its day. However, as it provided us with an example of a double-pile plan, diaper brickwork, crow-stepped gables and good plasterwork the niceties of 'polite' as opposed to 'vernacular' architecture were swiftly discounted.

Early features such as passing-braces, notched-lap jointings, and aisled construction are also missing from our studies, but as Shropshire is not rich in these delights it would be surprising to find them. The gaps in the typology tend to confirm the known distribution of building practices. For example, we found no evidence of aisled construction which is a dominating feature of south-east and eastern England, taking over from cruck-construction where that typically western form terminates. Neither did we encounter the Wealden house-form which, as its name suggests, is popular in Kent, Surrey and East Sussex, although it has a wider distribution than was once thought. Also absent were examples of the use of mathematical tiles—that form of hung tile-work designed to look like brick-work—which is another south-eastern speciality. These are three clear-cut examples, although in fact Shropshire has isolated instances of each. Another absentee, whose type could logically have been expected to survive had not the attrition rate mitigated against it, was the defended stone-built house with the hall at first floor level. We thought that we had an echo of the form at St. Mary's Cottage, but that was all it was, a reflection. However, there was great excitement when a hitherto unknown sketch of Whitchurch's missing castle was found. At last we had evidence of defence, a factor which must have played a great part in the town's early planning. As the local stone is a mudstone not suitable for permanent buildings, it is not surprising that there is little evidence of stonework at vernacular level, its use being confined largely to dressings. Stone has to be imported from Grinshill if it is to have any visual impact at all, even the Wilmslow sandstone at Ridgwardine is too soft for mouldings. Even the parish church is brick-built, but with an outer skin of the red Grinshill sandstone. The name 'Whitchurch' specifies a white church, and today this is a contradiction in terms.

Some features seem to be typical of Whitchurch and of north Shropshire in general. The timber-framing is robust but not spectacular. Scantlings are perhaps above average quality compared with some areas of Britain but not with south Shropshire. Crucks tend to be straighter than the well-tailored boomerang-shaped examples found south of the Severn, and the two examples where we were able to obtain dendrochronological dating, Ash Wood (1550) and Manor Cottage, Prees (1551) suggest that traditional cruck construction continued in north Shropshire after it had been abandoned in the south of the county. The use of stylobates was also noted, a practice not often found south of the Severn. Braces are not large, indeed those found in the solar wings in the High Street are uniformly small, cusping is no more than a token, mouldings are mostly plain and joints are unremarkable. But Whitchurch can offer its own specialities. The beautifully carpentered staircases are almost *de rigueur* and it is as though the town had a tradition for these, spanning, as they do, from the early 17th to the late 18th century. Admittedly, no handrail could compete with the elaborate inlaid serpentine example at Mawley Hall in the parish of Cleobury Mortimer in south Shropshire, but that must be exceptional by any standards.

Locally dug peat blocks were used as infill for framed houses, insulation, partition walls and presumably for fuel, and the cast-iron shop front in the High Street is a remarkable contribution from the 19th century. A phenomenon of north Shropshire, of which there are examples in Whitchurch, is the working of cement render to resemble weathered timbers. The practice does not seem to have a name, but the effect is realistic and we recorded two examples in 6 - 10 Dodington and in The Olde House, Dodington.

No elaborate moulded brickwork was noted either in walls or chimneystacks, and the diaper patterning at Alkington Hall was the nearest we came to any distinctive work. We pride ourselves that we can recognise the products of Fenn's Bank, a local brickworks which closed before the Second World War for economic reasons, being unable to compete with larger commercial firms. Its output must have been considerable, but we know of only one brick which is stamped with the manufacturer's name, and that occurs at Park Farm. Rat-trap bonded brickwork is also scarce, but the fact that we found a form of it used as infilling in the old Raven Inn (17 - 19 Watergate) and in 18 Green End, leads us to think that it was not unknown.

Several discoveries, we felt, had a bearing on social history generally, such as the emphasis on cock-fighting at Dodington House and the still not fully understood cages and hoppers in the attic rooms there. Another was the stencilled wall decoration at 60 High Street which could be compared closely with a published example in Worcester. Nothing like the beautiful Last Supper and Annunciation painting at the King's Head in Shrewsbury came our way, but we were delighted to discover that there were fragments of wall paintings in the long-lost hostelry, the Raven, at 17 - 19 Watergate. For Pat Gates it was a labour of love and her term's work to record them. The fact that we found so little evidence of wall-paintings should not be taken as proof that they were not widely used. The parish church and other ecclesiastic buildings were outside the scope of our survey, but the church occupies a dominating position and had a distinguished, if rather under-rated architect, William Smith, brother of Francis, the more famous 'Smith of Warwick'.

In the Dordogne area of France the farming pattern is geared to produce '*un peu de tout*'. The legendary soldier, Sir John Talbot, Earl of Shrewsbury, provides a link between Whitchurch and Castillon la Bataille in the Dordogne. We hope that in compiling this book we have echoed that formula and provided a 'little of everything'.

The Structure of the Book

The order of this book is so arranged that after the preliminary chapters the houses follow in their street settings, not necessarily in order of size, although it seems appropriate to deal with the major houses in Dodington first. Where only cursory surveys could be made these also are included in the appropriate area instead of being collected in 'Gazetteers'. The latter are reserved for outlying properties.

The lay-out of the individual chapters also attempts to follow a pattern with, where possible, a photograph of the building on the first page, with plans and/or sections often on the second page. Other illustrations (and sometimes plans and sections) are included adjacent to or as close to the relevant text as practical. Scales are included for many of the drawings, but in the text measurements are given only in feet and inches to save the text becoming too overwhelmed in minutiae. It was not always possible to recover much of the background history to the houses, but this is featured whenever success was encountered.

Like most English towns, Whitchurch did not develop according to a set plan, but we hope the arrangement of the book will help both visitors and serious investigators to follow a logical sequence.

Madge Moran
& Andy Johnson (Logaston Press)

An Introduction to the History of Whitchurch

Whitchurch, a market town of c.8,000 people and the only Shropshire town on an original Roman site, lies in a unique position in the north of the county. The northern boundary, the Grindley Brook, divides the parish from Tushingham, Shropshire from Cheshire, the diocese of Lichfield from that of Chester, and the archdiocese of Canterbury from York. The western boundary, the Red Brook, similarly divides Whitchurch from the Maelor, Shropshire from Clwyd, the diocese of Lichfield from that of St. Asaph and the ecclesiastical Province of Canterbury from the Church of Wales.[1]

The town itself stands on a low hill in the middle of the North Shropshire/Cheshire plain. The auxilliary fort built there by the Romans was known as *Mediolanum*, 'the town in mid-plain' and its situation has been compared with that of modern Milan.[2] Watling Street, the great Roman highway, passed through the fort on the line of the present High Street, and excavations have uncovered the foundations of stone buildings, the northern section of the town wall and pottery spanning the period from c.70 A.D. to the early fourth century—a rescue dig in 1977 found evidence of Roman military settlement dating from the first century. A few sandstone blocks outside the High Street Garage mark where a Roman wall was briefly uncovered. The cemetery at Sedgeford outside the town has yielded several cinerary urns, and a fine specular mirror (with a smooth polished surface), discovered in 1973, is displayed at the Civic Centre.[3]

Evidence of Saxon occupation comes from the place-name and from the church dedication. The new settlers called their village 'Westune' or 'west farmstead'. This may have been to identify the settlement as west of Hodnet where the Hundred court was held, or may simply have been descriptive of its position near the Welsh border.[4] Surrounding hamlets which later became townships such as Alkington, Edgeley and Tilstock are based on Saxon personal names, and Ash is descriptive of the topography, abounding in ash trees.[5] Dodington, the 'tun of Dodda's people', is now fully integrated with Whitchurch, and the term is used only as a street name; but it was noted as a separate manor at the time of Domesday, the boundary being the Staggs Brook.[6] Township stones still mark some of the boundaries of the 13 townships which make up present-day Whitchurch. (Apart from Whitchurch itself and Alkington, Edgeley and Tilstock mentioned above, these include Hinton, Hollyhurst, Chinnel, Broughall, Ash Magna, Ash Parva, Old Woodhouses, New Woodhouses and Dodington). Traditionally the church was founded in the early 10th century by Ethelflaeda, Lady of the Mercians and King Alfred's daughter. It is dedicated to St. Alkmund, a young Northumbrian prince who was killed in battle, regarded as a martyr

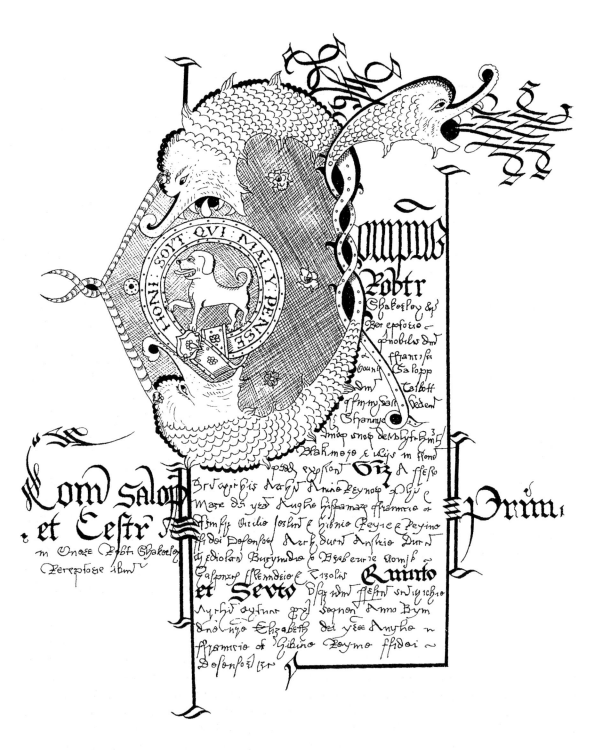

Introduction to the Manorial Court Roll for Whitchurch 1557-8

and subsequently canonised. It is a rare dedication; only six others are known in the country, one of which is in Shrewsbury, the county town.[7]

Westune and its satellite hamlets formed part of the Mercian kingdom of Offa, which later became the Earldom of Mercia under Leofric and his wife, Lady Godiva. In 1063 their granddaughter Ealdgyth married as her second husband Harold, Earl of Wessex, and *Westune* formed part of her dowry. Harold was crowned in January 1066 and *Westune* became a royal manor, but Harold's reign was short—he was killed at Hastings in October of the same year. After the Norman Conquest *Westune* was held by William de Warenne. He built a castle on Westune Hill, looking across to Wales, as part of a second line of defence in the Welsh Marches.[8] The castle has disappeared, but the street name 'Castle Hill' survives, traces of what was thought to be part of the boundary of the inner bailey were uncovered in February 1993, and a hitherto unknown 19th century drawing of the castle, or, more likely, a gatehouse belonging to it was recently found. The latter is reproduced on page 8.[9] William de Warenne is believed to have built the new church of white stone which gave the settlement its new name of Whitchurch, or as given in early documents— *Album Monasterium* or *Blancminster.*[10]

The Whitchurch estates, later linked by marriage settlements to Dodington, Alkington and Edgeley, were held by the de Warennes until early in the 13th century when they passed by marriage first to the le Strange family and in 1377 to the Talbots.[11] The manor thrived under the successive lords, despite the ravages of the Black Death; a market charter was granted by Richard I,[12] and another by John le Strange in 1362.[13] John Talbot, the sixth Baron and 1st Earl of Shrewsbury, played a prominent part in the history of Whitchurch. He was born *c.*1387 in the manor house at Blakemere where he spent his childhood. He fought under the Lancastrian kings Henry IV, V and VI in Wales and in Ireland and strove for 30 years after Henry V's death to hold back the French advance on English possessions in France. He fought against Joan of Arc at Orléans and became a legend in his own time. Shakespeare called him 'the great Alcides of the field', and made him play a major role of distinguished bravery in his play 'Henry VI, part I', where the battle-cry 'A Talbot!' conjures up images of a local war-lord who became a national hero. So fierce was his reputation that, according to Shakespeare, parents would threaten naughty children with Talbot, the bogey-man personified. Aged 70, he was killed at Castillon la Bataille, near Bordeaux in July 1453 when England lost to France in what proved to be the last battle of the Hundred Years War. His heart is buried under St. Alkmund's church porch, and his bones rest beneath a fine monument within.[14] By this time the white church of the Normans had been replaced by one built in the Early English style.

After the 1st Earl of Shrewsbury's death, the Talbot interest was devoted largely to their Yorkshire lands and from then on the estate was managed by stewards, although another John Talbot of that ilk, Rector of Whitchurch 1534 - 1550, left £200 towards the founding of a Grammar School in the town.[15] Eventually Sir Thomas Egerton, a successful lawyer and Chancellor to Queen Elizabeth I and King James I, bought the manors of Whitchurch and Dodington from the Talbot family in 1598.[16] Although his descendants, the Earls and Dukes of Bridgwater, were all absentee landlords, the little town prospered, becoming a centre for leather-working and shoe-making and with an estimated population of over 3,000 by the end of the seventeenth century.[17] Road improvements and the introduction

Town Map of Whitchurch in 1767 (traced by Pat Gates).
The original is in the Bridgwater Collection[19]

A lithograph of 1810 by W. Gauci, published by T. Gregory for the Shropshire Gazetteer—this comprised short descriptions of towns and villages in Shropshire, published by subscription and intended to build up into a book. The view is from what is now Jubilee Park, looking north-east. The area of Newtown is seen above the clearly defined burgage plots on the left. A year later an arm of the Ellesmere Canal was constructed along the foot of the plots, linking Whitchurch into the network. The house in the right foreground is Barkhill House, the subject of a later chapter

of turnpikes led to the town becoming a staging post for coach travellers, with several inns providing facilities by the early years of the 18th century.[18]

Whitchurch developed much of its present appearance at this time. The medieval church tower collapsed in July 1711 and it was not thought worthwhile to save any of the remaining fabric.[20] The present church, which dominates the town, was built in the classical style and dedicated in 1713, a joint effort between two architects of note, John Barker of Rowsley, Derbyshire and William Smith of Warwick, the lesser known brother of the famous Francis Smith who was responsible for Mawley Hall, Davenport and Kinlet in Shropshire.[21] Two years later a new Market Hall (now Barclay's Bank) was built in the High Street, after a public petition to the lord of the manor for permission to replace the 'little place in Whitchurch Towne where poore people may sit dry to sell butter, cheese and other comodity' which had been built by the bailiff Richard Hyde in 1638.[22] Many of the timber-framed buildings in High Street were refaced in the then fashionable brick, and street encroachment, noted in some of the buildings of this survey, took place with the effect of narrowing the High Street. Few, if any, traces of pre-15th century buildings remain. Owain Glyndwr's forces are reputed to have sacked the town in 1404 and to have destroyed the town mill. Indeed, there may have been an earlier attack as there is an account of the mill's rebuilding in 1402. Mills were frequently an object of systematic destruction by the Welsh.[23] In the 18th century several new houses in the elegant Georgian style were built at the southern end of the High Street and in The Bull Ring. In Dodington houses were either remodelled or built from new. Dodington especially became a fashionable residential area, the equivalent of Abbey Foregate and the St. John's Hill area of Shrewsbury, and boasted the 'most ambitious private house' in 'the best street'.[24]

By the late seventeenth century dairy farming had became popular and profitable in north Shropshire, and Whitchurch was the natural centre for activities associated with milk processing, particularly the production and marketing of Cheshire cheese, and these trends continued throughout the 19th century and well into the 20th.[25] But at the same time there were many changes which affected the appearance and the function of the town. The Town Mill was demolished in 1811 to give access to a newly-built arm of the Ellesmere Canal, an enterprise by the 3rd Duke of Bridgwater which encouraged trade.[26] The pool which had served the mill was drained and filled in, and the area is now occupied by the main car-park and bus station, a large supermarket, some smaller shops, and the Youth Club. In 1858 Whitchurch railway station was opened as part of the Crewe to Shrewsbury line of the L.N.W.R.[27] The greater ease of travel and transport of goods ended the rural isolation of the town and ushered in modern times. The building of a new road, the town's first by-pass, in 1875 meant that suitable land was available to build a Smithfield, or livestock market, (1877), a Cottage Hospital (1886), a Fire Station and Public Baths (1891) and a new Weslyan Chapel (1877). A neo-gothic Town Hall with Assembly Rooms, Market Hall and Corn Exchange was built in the High Street as the 18th century building was too small to cope with the increased trade, and stall-holders had begun to obstruct the street.[28] The complex was opened by Lord Brownlow on 25th October 1872 when, as Lord of the Manor, he gave the Market Rights to the town. The building was badly burned in 1941 and was replaced 30 years later with the present Civic Centre. The most recent improvements include the provision of a modern by-pass (opened in 1992) and the re-paving and one-way traffic system introduced into the High Street (1993).

Improved road and rail transport during the last 100 years has had much the same effect as in other towns, with less reliance on self-sufficiency and more people commuting elsewhere to work. The population, about 6,000 from 1841 to 1951 has risen to 7,500, but the majority find work out of town and increasingly Whitchurch is becoming a dormitory town.[29] Apart from cheese-making and distribution Whitchurch had two industries for which it was nationally famous—clock making and ironfounding. Forty-five clockmakers are listed in Whitchurch between 1696 and 1886, the firm of Joyce being world-famous, whilst Dutch barns with their characteristic blue label indicating their origins in W.H. Smith's foundry in Dodington are still a familiar sight on many farms in the area. James Joyce moved to Whitchurch in 1782 and the firm is still in business, though merged with John Smith & Sons of Derby. The firm of W.H. Smith became specialists in steel construction work but went out of business about 1983.[30]

Apart from John Talbot, Whitchurch is associated with several famous people, not all of whom were natives. The nonconformist movement produced pioneers such as Nicholas Barnard, at one time rector of Whitchurch, and Philip and Matthew Henry whose associations with the town are reported in the chapters entitled Dodington House and 7 Dodington (The Olde House). The famous hymn-writer Reginald Heber had tenuous connections with Dodingon House and attended the Grammar School while Randolph Caldecott, the 19th century caricaturist and well-known illustrator of childrens' books worked as a bank clerk in the town and used local topography in much of his work. Lastly, Sir Edward German, the composer, conductor and instrumentalist was born, lived, died and is buried in Whitchurch.[31]

Whitchurch Castle & The Star Hotel

That there was a castle at Whitchurch is evident from the many documentary references to it, and the street-name 'Castle Hill' remains as well as the more modern 'Castle Court'. Nothing now remains above ground and opinions differ regarding the siting of the keep. The 1880 version of the OS map has the castle site marked at the junction of Castle Hill and Pepper Street; by 1910 it is shown further north but still along the west side of Newtown. In 1976 an OS correspondent identified the possible remains of a motte within the large coal yard which is bounded for the most part by Pepper Street, Castle Hill, The Bull Ring and the southern end of High Street, a site, incidentally, traditionally held to be correct by many local inhabitants. But it is argued that the higher ground suggested on the 1910 map and repeated on the present (1988) map would provide a more elevated position and would give better views westwards towards Wales from which the most obvious threats would come. This theory has received some slight support recently from a small archaeological excavation which uncovered a curving corner of a boundary ditch near the junction of Newtown and Castle Hill.[1] In such a position one possible interpretation is that it represents the boundary of the inner bailey, and as the enclosure is clearly further up the hill, the site of the keep on the higher ground to the north is, at present, the favoured choice.

The report of the excavation cites various documentary sources for the castle's existence, the earliest of which makes it clear that it was there in 1119, was held by William Fitz-Randulf and was in need of repair. Further twelfth-century references in the Pipe Rolls occur, by which time the Fitz-Allens were in possession, and by 1282 it was commanded by Roger le Strange.[2]

In 1384/5 work was being carried out at the castle. The term 'Turris' (tower) is specified and this probably refers to the keep.[3] It was roofed with timber (shingles?) and the carriage of 98 loads of timber cost 32s 8½d. John Gyll, a stonemason, was paid £6 13s 4d for his work, and 69 loads of stone were brought from the quarries at Grelushill (Grinshill).[4] Other items included 68 loads of lime at 53s 2½d, 12 lbs of lead at 8d (per lb?), a hempen rope at 10s 6d, whipcord 2d, a key 1d, two wooden vessels 16d, hurdles for scaffolding 4s 8½d, a 'forma' 15s, iron 12s 1½d etc. The account indicates that this was a substantial programme of reconstruction/repair work undertaken at the time when Richard and Ancaret Talbot were in possession of Blakemere and when the castle at Whitchurch still formed an important link in the chain of defences along the Welsh border.[5]

John Leland, Henry VIII's chaplain, librarian and antiquary, noted the castle at Whitchurch during his travels in 1538, but those inveterate travellers, Celia Fiennes and Daniel Defoe make no mention of it.

Brief as it is, the only known written description of the location of the castle states 'Part of the old walls of the castle of Whitchurch was standing in 1760 on the castle-hill, on the side next the mill, just above the brook that now runs under what is called the Lock-up house.'[6] The mill, the brook and the lock-up house were all located at the junction of Mill Street, Castle Hill, The Bull Ring and Watergate and it is possible that the Rev. Nightingale was describing part of the boundary wall of the outer bailey.

In a collection of drawings of Shropshire buildings there is one captioned 'Whitchurch Castle' (see below).[7] Its form bears a striking resemblance to that of the Layerthorpe postern tower which, before demolition in 1829-30, was one of the gateways into the city of York. Layerthorpe measured 26ft. x 20ft., had been converted to a house in the early 17th century at which time, presumably, its flat roof and crenellated parapet were replaced with a pitched roof and provision made for a chimneystack.[8] The Whitchurch drawing shows a building of similar size but retaining its flat roof and crenellated parapet. It appears to be a gatehouse tower rather than a keep, and, like Layerthorpe, it may have related to town defences, although there is, as yet, no evidence that Whitchurch was ever a walled town. Both towers are stone-built, three stories high, have buttresses at each corner and a two-centred arched entrance. The fenestration on the Whitchurch drawing is more detailed, and shows above the entrance a two-light square-headed window which has a pronounced square-headed drip-stone with labels. The inner faces of the twin lights may have had foiled heads. A trefoil form is clearly shown on the single-light window in the third storey, and this also has a similar dripstone. On the left of the picture is a lean-to structure with upper and lower windows of twin-light form which seem to be fitted with leaded lights, and to the left of the lean-to the start of a tall wall is shown. This

'Whitchurch Castle'

has a single lancet-type opening. As at Layerthorpe, most of the architectural details suggest a 14th century date, although the basic structures could be earlier. Similarly, it appears that both drawings depict the inner faces of the structures.

The similarity between the two buildings is interesting and provides a valuable comparative study, but arising from that is the question of whether the Rev. Nightingale's description relates to the Whitchurch illustration. The most likely position for such a gate-house entry into the outer bailey would be where he stated. Such a site would control the junction of important routes and the abundance of water in the area would increase the potential for defence. Two references to a gatehouse occur in copyhold surrenders and it is worth quoting from these:

1) (Dated 1726) 'Thomas Deaves, Mercer, and Catherine his wife doth surrender into the hands of the Lord of the Manor all those two dwelling houses with rooms, chambers and brewhouses in High Street near the Pool Dam and also the *chamber over the Gatehouse*, the cellar and appurtenances to the said two messuages (the shop now erected and now standing within the said gatehouse) all of which are now in the occupation of Richard Meadlove, skinner and Mary Jenkin, widow, the front towards the street from the corner post of the gatehouse to the corner post next the lands of Thomas Robinson in length 41 feet together with 1 foot formerly forward of the lands of the said Thomas Robinson - in whole 42 feet or thereabouts. Also all that other outbuilding joining to and extending the cellar with brewhouse - the said brew and colehouse stand in from part of the said gatehouse 81 feet and breadth of lower part of colehouse 11 feet or thereabouts - now in occupation of Thomas Payne, adjacent lands of Thomas Robinson and Ambrose Nickson on the one side and the said Thomas Deaves on the other.'[9]

2) (Dated 1772) '... And also that shop adjacent to a certain copyhold messuage in High Street late in the possession of Daniel Wycherley now in possession of Peter Massey and which shop adjoins *the entry or Gatehouse* (leading into the yard or court of the George Inn) on one side and on the other to a certain room called the "Street Parlour" belonging to the aforesaid messuage and shop sold to Richard Hayes to use of his only son Richard Hayes Junr.'[10]

Although the phraseology is tortuous, particularly in the earlier document, several points may be noted. The 'corner posts' mentioned in the 1726 surrender suggest a wooden structure, but this is not necessarily the case; the reference may be to the buttresses of the gatehouse. The inclusion of the 'Pool Dam' certainly suggests that the properties were in the vicinity of the junction of Mill Street, Castle Hill, The Bull Ring and Watergate. The 'George Inn' occupied the large block of land shown on the 1761 map at the southern end of the main High Street on the western side. Part of its frontage cut obliquely across the corner and this is perpetuated in the present properties.[11]

Finally, it may be pure coincidence but the frontage of the 'Star Hotel' in Watergate measures exactly 41ft which was the distance between the two properties specified so carefully in the first surrender. The entry on the eastern side is 10ft wide and this may relate to the '11 feet or thereabouts' which apparently adjoined the property. The cellar of the

The Star Hotel

Star Hotel is partly brick-built but the walls on the east and west sides consist of blocks of dressed sandstone which vary in length from 6ins. to 2ft., but have a reasonably uniform height of 11ins. In the south-west corner the stonework makes a return onto the street front and in the eastern wall there is the suggestion of a former arch, now blocked. While it is acknowledged that the drawing shows a building which cannot be 41ft. across the possibility remains that perhaps the gatehouse was contained within the western half of what is now the Star Hotel and that the stonework in the cellar represents the tangible remains of it. The cellar has an internal width of 14ft. 10ins. which further emphasises the similarity to Layerthorpe.[12]

About a mile to the east of Whitchurch is Blakemere, the site of the old manor house of the Talbot family, and from the mere rises the Staggs Brook, now culverted for most of its course through the town. At one time the brook was dammed to provide power for the mill whose site is clearly shown on the 1761 map, and the brook still carries the overflow from Blakemere.[13] As the householders and shopkeepers in the area know to their cost, drainage in the cellars is a problem and The Star Hotel is no exception; fresh water flows freely through part of the cellar and special drainage arrangements have had to be made. It may be a fanciful suggestion, but perhaps the gatehouse on the drawing represents Whitchurch's original Watergate.

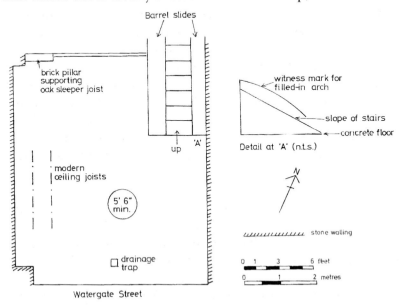

Cellar Plan of the Star Hotel

Cruck Construction in Whitchurch

Whitchurch presents a general impression of brick building, much of it dating from the 19th century, but, in common with many small market towns, it has a legacy of timber-framing concealed behind the brick façades. Most of the timbered buildings are of the box-framed variety, that is to say a series of posts and beams form a box-like structure which supports the roof, the walls forming an integral part of the whole. The alternative technology was to build with crucks. This technique required for each main bay division of the house two long curving timbers, known as 'cruck blades', preferably taken from one oak tree, and shaped to form a monolithic arch joined at the apex. The backs of the blades would support the weight of the roof directly and the walls would be independent of both the basic frame and of the roof. Cruck-built houses were not easily adapted for changing conditions in towns—it was difficult to add to the height and width because of the restrictions imposed by the size of the blades, whilst plot sizes would preclude increasing the length of such houses if they were set parallel to the street. Where good oaks were at a premium, as in north Shropshire, crucks were used for small dwellings and, within the basic chronology of the genre, tended to be of a late date. Where dendrochronological dates have been obtained the large substantial crucks of south Shropshire are of the 14th and 15th centuries, while those in north Shropshire are producing 16th century dates.

It is unsurprising, therefore, to find little evidence of existing cruck structures within the town. The 'Old Eagles' in Watergate is exceptional in that it represents an up-market variation of the genre, known as base-cruck construction. But the only full-cruck to come to light is within 6 Dodington, and, as that chapter relates, it is difficult to relate this single truss to the rest of the structure. The examples of upper-cruck construction at 25 Dodington and at the 'Horse and Jockey' are less surprising as they represent late-comers to the tradition and were effective for gaining height particularly in upper stories and in ancillary buildings.

However, it should be borne in mind that Whitchurch, like many other historic towns, was subjected to ruthless programmes of so-called 'slum clearance' in the 1930s and 1950s, with no architectural records being made. This has left unsightly gaps and waste land in many areas of the town. Cottages classed as 'unfit for human habitation' were demolished with no regard whatsoever either for their historic structural interest or their possible reha-bilitation. It is, therefore, very fortunate that one gentleman, Mr Geoffrey G.J. Owen, (d.1982), left among his notes a list of those cottages which he recognised as being of cruck construction. His daughter, Mrs Mary Perry, has made her father's notes available to

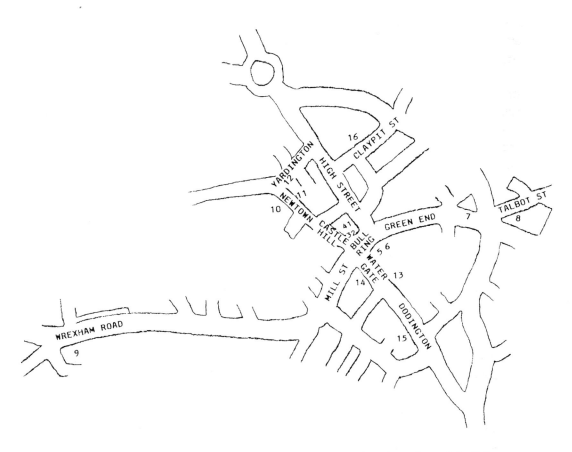

Simplified map of Whitchurch town centre showing location of cruck buildings.
Nos. 1 - 12 have been demolished; No. 13 is 6 Dodington (full crucks);
No. 14 is the 'Old Eagles' (base crucks); no. 15 is 25 Old Dodington (upper crucks);
and No. 16 is 'The Horse & Jockey' (upper crucks)

the class, has shown us the sites and plotted the location of the demolished crucks on the map above. Where we have been able to check Mr Owen's statements, he was invariably correct, and there is no reason to doubt his assertions.

Mr Owen's schedule of the demolished crucks follows. The comments are entirely his, with editorial notes in brackets added by Mrs Perry. The existing crucks are also shown on the map (nos. 13 - 16).

1) Porter's Yard, motor cycle and bicycle repairs and sales. Store-room behind. Workshop at rear of Porter's shop. Demolished for the National Provincial Bank. (*c*.1923. 'Well meaning but presumptuous' - Pevsner) Entry through to Castle Hill. 3 pairs of crucks, Beams, carved and shaped. (One local person said 'It was a row of cottages.' Another said 'the wood was that hard you couldn't knock a nail in it.')

2. Storeroom/Stable at rear of 'White Bear'. Demolished 1937-8, reused cruck at the end.

3. Small cruck cottage behind Whittingham's. Entry from Watergate and Castle Hill. Roofless in early 1930s. 2 pairs of crucks. Collapsed in a strong wind in the mid-1930s. (The site is that of the first Tesco building next to the 'Star Hotel' in Watergate.)

4. Rear of 'Swan Hotel', alongside Castle Hill, long open-sided building, 4 pairs crucks, red raddle on walls, packed earth floor. Demolished after World War I. (The 'Swan' was demolished in 1968. The building can be seen on a 1938 aerial photograph in *Whitchurch Remembered*, p.9. Red raddle was the earth-based mineral, ground to a powder, mixed with water and used extensively to colour buildings in the area.)

5. Behind Cooper's Toffee shop. 2 or 3 rooms behind the Bull Ring Vaults, very low and dark. Crucks visible in centre and end wall. Demolished for Lloyd's Bank (2 Watergate Street.)

6. 'White Lion'. Small cruck building used as storeroom and for washing glasses. 2 pairs crucks. Demolished to extend car park in late 1930s. (This and no. 5 must have been close together. An elderly lady said 'Bent beams holding it up, no straight wood in it anywhere.' She worked in it for two years during World War I.)

7. Three cottages behind Fountain House, Green End. Used as a garage and chauffeur's house. Crucks in wall between garage and cottage. Demolished for Fountain car park.

8. 1½ pairs crucks visible internally in Mr. Tapley's cottage, Paradise Row. Down two steps into a room. Demolished in late 1950s. (Paradise Row is now Talbot Street. The cottages may be those shown in *Whitchurch Remembered*, p.67. The end gable shows a box-framed truss, but they may have been similar to 6, 8 & 10 Dodington which has one cruck truss in an otherwise box-framed row.)

9. Hovel at the top of Wrexham Road. 2 pairs of crucks about 15ft. x 12ft. Loft over. Condemned and demolished late 1940s. (Here my father is using the term 'hovel' to mean a poor dilapidated cottage. It housed a couple and their nine children who were rehoused in two houses in George Street when the house was demolished. The cottage had thatch under a tin roof, and wattle walls.)

10. Newtown - condemned and demolished. Inhabitants rehoused in council houses after World War II. 6 pairs crucks.

11. Newtown - 'Not worth repair' (Treasurer of U.D.C.).

12. Yardington - 4 crucks in 2 or 3 houses.

Mr. Owen's list provides a rough estimate of 28 pairs of demolished crucks. This does not take into account others which may have escaped his notice or those demolished before his time. It is very difficult to assess the ratio of box-framed structures to crucks that existed when Whitchurch was largely timber-framed, but the general impression is that box-framing was used for the more prestigious buildings, such as the hall-houses in the High Street, whilst crucks were used for lesser buildings including single-storey cottages. The rate of attrition certainly accelerated in the periods before and after World War II. It would have been very helpful to know more about the form of the lost cruck cottages, whether any of them represented medieval hall-houses later sub-divided into cottages, and especially whether there were any blocks built as whole terraces of crucks. Only one such terrace has been identified in the British Isles and that occurs in Much Wenlock, but the record of six pairs of crucks in one block in Newtown, four pairs in Yardington and the description of those in Porter's Yard as 'a row of cottages' certainly raises the possibility that Whitchurch could have produced other examples.[1]

The Use of Peat in Whitchurch Buildings

Several meres and mosses are located to the north-east and east of Whitchurch, while to the south-west Fenn's Moss and Whixall Moss cover large tracts of land. In common with many of the wetlands in the area the latter were artificially drained in the 19th century, but because they were not suitable for cultivation they were left for peat cutting. Ranging in depth from 9 to 25ft the peat beds produce horticultural material of excellent quality.[1] Peat was recognised as a useful natural resource long before the 19th century, however, and in addition to its use as fuel and as a fertiliser it was used in buildings. No complete building with peat walls has been found, but at Aston Bridge Farm near Wem, a house whose origins may lie in the longhouse tradition, the older cruck-built range was found to have peat blocks forming the infilling of the timber-frame, both in the walls and in the cruck truss.[2]

In Whitchurch there appears to be a long tradition of peat walling, although very little survives. The discovery in 1991 of peat blocks used for a partition wall in nos. 1 and 3 Church Street led to one of the class members, Mrs. Mary Perry, reporting the gist of a conversation she had with Mrs. Penlington, an elderly lady living in Nantwich who was born in Newtown, Whitchurch: 'There was a lot of peat used for walls in Whitchurch. I remember particularly Newtown and Yardington. They were healthier than mud and straw [wattle and daub]. They took away the damp, so people didn't get rheumatism. There were no bed bugs or cockroaches either, so we didn't need gas-water and they were warmer as well, not noisy and quite strong. My father wanted to make a doorway through a peat wall once and had to use a sledge-hammer.' ('Gas-water' was a residue from the filtering of gas at the gas-works used as a form of disinfectant. Householders would wash down the inner walls of houses with it to destroy bed-bugs and other lice, but the whole row of dwellings had to be treated simultaneously, otherwise the pests simply moved to the next house in the row.)

Another class member, Mr. Brian Edwards, a native of Whitchurch, reported on a cottage in Bargates which had outer walls of brick but peat partition walls: 'Alderman Robert Wragg lived there or nearby as a boy. He became a barrister at the age of 40 and was the first Lord Mayor of York to serve for three consecutive years since 1403 [the date of the battle of Shrewsbury]. He served again to host the centenary of the British Association in 1932 and was Recorder of Pontefract for 27 years.' The cottage was demolished *c.*1960. Mr. Edwards also commented that during a severe fuel shortage in about 1947 cottagers were driven to recover the peat from internal walls and use it for firing.

When no. 42 Watergate was being renovated in 1991 it was discovered that peat blocks, laid with a mortar of fine-textured mud, formed the infill of the framing of the partition walls. The class was given a block for record purposes, and now that it has dried out it weighs only 2ozs (50grams). The blocks measure on average 7ins. x 2½ ins. x 2ins., and in many respects are a natural alternative to manufactured bricks.

How widespread was the practice of peat walling in the area and how many of the demolished cottages and houses were so built? When peat blocks were clearly known to be strong, durable, damp-absorbing, warm and sound-proof why were they regarded as inferior and could there be a future for them? There is a fine irony in the fact that 42 Watergate, when renovated, was occupied by a firm of heating appliance suppliers called 'World of Warmth'.

The Whitchurch Inventories

The value of wills and especially the accompanying probate inventories as source material for local history studies has long been known, although their survival rate varies considerably throughout the country. Because Shropshire was divided between three dioceses the wills and inventories are deposited in the Lichfield Joint Record Office, The Hereford Record Office and The National Library of Wales. If a person owned property in more than one diocese the will was proved in the Prerogative Court of Canterbury, and these records are held in the Public Record Office, Kew. Until 1858 the Church was responsible for the administration of Probate matters, that is to say, the proving of a deceased person's last Will and Testament, but after that date civil districts were established. In 1529 Henry VIII decreed that if a deceased person's goods and chattels were worth more than £5 two or more 'honest and skilful persons', usually neighbours or fellow parishioners, should be appointed to make an inventory of the goods and an assessment of their value.[1] Duty was payable to the Church and, after 1858, to the state.

The 'honest and skilful persons' were called 'appraisers', although the spelling varies on the actual documents. They were not obliged to go through the house systematically, naming the rooms as they did so, but in the most useful examples this is what occurred, and so the size and plan of the house can often be deduced from the inventory, although certain reservations must be made. For example, if a room was empty at the time of the appraisal there would be no point in naming it, similarly rooms can be inferred from 'chambers over', though the lower rooms may not be named, and in many cases it is clear that only some of the rooms are mentioned. Some begin methodically, but trail off as the appraisers lose interest.

Unless there is a history of continuous occupation by one family or some other documentary evidence as is sometimes the case with licensed premises or a large country house, it is rarely possible to relate an inventory to a standing building. Addresses as such were not used, for everyone in the community knew where a person lived. But the study of the inventories of a particular area will provide much useful information regarding relative wealth, the social structure, agricultural practices, occupations, trades, money-lending and borrowing, standards of living, and much besides.

Where the Whitchurch inventories are concerned, those held in the Lichfield Joint Record Office and dated between 1535 and 1650 have been extracted and transcribed by Sylvia Watts, a Ph.D. student from Wolverhampton University.[2] They require detailed analysis and comparison with other collections, which is, perhaps, a task for a future extramural class. For the present a few basic statistics are included which will, hopefully, provide a starting-point.

434 inventories were transcribed, 52 (12%) of which name the rooms in a useful manner. This compares poorly with those of Telford (57.2%) analysed by Drs. Trinder and Cox.[3] A list of those with named rooms is given below, followed by a breakdown of the room figures, giving, by analogy, the comparative sizes of the 52 houses. Three have not been included in the analysis because the information appears to be incomplete. There may be good reasons for the discrepancies, but they are discounted because of the scanty and probably misleading information they present. James Beard (1638) and Roger Eddow (1648) are shown with only two-roomed houses, but their goods total £12 11s and £54 5s respectively, and Peter Hopkin (1648) of Black Park, worth £225 13s 10d, is shown as having only three rooms. On the other hand the three inventories relating to members of the Burghall family have been included because those of George (1562) and Thomas (1641) show 'The Swan' before and after extensions were made which can be identified in the standing building (21 and 23 High Street, 'Walker's'), included as one chapter. The 1626 inventory of another George is included because it appears to relate to a different property.

Although the two inventories of the Penkethmans are listed, only one is counted for analysis. This is because they appear to relate to the same property. It would be interesting to know what lies behind these deaths. William Penkethman is shown with 'Elizabeth his wife' appraised on 30th June 1632 and worth £26 11s 8d, followed swiftly by another William and Elizabeth Penkethman on 31st October who were worth £15 12s 2d. Another Penkethman, George, died in 1634, but apparently he occupied a different house. His inventory included 'One joyned standinge bed seised for a haryott [heriot] by the Countess of Derby, her officer.' The bed was worth £1 15s, and his total goods £20 8s 2d.

The report of Ash Wood contains the inventory of Richard Hughes, and its contents are analysed. It is not included here because its date, 1727, puts it outside the range of Mrs. Watts' study.

In the list below the spelling has been modernised, and rooms which are positively implied, though not listed, are included.

References to Rooms in Whitchurch Inventories 1535-1650[4]

Richard Torperly 1537
Hall, kitchen, buttery.

Philip Tonay 1539
Hall, kitchen, servants' chamber, best chamber.

Thomas Wyn 1549 (Innkeeper, 'Crown Inn')
Great chamber, chamber over gate, hall chamber, chamber over cellars, parlour, chamber over, chamber next to parlour chamber, hall, inner parlour.

George Borghall 1562 (Innkeeper, 'Swan Inn')
Hall, chamber over, parlour, chamber over, chamber over the gate, shop, chamber over the shop.

William Aston 1576
Hall, chamber.

Richard Mericke 1583
Hall, higher parlour, solar, little parlour.

John Kettle 1588
House, parlour, kitchen, buttery, great chamber, little chamber, middle chamber, privy chamber.

Thomas Stockton 1591
Hall, chamber over, parlour, chamber over, buttery, chamber over, shop, chamber over.

Richard Tayler 1592
Hall, chamber over, parlour, chamber over, buttery, chamber over, kitchen, chamber over, two chambers over the gates, brewhouse.

Joan Paynter 1593
Parlour, chamber over, hall, chamber over, buttery.

Edward Probyn 1613
House, chamber over, parlour, chamber over, buttery, chamber over, kitchen, chamber over, bolting house, storehouse, (one room indecipherable).

John Rhodes 1617
Great chamber, little chamber, privy chamber, loft over, lower parlour, hall, chamber over hall, upper chamber over the hall, mens' chamber, kitchen, buttery, chamber over the parlour, upper chamber over parlour.

Robert Richardson 1618
Hall, chamber over the hall, new chamber, kitchen, chamber over.

Ferdinand Wynne 1624
Hall, great chamber, ladies' chamber, street chamber, chamber next the store house, store chamber, kitchen, milkhouse.

Jane Waring 1626
Hall, chamber over, buttery, chamber over, kitchen, chamber over, parlour, chamber over, two chambers over the gatehouse, (plus ostler's lodging).

George Burghall 1626 (Innkeeper)
Hall, chamber over, lower parlour, chamber over, little chamber, kitchen, chamber over, bolting house, higher parlour, chamber over, little chamber, buttery.

Margery Willaston 1628
Hall, chamber over, parlour, chamber over, chamber over the gates.

Margery Greatbache 1629
House, great chamber, parlour, shop, study, chamber over the entry.

Robert Podmore 1631
House, parlour, loft, buttery, store chamber.

William Penkethman and Elizabeth his wife 1632 (30th June)
House, chamber over, chamber over the entry, room next the street, back room, buttery, kitchen. (Total value £26 11s 8d).

William and Elizabeth Penkethman 1632 (31st October)
House, chamber over, chamber next the street, little back room, buttery, kitchen (Total value £15 12s 2d).

Thomas Sympson 1632 Alkington
House, chamber over, parlour, menservants' chamber.

William Higginson 1632
Best chamber, little chamber, cockloft, lower parlour, house, shop, bolting house, kitchen, (plus old cockpit).

Andrew Bostock 1633
House, little parlour over house, great parlour, chamber over, little chamber over house, loft over little parlour, lower parlour, kitchen, buttery.

William Rigby 1633 (Vintner)
Parlour, chamber over, house, loft over, kitchen, loft over, cellar, buttery, bay below kitchen.

William Constantine, 1633
Hall, room over, parlour, room over, lower parlour, kitchen.

George Penkethman 1634
House, chamber over, parlour, loft over, buttery, kitchen.

John Byrd 1634
House, buttery, shop, chamber over, next chamber, parlour, best chamber.

William Lloyd 1635
Parlour, chamber over, hall, chamber over, kitchen, chamber over.

Robert Leech 1635
Spence (buttery), house, room over hall, over the entry, shop, little chamber over the shop, farthest chamber, cocklofts.

William Richardson 1636
Hall, chamber over, kitchen, chamber over, odd room.

John Hopkin 1636
Dyehouse, shop, hall, loft over, chamber.

Humphrey Rowley 1637 (Yeoman)
Parlour, chamber over, buttery, chamber over, house.

Thomas Rhodes 1637
Parlour, chamber over, hall, chamber over, beer house, chamber over, buttery, chamber over, kitchen.

Alice Morhall 1638 Black Park
Parlour, chamber over, kitchen, chamber over, milkhouse, chamber over, old house, chamber over.

John Bentley 1638
Hall, chamber over, parlour, chamber over, buttery, kitchen, chamber over, storeloft.

Randall Judson 1638
Great chamber, little chamber, cockloft, parlour behind the kitchen, parlour next the street, chamber over, hall, chamber over, higher chamber over the hall, high chamber over the parlour, high chamber over the gates, kitchen, little chamber at the stairhead, cornloft.

Thomas Bromfield 1638
Hall, chamber.

William Wickstead 1639
Hall, chamber over, parlour, chamber over, little chamber, kitchen, chamber over, buttery, chamber over, gallery at stairhead, store chamber, kiln chamber, milkhouse, servant's chamber by the kill (kiln).

Wilfred Bumbie 1639
Shop, chamber over, kitchen, chamber over, house, chamber over, buttery.

William Gregory 1639
Chandling house, shop, chamber over, lower parlour, kitchen, buttery, servants' chamber.

Elizabeth Bostock 1640
Hall, little chamber over house, great parlour, chamber over, little parlour over house, lower parlour, chamber over little parlour, kitchen, buttery, store loft, chamber next the buttery, chamber over the parlour.

John Barrow 1640
House, chamber over, chamber, buttery, kitchen.

William Barrow 1640 (Butcher)
Parlour, house, chamber over.

Arthur Dudley 1640
Parlour, chamber over, kitchen, chamber over, study, buttery, chamber over the entry.

William Barrow 1641 (Butcher)
House, chamber over, next chamber, shop, chamber over shop & buttery, buttery, kitchen.

Thomas Burghall 1641 (Innkeeper, 'The Swan')
Hall, chamber over, parlour, chamber over, new chamber, chamber over the gates, dark chamber, further chamber, chamber over the shop, buttery, kitchen.

John Corbishley 1642
House, chamber over, store loft, little parlour, chamber over, buttery, room over the entry.

Thomas Dickin 1643
Hall, chamber over, parlour, chamber over, kitchen, buttery, chamber over, cockloft, chamber over entry, chamber over shop.

John Symcocks 1643
Great chamber, gallery chamber, cockloft, parlour, chamber over, kitchen, chamber over, house.

Margaret Murhall 1644 Black Park
Hall, chamber, chamber over, further room.

Robert Hawkes 1646 Woodhouse (Cooper)
House, chamber over, chamber, new chamber, cheese loft, kitchen, chamber over, two butteries.

James Grindley 1648
Hall, chamber over, best chamber, parlour, kitchen.

	No. of houses
2 roomed houses	2
3 " "	2
4 " "	4
5 " "	9
6 " "	4
7 " "	8
8 " "	7
9 " "	6
10 " "	2
11 " "	3
12 " "	2
13 " "	1
14 " "	2
	Total 52

1-5 rooms, 17 houses
(32.6% of the total)
6-10 rooms, 27 houses
(51.9% of the total)
over 10 rooms, 8 houses
(15.3% of the total)

	No.	% of houses
Hall or House	50	96
Great Chambers	11	21
Great & Little Parlours	46	88
Solars	1	2
Kitchens	34	65
Butteries	31	60
Chamber over Hall	36	69
Chamber over Parlour	31	60
Chamber over Buttery	8	15
Chamber over Gatehouse or Entry	9	17
Other Chambers	71	137
Shops	10	19
Lofts	18	35
Milkhouses (Dairies)	3	6
Bolting Houses	3	6
Cellars	2	4

There are also single entries for: Dyehouse, Chandling House, Brewhouse, Beerhouse, Storehouse, Study, Bay below kitchen, and Gallery at Stairhead.

Tables showing (above left) the size of the houses mentioned in the inventories, and (above right) the named rooms in the 52 houses

From the figures in the above tables it is possible to deduce certain trends characteristic of Whitchurch between 1535 and 1650, although it should be remembered that 52 represents a small proportion of the whole housing stock. The term 'house' or 'houseplace' means the main living-room and should be regarded as the equivalent of the medieval 'hall'. It is clear that the 'hall' or 'house' was still used as such, and that most were floored over. The 'great chamber' and the 'chamber over the hall' may be synonymous terms, and if so indicates that 47 out of the 52 (90%) had floored halls. 34 kitchens are listed, implying that in 18 cases the cooking was done in the 'hall' or 'house'. The small number, eight, of chambers over the buttery, so precisely defined, implies that many butteries were single-storied, although it is possible that they are included in 'other chambers'. Similarly, in 21 cases chambers over parlours, though not listed, may be included in 'other chambers'. The 'storehouses' in Ferdinand Wynne's inventory of 1624 are probably butteries.

Only 10 shops appear to be included in the 52 examples, and in two cases these are only inferred from the inclusion of a 'chamber over the shop'. Also surprising is the small number, three, of 'milkhouses' (dairies). Some of the inns which offered accommodation are discernible, and the multi-roomed inventories and those with 'chambers over the gates' are likely to include other examples. The inveterate traveller, Celia Fiennes, stayed at 'The Crown' in 1698 and left a graphic record of two remarkable gardens in Whitchurch. That at the 'Crown' contained 'oring and lemmon trees mirtle striped and gilded holly trees box and filleroy finely cut and firrs and Merumsuracum which makes the fine snuff, and fine flowers, all things almost in a little tract of garden ground.'[5] Thomas Wyn's inventory of 1549 shows that he was landlord of the 'Crown' a century and a half before Celia's visit, and the site has been identified as that of Bradbury's butcher's shop, 42 High Street.[6] The Burgall family at the 'Swan' (21 and 23 High Street) has been mentioned and that property is included in the surveys.

Chambers over Gates, Gatehouses or Entries are mentioned in nine cases, most of them clearly associated with inns, suggesting that Whitchurch, in common with many other market towns, had many yards or courts behind the main streets which would contain gardens, cottages and back buildings.

Three bolting houses are mentioned, and there were probably many more. This was where flour was sifted to separate the bran and indicates the importance of having a year's supply of flour to hand. Two appear to relate to inns, the other may have been a merchant.

In 18 cases 'lofts' of one kind or another are listed. The question arises as to whether some of these are 'crogloffts'—sleeping platforms, an example of which was found and recorded at 38 Watergate. Cocklofts (attics) and storelofts are distinguished, as is the one 'cheese loft' of Robert Hawkes at Woodhouse (1646). The latter had two butteries and a 'new chamber'. Could this be seen as indicative of the beginning of the boom in cheese production in north Shropshire? Cheeses feature among the contents of houses in a number of cases, John Bentley's (1638) storeloft containing 21.

Even a cursory examination of the inventories shows that numerous people acted as moneylenders. William Barrow (1641) had £123 out in debts, nearly half of his total value. The three Barrow inventories are included in the analysis as they appear to relate to different properties.

As mentioned earlier, detailed analysis of the inventories has still to be done, but it is evident that painted cloths were popular. These, of course, were regarded as 'the poor man's tapestry'. Their value was not high, ranging between 4d and 4s, but because their survival rate is so low they have given rise to a culture study of their own. James Wyn, an innkeeper, possibly at the 'Crown' where Celia Fiennes stayed, had some in a chamber over the kitchen in 1587. Munslow Farm is one house in Shropshire which contains a complete set. None has been found in Whitchurch, the oldest wall decoration remains the painted motifs in the upper chambers of 17 - 19 Watergate (The Old Raven Inn).

Dodington House

Dodington House is situated in a part of Whitchurch which was once a separate township with its own manor but is now an integral part of the town.[1] Dodington forms, in effect, a staggered continuation of the High Street and contains a mixture of shops, chapels, inns and houses, some of the latter retaining elements of refinement which suggest that in the 18th and 19th centuries this was an area of gracious living. Dodington has been described as 'the best street in Whitchurch' and the Mansion House, which adjoins Dodington House, as 'the most ambitious private house in Whitchurch.'[2] Since the later mutilation of the Mansion House and its conversion first to a petrol station and workshop and later to a short-lived super-market, that distinction no longer applies. Arguably it now belongs to Dodington House.

The Exterior

A totally symmetrical front elevation, with a recessed entrance between balanced projecting wings, as well as a Tuscan porch, whitewashed stucco, raised quoins, rectangular sash windows, a continuous eaves level and twin triangular pediments give the impression of a simple, though elegant, late Georgian or Regency residence with overtones of the Greek Revival movement. However, the internal plan is not symmetrical, there is a marked difference in wall thicknesses, some timber-framing survives in the northern wall and there is evidence for at least three different building phases.

Dodington House

Dodington House appears to occupy five burgage plots that have a marked bending towards the south-west. The overall width of the five plots, measured from the end of the garden, is 82ft. 6ins. and the house basically follows the

25

plan of an inverted L with a projection towards the western end of the long northern wall of a service unit which may have been a game larder. This encroaches into the adjoining plot and makes it difficult to examine the surviving timber-framing on that side. On the southern side there is sufficient width for a carriage entry to the stable and coach-house. Any early features on this side are thoroughly disguised with stucco, although the addition of a large drawing-room in the south-west corner of the plan may be discerned by changes in the wall surface and in the roof line. The drawing-room block adds a hipped roof to an already complicated roof-plan and effectively turns the house into a double-pile plan.

All sense of symmetry is lost at the rear of the property where windows and doors appear at odd intervals in seemingly haphazard fashion and with no consistent style. Even the elegant drawing-room with its shuttered sash windows fails to maintain regularity with the fenestration above.

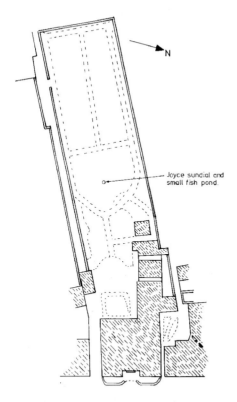

*Site plan of Dodington House
(based on OS 1880. n.t.s.)*

Phase 1

The timber-framing on the long northern wall appears to represent the survival of part of an early 17th century house, although its extent and orientation are impossible to determine. No wall-framing is visible from the inside and because of the restrictions imposed by the property boundaries it was not possible to measure from the northern side. However, from the vantage point of the game-larder the framing could be seen to consist of large rectangular panels, two above and two below the girding-beam. The size of the panels is not entirely consistent, and the timbers are of average dimensions (*c.*6ins. wide giving panels of *c.*22 ins. x 46ins.) apart from the substantial continuous posts which mark the bay divisions. The panels are infilled with brick nogging, but

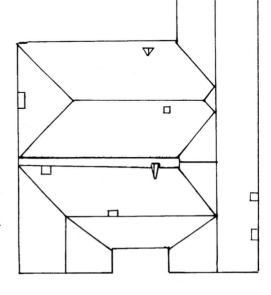

Roof plan

26

it would be reasonable to assume that this is a replacement for original wattle and daub. Some features in the roof structure on this side relate to timber-framing, notably a roof truss with V-struts above the collar-beam in the western gable end and associated purlins with plain, straight windbraces. The windbracing is confined to the eastern half of the wing and it is perhaps significant that it runs through to the front of the house. One windbrace remains on the southern wall of the opposite wing, but is located level with the line of the recessed front.

Phase 2

The house stands back slightly from its neighbour but the extent and location of the wind-braces suggests that the timber-framed house, whatever its form, extended to the present building line, at least on the northern side. However, the thick wall which now forms the main transverse division of the house at ground level suggests that the accommodation to the east of it, in particular the hall, the main staircase, the small front parlour or waiting-room and at least the front part of the dining room (once a billiard-room) in the southern wing are the result of a major re-modelling in the late 18th century. It was at this time that the front of the house assumed its present appearance and perhaps when the present kitchen was created from a rear service wing of some kind. The hall is itself divided by two flat-arched openings with a central wooden fluted circular pillar on a square base, and there are other Regency features in the form of moulded doorcases, a large gilt mirror and fluted pilasters. The dog-leg staircase is rather tucked away between the small parlour and the study or consulting-room and lacks the style and flair of other staircases in Whitchurch, although it is in keeping with the suggested date. The fact that it is not a prominent feature and is located away from the hall supports the suggestion that the re-modelling was constrained by what already existed on the site and was, of necessity, retained.

Phase 3

The addition of the drawing-room with bedrooms above it fills in the south-west corner of the plan. It was probably built in the early 19th century and may coincide with the occupancy of Mrs. Heber, a point which will be discussed later. The hap-ç hazard arrangement of the bedroom windows above suggests that perhaps it was adapted from part of the older house, but there are equally strong indications that it was a new extension. Its hipped roof has a higher ridge-line than the kitchen wing but lower than the southern wing which was altered to accommodate it. The drawing room has an unusually high ceiling and its dimensions suggest that it may have been used as a ballroom on occasions. Certainly it was a room designed for entertaining on a fairly large scale. The fireplace has a fine marble overmantel which was brought from Emral Hall, Worthenbury when that house was demolished in 1936.[3]

Internal features

Apart from the stylish features noted above there are two others which add interest to the house and are still not fully understood. One is a cage-like contraption made from posts and wooden laths in an open criss-cross design. This measures 11ft. 8ins. x 6ft. 10ins. and is 7ft. 7ins. high. It is located at attic level above the recessed front of the house and has a

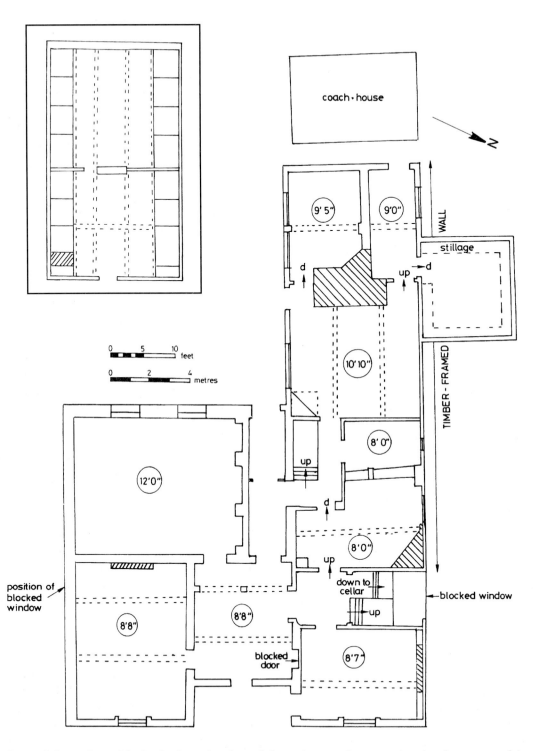

Ground floor plan with, in the box, the plan of the attic over the west wing (to the same scale) showing the grain bins

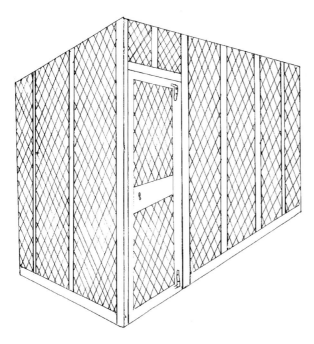

The cage in the attic over the central bay (n.t.s.)

door constructed of the same open lattice-work and fitted with a mortice lock. Inside the cage there are thirty-six strong metal hooks arranged in three rows on the ceiling beams. There is a strong tradition of cock-fighting attached to Dodington House; pictures and exhibits such as silver spurs abound, and it is said that the cage was where fighting-cocks were kept when cock-fighting became illegal. Whenever discovery threatened they were suspended by the feet from the hooks and hooded to prevent them making a noise. However, to present-day keepers of exotic birds this seems improbable and a more rational suggestion is that it relates to experimentation in indoor winter breeding of poultry for the table. A similar cage is illustrated in a mid-18th century book on poultry keeping, but only one hook is shown and it supports a basket containing a solitary egg.[4] Perhaps the multiplicity of hooks at Dodington House indicates that here the experiment was more successful. However, there may be a completely different reason for the presence of the cage.

The other feature is located at attic level above the kitchen wing. Here the space between the lower purlins and the floor in both bays is sub-divided by wooden planks of diminishing lengths to provide 16 compartments, each with grooved uprights at the front so that a retaining board could be slotted in. Clearly the compartments were for storage of some kind. They are not vermin-proof, although this does not rule out the possibility that they were used for grain storage. They may have been designed for the storage of seed corn, bread corn, hops or for a completely different and, at present, unknown commodity. Again, the house tradition says that this is where the corn was kept to feed the fighting-cocks. However, the area is not directly accessible from the cage level and can only be reached by the secondary staircase shown on the plan.

The Firemark

In the south-east corner of the house, under the eaves and difficult to see from ground level is a firemark of the Birmingham Fire Office which operated between 1805 and 1867. It is unlikely to be in its original position. Although there are several firemarks still to be seen in Whitchurch, most of them relate to Shropshire-based companies. However, 26 Barkhill in Whitchurch also displays a Birmingham plate.[5]

The Social History[6]

The freehold of Dodington House carries with it the right to moor a boat on Whitchurch Mill Pool and to fish therein.[7] These aquatic privileges have no modern relevance as the mill was demolished in 1811 and the pool filled in soon afterwards. Until recently the area was known as 'The White Lion Meadow' and now serves as the town's main car-park.[8]

From the second half of the 19th century Dodington House has been home to a succession of Whitchurch doctors who

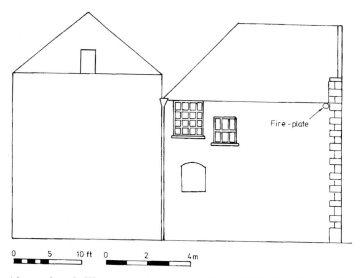

Above: South Elevation showing position of the fire plate with, below, the fire plate itself (n.t.s)

practiced from there. The first was Dr. John Brown and it was he who transferred the oak panelling in the consulting room from his house in St. Mary's Street when that was demolished *c.*1870. On the plan this room is the one shown with a corner fireplace. At the same time he inserted a door in the south-eastern corner of the long northern range to give patients direct access from the street into the waiting room.[9]

There is a strong local tradition that in earlier centuries Dodington House was home to three men of national importance: Philip Henry, Matthew Henry and Reginald Heber, all ecclesiastics. In the case of the Henrys, though their tenure was short, the story could be true, but documentary research has failed to connect Reginald Heber directly with the house. The legend probably stems from the fact that his mother, when widowed, bought the house and occupied it until a year or two before she died.

1) The Rev. Philip Henry[10] (1631 - 1696)

Philip Henry was one of the first and subsequently most respected nonconformists of the 17th century. He was born in Whitehall and brought up at the court of Charles I where he was an attendant to the sons of the monarch, the young princes Charles and James. He watched the execution of the king in 1649. Educated at Oxford and ordained at Prees church under the Presbyterian order in 1657, he became tutor to the sons of Judge and

Lady Puleston at Emral Hall, Worthenbury, Flintshire and was also vicar of Worthenbury. Despite his royalist upbringing he held firmly to his dissenting beliefs, refusing to obey the Act of Uniformity passed by Charles II in 1662. Forced to leave Worthenbury, he went first to Broad Oak farm, in the parish of Whitewell, some four miles due west of Whitchurch (from where in 1660 he had married Katherine Matthews, the daughter and heiress of Daniel Matthews); and, on March 8th 1667, to Whitchurch. This was after the passing of the Five Mile Act which stipulated than no nonconformist minister could come within five miles of any place where he had preached or taught since 1660 unless he subscribed to the Act of Uniformity. He wrote in his diary 'In January [1667] we removed to Whitch. in Shropshire partly to satisfy the law, ptly to have convenient schooling for him [his son John] and his brother...' A later note to the entry for 9th March 1667, added by the editor, reads 'the house now occupied by Philip Henry is said to be the one opposite to the new Independent Chapel in the street of Doddington.' The chapel, opened in 1798 and now the United Reformed Church, is diagonally opposite to Dodington House, and while such a description leaves room for some doubt, local tradition has always associated Dodington House with Philip Henry. In May 1668 the family moved back to Broad Oak, having demonstrated that the farm was five miles and 70 yards from Worthenbury church, the scene of Philip's earlier ministry. On modern maps it is considerably more. At Broad Oak in 1672 he built a Presbyterian chapel as an outbuilding to the house. This was superseded in 1707 by one built at the rear of no. 7 Dodington in Whitchurch.[11] Philip Henry was buried in Whitchurch and has an inscribed marble memorial in the parish church.

2) Matthew Henry (1662 - 1714)

Matthew Henry was Philip's second son, born prematurely in 1662, only two weeks after his father was ejected from the living at Worthenbury. When the family moved to Dodington House Matthew, then five years old, attended Whitchurch Free Grammar School for a few months with his elder brother John, whose death from measles in April 1668 was one reason for the family's return to Broad Oak. Afterwards he was educated privately before being ordained as a Presbyterian minister in 1687. Twelve years later he officiated at the ordination of Samuel Benyon as minister to the nonconformist congregation at Broad Oak. When the first Presbyterian chapel was built in Dodington in 1707 Matthew Henry preached the first sermon.

He is, perhaps, best known for his six-volume *Commentary on the Bible* which remains a major work of reference for present day clergy and is still in print. Generations of theologians have been influenced by it, including such notable individuals as George Whitfield and John Wesley. It is regarded as one of the great classics of English literature.[12]

3) The Rev. Reginald Heber (1783 - 1826)

In several publications and written sources Dodington House is quoted as a childhood home of the Rev. Reginald Heber who was born in Malpas, Cheshire, became rector of Hodnet (1807) and later bishop of Calcutta (1823), but whose chief claim to fame is as the writer of such enduring hymns as 'From Greenland's Icy Mountains' and 'Holy, Holy, Holy, Lord God Almighty'. Unfortunately, all the published references seem to be based on heresay.[13] He attended Whitchurch Grammar School and it has been assumed that he lived at Dodington House at the time. This seems unlikely as the school had its own 'commodious house for the reception of a moderate numbers of genteel boarders' and it is known that the headmaster, William Kent had as many as 30 boarders or 'tablers' as they were known, some of them from prominent local families like the Hebers of Hodnet and the Hills of Hawkstone.[14] A letter from the Rev. Reginald Heber, senior, to his son Richard, dated 29th December 1792 and written from Malpas states 'Mama went to Whitchurch to fetch Reginald home ... on account of the sickness that he complained of.' A description of a mischievous episode follows in which it is reasonably clear that Reginald junior was not boarded out privately.[15]

The rectory at Malpas was either built or rebuilt for his father in the 1770s when he became Higher Rector of Malpas.[16] (Malpas was unusual in having a Higher and Lower Rector. Presumably the Lower Rector was a glorified curate.) Local tradition in Whitchurch maintains that the family occupied Dodington House while the building work was in progress, but, as mentioned above, the legend of the Heber connection has firmer foundation in the fact that Mary Heber, second wife of the Rev. Reginald Heber (d.1804) (parents of bishop Heber), went to live in Dodington as a widow in a house that she bought from a Mrs. Knight who was also, presumably, widowed. This was in 1824, by which time her son was in India. From letters that she and her daughter wrote it appears that Mary had never lived in Whitchurch previously and that, in her younger days, she would have considered it beneath her social status. However, she settled happily and had 'respectful attention from all the inhabitants of Whitchurch' who were 'the best set for a little town I ever saw'. But she had to make 'a few trifling alterations in the disposal of rooms for Mr Knight had a marvellous bad taste.' As mentioned above, the 'few trifling alterations' probably included the addition of the drawing room and bedrooms above. Though widowed, it seems that she continued to entertain in some style, and the letters make it clear that she hoped to receive her son Reginald and his wife Amelia ('Emily') in her new abode. With nearly eight acres of land behind the house she was 'able to to keep a cow and carriage horses.'[17] In fact, Reginald never returned from India, dying there in 1826, aged 42. There can be little doubt that Mary Heber occupied Dodington House. In the Church Lewns of the time two houses in Dodington are rated above the others. One was clearly the Mansion House, occupied by W.W. Brookes and later by the Downward family, and the other by Mrs. Heber. Mostly Mrs. Heber paid less than Mr. Brookes, but some of the returns show her paying more. In 1831/2 her house had passed into the ownership of Mr. Brookes.[18] She died in 1834, aged 82, and was buried at Hodnet. The Poor Law levy for 1827 shows her more highly rated than Mr. Brookes, but she also paid rates on a tanyard and two gardens.[19]

There is a gap in the deeds of Dodington House between 1772 and 1849, but they record that in 1772 it was bought by J. Knight from the Duke of Bridgwater. By 1849 it was in the possession of Edward Jones and his second wife, née Martha Piggott. He was a grocer and wine and spirit merchant with premises on the corner of High Street and Pepper Street. It is thought that he was an ancestor of the composer, Edward German (Jones). In 1849 the property is described as 'late in the tenure of R. Darwin Vaughton and the Rev. William Tyler' before it passed to Edward Jones.[20] The Church Lewns for 1833 show D.R. Vaughton as succeeding Mrs. Heber and paying a higher rate than W.W. Brookes.

23 & 25 Dodington (The old Manor House)

Nos. 23 and 25 Dodington are a pair of semi-detached houses, on the south-western side of the street facing the entrance to Bridgwater Street. The street frontage is of brick and applied timber-framing, clearly the result of early 20th-century remodelling, but the form is that of a $1^1/_2$ storied 'hall' block, flanked by a two-storied crosswing on either side. For this reason alone it was decided that the houses would repay investigation. In addition, in some documents they are referred to as 'The Manor House' and as Dodington was, from early times, a separate manor from Whitchurch, it was interesting to see whether there were any structural details which could possibly relate to a building of that status.[1] The only early timbers visible on the exterior are a short stretch of closely set verticals at the upper level on the rear of no. 23. These relate to the framing of the rear wall of a hall, and fortunately they continue and appear with the rafter ends as an internal feature within a later extension. The house appears to have been divided into two dwellings between 1861 and 1871.[2]

At ground level each house has an entrance hall, and the distinctive curve of the division is shown on the plan. Presumably this was done in order to retain the elaborate late

No. 25   No. 23

The east elevation (n.t.s.)

18th century staircase with its accompanying pillared approach in no. 23. Some structural alterations were necessary to accommodate this staircase which seems to have replaced a mid-17th century staircase with shaped flat balusters. A section of the earlier staircase was re-used in the cellar of no. 25. Details of both staircases are shown on the drawings. Following the 19th century divi-

The east elevation

sion each hall was given a decorative tiled floor, probably from the works of George Maw at Jackfield. In no. 25 the special border tiles which follow the line of the curved partition are still visible, but in no. 23 they are obscured.

During the investigations it became clear that, although no. 23 now has the larger share of the space, the properties are interlocked and the roof space was never divided. Furthermore, some subtle differences in the structural details suggest that no. 25 contained the upper or superior wing and no. 23 the lower or service wing. The original hall was a two-bayed unit with a first floor level, and that is now shared equally,

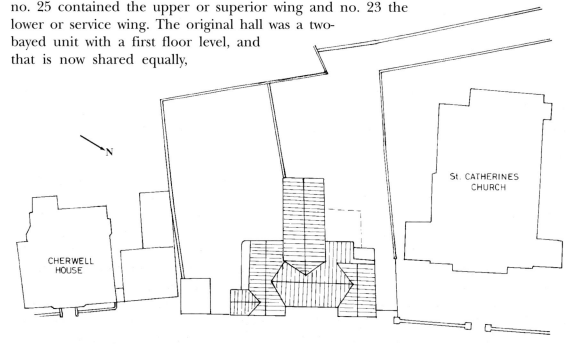

The site plan also showing the roof plan of 23 & 25 Dodington

34

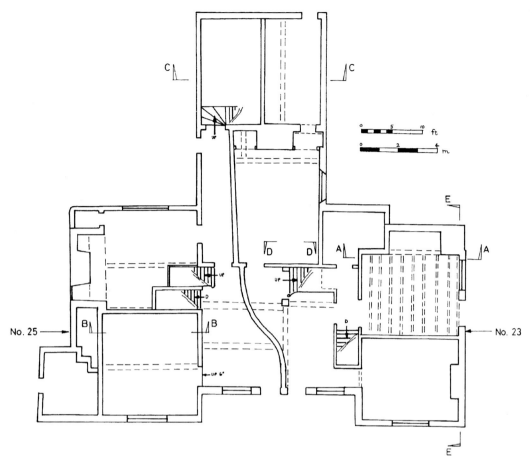

Ground floor plan

but there is no indication of where the original entrance was located or how the hall was heated. Within the roof space there is evidence of piecemeal redevelopment of the block as a whole as well as the anticipated differences between the two wings.

The Building Sequence

Presumably there was a house on the site before the present structure, but nothing remains of this. Visible only from the roof space there is a gap of *c*.1ft. 4ins. between the north wall of the crosswing of no. 25 and the start of the hall unit. Lower down the gap is masked by coving which appears as a feature in no. 25, but it is clear that the crosswing stood as a detached unit at some time, though not for very long. There seems to be a slight amount of weathering on the framing and there is flush-jointing on the northern face. In addition the purlins and the roof ridge relating to the hall range extend in a random fashion into the 'air space' of the crosswing, suggesting that the earlier house was replaced from the southern end, beginning with the crosswing at the upper end. Then presumably there was a hiatus before the remainder of the earlier house was taken down and the hall and the lower crosswing were completed. There can be little doubt that the hall and lower crosswing were erected in one phase as the junction is not marked by a gap and the southern wall of the crosswing does double duty as the north wall of the hall.

Although the roof trusses have much in common there are subtle differences which seem to distinguish the upper and lower wings:

Upper Wing (in no. 25)	Lower Wing (in no. 23)
Intermediate trusses divide space into 4 half-bays	No intermediate trusses
No Ridge Purlin	Ridge Purlin
Windbraces tenoned at both ends	Windbraces cross on back of principal rafters
Collar is slightly cambered	Collar is straight
Purlins are threaded	Purlins are trenched
Has single and double pegging	Has single, double and triple pegging
Principal rafters are 10ins. wide	Principal rafters are 1ft. 2ins. wide
Ovolo moulded beam in front room	Plain chamfered beam in front room
Panelling in front room	No panelling in front room

It may be thought that the pattern of the pegging and the difference in the scantling of the principal rafters argue against the hypothesis, but most of the points made support it. There is very little difference in the overall pattern of the roof trusses. With the exception of the intermediate trusses in the upper wing and those over the hall they are all closed trusses, each consisting of a tie-beam, collar-beam and two queen-struts, and are filled with wattle and daub. The windbraces are straight and are present in each unit, the only difference being that in the wing at the lower end they are simply crossed on the backs of the principal rafters though tenoned into the soffit of the purlins like the others (see illustration on p.38).

There is no smoke-blackening on any of the roof timbers, and while the crosswings would be heated from chimneystacks located much as they are at present, the hall and the chamber above it have no evidence of a stack. However, there could have been an external stack against the rear wall, which would have been taken down when the present large rear wing was built. In the upper level of no. 25 the remains of a panelled plaster ceiling, which, although probably of 18th century date, echoes the importance of the 'great chamber'.

In addition to the introduction of the hall staircase with its pillared approach and the plasterwork described above, remodelling in the 18th century included panelling the ground floor room of no. 25 and adding the large two-storied rear wing. No. 25 has two

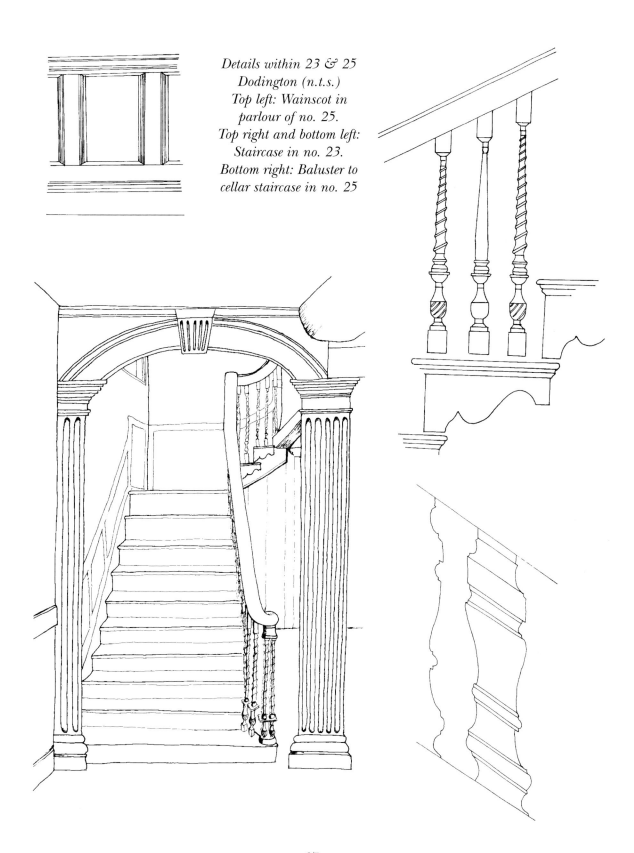

Details within 23 & 25 Dodington (n.t.s.)
Top left: Wainscot in parlour of no. 25.
Top right and bottom left: Staircase in no. 23.
Bottom right: Baluster to cellar staircase in no. 25

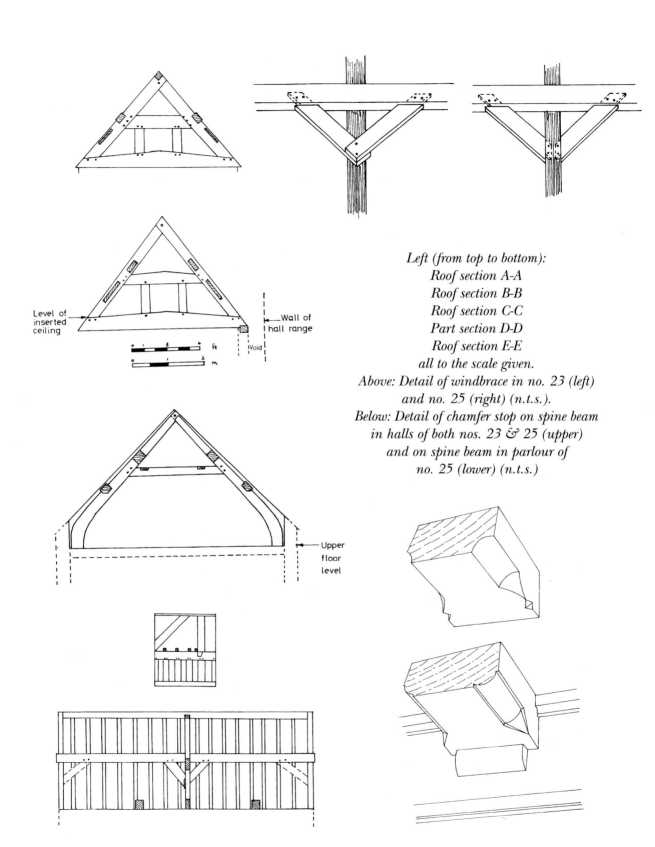

Left (from top to bottom):
Roof section A-A
Roof section B-B
Roof section C-C
Part section D-D
Roof section E-E
all to the scale given.
Above: Detail of windbrace in no. 23 (left)
and no. 25 (right) (n.t.s.).
Below: Detail of chamfer stop on spine beam
in halls of both nos. 23 & 25 (upper)
and on spine beam in parlour of
no. 25 (lower) (n.t.s.)

Level of
inserted
ceiling

Wall of
hall range

Void

ft

m

Upper
floor
level

further 'status symbols', an extension southwards of the front elevation, complete with its mock timbering, which at present houses the heating boiler at ground level and provides a small ante-room to the chamber above, and a brick-built heated tack-room at the end of the rear extension which has an unheated chamber above it containing a roof truss of upper crucks.

Conclusions, dating and historical note

When it became clear that nos. 23 and 25 Dodington were originally one house and that the building sequence could be established, the interpretation of the site became much easier. The structural form and details, as described above, suggest that rebuilding began *c*.1550 and was probably finished by *c*.1570. There is surprisingly little evidence of the re-use of timbers, and none at all in the main trusses. The impression is one of striving for the latest fashion, for example in the two-storied hall, up-to-date heating arrangements and privacy within the house. The house seems to have had a major remodelling in the late 18th century when the hall was given its prestigious staircase and another in the 19th century when the mock timbering was applied. An old illustration, prior to 1836, shows no. 23 with a mixture of herringbone work, close studding and rectangular framing on the front. This is probably the pattern of the original 16th century work, the use of herringbone work emphasising the up-to-date thinking of the builders.[3] In the winter of 1992 some plasterwork on the front of no. 23 fell away revealing earlier timbers 9ins. behind the mock framing.

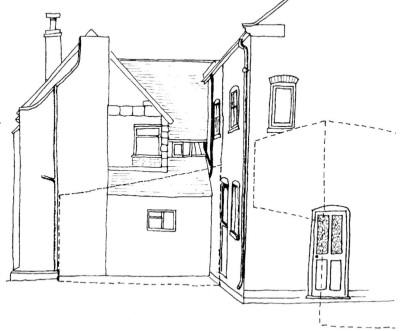

In 1255 the lord of the manor of Dodington was Ralph de Botiler and in 1261 his son William married Ankaret, a niece of James de Audley. Ralph gave the young couple the manor of Dodington as a wedding present, but the king, as overlord, levied an annual token rent on William of a 'mutilated' goshawk.[4] Their house may have been the predecessor of the present property.

As mentioned earlier, the house was divided between 1861 and 1871. St. Catherine's church

West elevation of no. 23 (n.t.s.)

had been built on the adjoining plot in 1836 and the rector's curate occupied the house *c*.1860.[5] The census returns show that in 1851 John F. Wood, described as a 'landed proprietor', his wife, their daughter and three servants were in occupation, and in 1861 Thomas H. Urry, a solicitor, his wife, their six children and one servant were in residence. In 1871 the occupiers of the two houses were Mary Groom, a widowed landowner and her servant in no. 23, and William E. Jones, a solicitor's clerk and his servant in no. 25.

Ellesmere House, 28 Dodington

Ellesmere House stands on the eastern side of Dodington opposite to the large 18th century house known as 'The Mansion House'. It takes it names from its connections with the Bridgwater estate, members of which family were great landowners in north Shropshire. Their successors, the titled family of Brownlow, were benefactors to Ellesmere, particularly in the mid-19th century, and it is thought that Lord Brownlow's agent occupied Ellesmere House at that time. Like its classical neighbour, Ellesmere House has a five-bay frontage, but its proportions are more modest and it has only two stories, although full use is made of the roof space. It is earlier in date than 'The Mansion House', and is something of a rare phenomenon in a town: a relatively unspoilt example of a building genre, in this instance of the crucial transitional period when timber-framing was on its way out, but houses built entirely of brick were not common. The compromise as shown here could not be more clear. The suggested date is within the early decades of the 18th century. There is no evidence of an earlier building on the site, and part of its contribution to the building history of Whitchurch is its relatively unaltered form.

The Exterior

In about 1930 the front elevation was stuccoed in an attempt to combat penetrating damp, but an old illustration shows a brick plinth, about 5ft. high, above which is a fully timber-framed frontage. When, from time to time, pieces of stucco become dislodged, this framework again became visible. The style of the framework is consistent with that of the late stages of the technique when it had passed through the flamboyant and highly decorative phases and returned to

The front elevation as it is today

Dodington in c.1830 from a lithograph by W. Crane.
Ellesmere House is the timbered building on the right

a purer and simpler form. Two dormer windows are shown on the old drawing, but these were removed and the attics then relied mostly on artificial light. In the roof space there was found structural evidence for a third dormer window which would contribute to a more balanced front elevation, and this is how the house has subsequently been restored.

The rear elevation retains its framework, and although later extensions obscure much of it, a pattern of plain rectangular panels is discernible at the upper level. This contrasts with the relatively close-set timbers on the front, and illustrates how the practice of using expensive timbering on the front, where it would be seen, and more economical work at the back continued in favour to the end of timber-framing itself. Of the extensions, the largest consists of a complete two-storied brick-built wing, and there are two smaller ones, an extension to the present kitchen and a small tower-like structure which provides a rear porch and facilitates access to the rear wing at the upper level.

Both gable walls are brick-built and show no sign of ever having been timber-framed. Gable stacks are incorporated on either side, that on the northern side is much larger than its counterpart and it seems likely that it served the original kitchen, while the smaller one on the southern side served a small front parlour.

The Interior
The plan of Ellesmere House is very simple. A central entrance gives access to a hall from which a quarter-turn staircase rises. To the right of the entrance, that is, on the southern side, are two rooms: a small front parlour with a larger dining room behind it. On the opposite side the original kitchen occupied all the space. This was later sub-divided into two rooms but has now been restored to its original size.

Ellesmere House

Top left: Front elevation when plastered over in 1930.
Top right: Front elevation as shown on 1830 lithograph.
Middle left: E. elevation.
Middle right: N. elevation.
Lower left: Ground floor plan.
Lower right: Cellar plan

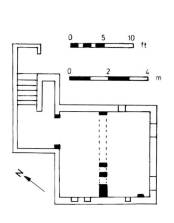

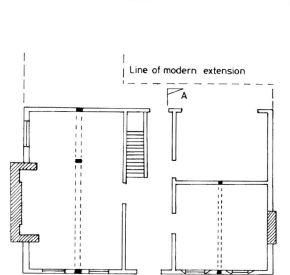

Line of modern extension

A

At first-floor level there are bedrooms above the ground-floor rooms, but the staircase continues and gives access to the attic rooms.

The oak staircase, though not as elaborate as some in Whitchurch, is well-carpentered and has turned balusters set between a wide handrail and a string. There is a square newel-post, modestly carved, and the treads are all of polished oak. Where the ascent changes to the attic flight the form of the balusters changes to shaped flat examples of a more old-fashioned and less expensive form.

All the internal partitions are timber-framed, and the modern practice of uncovering suspected framing has exposed much of it. The combination of irregularity and highly eccentric jointing on some of the timbers reinforces the point that such framework was never intended to be seen and would have been decently obscured with plaster.

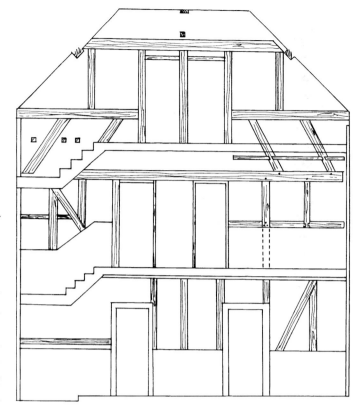

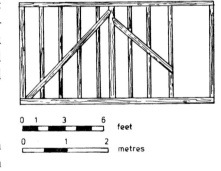

0 1 3 6 feet

0 1 2 metres

*Above:
Section A - A
Left: Partition
in Garret*

The Kitchen Sequence

As mentioned above, the large stack on the northern side serves a room containing a fireplace which seems to have been designed for cooking. Its high jambs and mantel-beam and the deep inglenook suggest that this room was the original kitchen. Its function changed when the large brick wing, accommodating a kitchen at ground level, was added at the rear. This arrangement, in turn, was superceded when the original dining room was extended and given an enlarged fireplace to serve as the kitchen.

When the original kitchen became a sitting-room it was panelled to within 1ft. of the ceiling, but all the panelling and most of the plasterwork has been removed. A scarf joint on the spine-beam has failed and is at present supported by a cast-iron post and a wooden pad.

44

The Small Parlour

This room, to the south of the hall, faces Dodington and is the least changed. If not contemporary with the building, it was probably fitted out about 1730-40 and is fully panelled in a style incorporating square panels surmounted by larger rectangular ones, the two divided by a dado rail which does not project. All the panels are slightly raised and fielded and have carpenters' mitres at each corner; whilst a moulded plaster cornice completes the wall treatment. The room is fitted with a corner cupboard with open shelves for the display of porcelain; and the panelled door with its angle-hinges is also likely to be a contemporary feature. The fireplace, however, is in the 'Adam' style and is probably a replacement of *c.*1800. A homely touch is imparted by the error in the fitting of the decorative tiles in the cheeks of the fireplace. Like the single baluster, they are upside-down.

Sketch showing the turned balusters on the ground floor staircase

The Attic Rooms

The strongest sense of family life remains at attic level where there is evidence for a safety gate on the stairs. There are four rooms, two on either side of the landing. One room retains its original panelled door. Another, perhaps that assigned to the housekeeper or the nanny, is furnished with a small fireplace. The partitions are free-standing wooden frames which were originally plastered over. Although they are not an integral part of the

The fireplace in the small parlour

*Sketch showing flat balusters
in the garret*

structure they could not be moved easily and were probably seen as an inexpensive way of sub-dividing the space. One has had the plaster removed. In the attic space two large horizontal beams appear about one foot above the floor level. In effect they provide additional tying and, by coincidence, a play feature for children. Similar beams were found in 23, Dodington, but they were not present in no. 25.

Recent History

Little is known about the early history of Ellesmere House. Throughout most of the 19th century it was used as a boarding school/seminary for young ladies. An advertisement in 1818 reads: 'The Miss Cooks respectfully inform their friends and the public that their school re-opens on Monday 27th instant. Terms: 25 guineas per annum. Parlour boarders 30 guineas per annum. A single lady may be accommodated with lodgings.'[1] In 1868 it was run by Miss Sophia Veale and later by two sisters, the misses Mary and Jane Hindmarsh.[2] In 1894 Miss Ada Keitley took over and continued to run the school at Ellesmere House until, sometime between 1902 and 1905, she moved to the Mansion House opposite. Here she had larger premises and could offer more extensive boarding facilities. Born in 1862, she had been privately educated at a school near Paris, but 'had not been allowed to sit for examinations on account of delicate health.' At the Mansion House she added a preparatory form for boys and in 1904 sold the establishment to Salop County Council who continued to employ her as headmistress of Whitchurch Girls' High School as it became.[3]

In about 1929 Ellesmere House was bought by Mr. Gerald Hoban, M.R.C.V.S. who added a surgery, since demolished, at the end of the drive on the northern side. At that time the original kitchen had been subdivided and he used the smaller rear part as a dispensary and had an access door inserted into the north wall. The front part of the room was used as a sitting-room and the kitchen was housed in the large brick extension. Mr. Hoban was responsible for plastering the front elevation and he painted the panelling in the sitting-room a cream shade to lighten the effect. In 1949, after her husband's death, Mrs. Hoban sold the house and the practice. Apart from removing the panelling in the hall and in the original kitchen and exposing timbers which have more structural interest than aesthetic appeal, subsequent owners have shown care and respect for this building, and it continues to add dignity to the townscape, unlike the unfortunate Mansion House, opposite.[4]

The Mansion House, 21 Dodington

The Mansion House in Dodington is an early 18th century house of double-pile plan form. With good reason it has been described as 'the most ambitious private house at Whitchurch.'[1] When the late Nikolaus Pevsner saw it in the 1950s it had already suffered severe abuse, and the wings had been reduced to single-storied structures. But worse was to follow when it became a short-lived supermarket; the ground floor was gutted, the roof removed and replaced with a flat one, the ground-floor windows, which had been enlarged in the 1930s, were replaced with large commercial lights, the staircase was mutilated and the fireplaces destroyed. At present it stands violated and empty. But there is sufficient evidence to reconstruct the front elevation, details of the staircase and the plan at first floor level. Other features relating to its former elegance are illustrated.

The Front Elevation

Brick built, three stories high and five bays wide, the house has stone quoins and window dressings, a plain brick modillion eaves cornice and a full length parapet. Emphasis is given to the central bay in the form of a projection in the brickwork, a triangular pediment, consoles to the windows which have eared and decorated surrounds, and another triangular pediment to the doorway. The doorcase itself may not be original. Witness marks on the brickwork suggest that it was larger and that the pediment had a canopy of some kind which reached the soffit of the window sill above. Although the present doorcase is enriched and has carved brackets supporting the pediment, the impression is that of a slightly debased feature, and this is extended to the door itself and to the fanlight. The flat-headed sash windows are set into the normal recess of brickwork and have keystones

The front, or east elevation of the Mansion House today

47

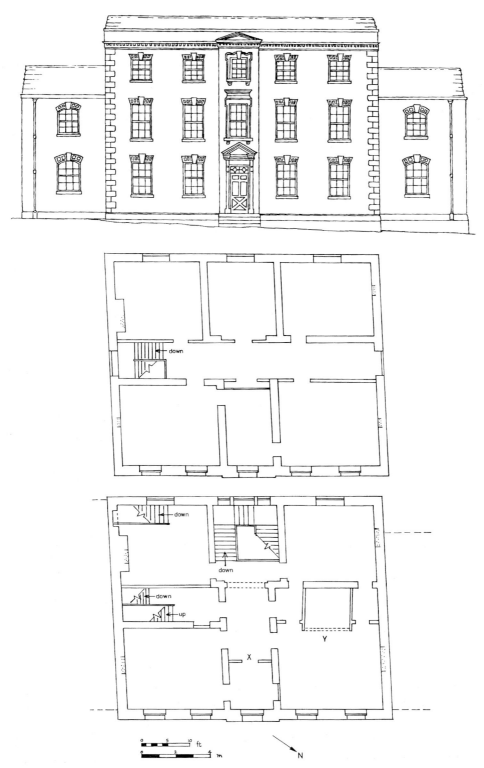

The first floor plan (above) and second floor plan (centre) both based the R.C.H.M. survey carried out in 1991, together with the east elevation as it was in 1905 (top)

48

Carving on stair tread ends

and raised voussoirs. Only the windows on the top floor retain their original lights; when the building was recorded those on the ground floor related to the supermarket era (since replaced), and those on the middle floor have Victorian-style glazing bars giving four lights instead of the original twelve.

On either side of the main block were two-storied wings which presumably provided service rooms. During the change to commercial use these were reduced to single-storey ranges. There are traces on the side walls of the main block, indicative of their original height and form.[2]

The Interior

It was impossible to reconstruct the plan at ground level, but the structural divisions on the first floor suggest that the arrangements on both floors were similar and that the ground floor would have accommodated a drawing-room and a dining-room at the front and a small parlour and perhaps a study at the rear. Of the four chimneystacks only that to the south-west projects into the body of the house, suggesting that the kitchen was housed in the south wing.

Considering the treatment that the property suffered under commercial enterprises, it is amazing that the imposing archway to the staircase survives at all, but it is relatively intact with decorative plasterwork on the soffit of the arch. Most of the components of the open-well staircase were found lying in an upper room, and after much patient fitting together of the parts the pattern emerged. As originally designed each tread had three turned balusters and the tread-ends were carved with a design of flower-head and acanthus leaf foliage. The bottom step had ten balusters curving round the newel post. The handrail was wide,

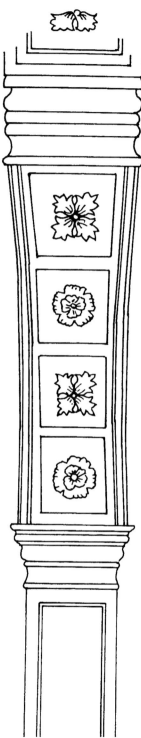

Detail of arch soffit in hall (n.t.s.)

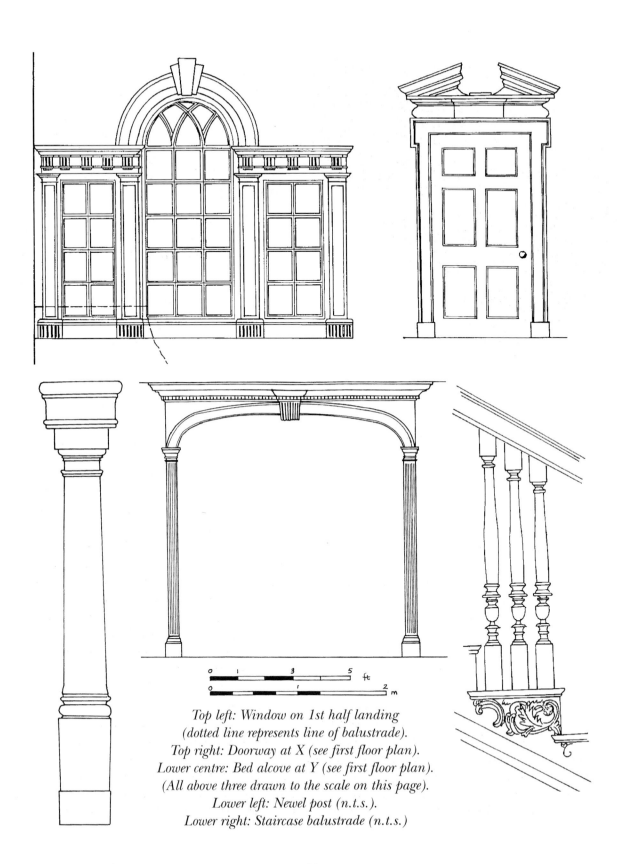

Top left: Window on 1st half landing
(dotted line represents line of balustrade).
Top right: Doorway at X (see first floor plan).
Lower centre: Bed alcove at Y (see first floor plan).
(All above three drawn to the scale on this page).
Lower left: Newel post (n.t.s.).
Lower right: Staircase balustrade (n.t.s.)

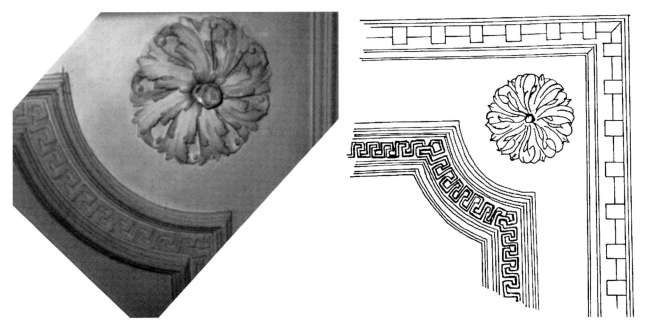

Detail of plaster ceiling on the landing

moulded and ramped, matching the ramping on the panelled dado on the wall. At the turn of the stairs a second ramping to the dado obscures some of the features of the Venetian window which lights the staircase. This suggests that either the dado is an added feature or that the Venetian window replaced a smaller window, probably of the type postulated for the front elevation. The latter seems to be the most likely solution. Such a large staircase would require a lot of light, and an ordinary twelve-light sash window would hardly be adequate. The Venetian window would also provide a fashionable up-market feature. It occupies virtually all the available wall-space at landing level.

The first floor contains more features relating to the age of elegance. The ceiling over the landing has a moulded plaster cornice, a central panel with a Greek key surround and medallions in each corner; the doorcase to the small room over the front door, presumably a dressing room to the south-eastern bedroom, has an eared surround and a broken pediment, and there is an open-fronted cupboard on the north wall of the room containing typical 18th century shaped shelving. The north-eastern bedroom has a bed recess enclosed on three sides with an arched and pillared entrance. Free access to the bedroom behind is from closets on either side of the bed recess; the closet on the south side also afforded a secondary access onto the landing. From the walls of this closet a piece of wine-coloured flock wallpaper with hand-painted inserts was recovered.

Between the south-east and the south-west bedrooms is a corridor which houses the service stairway. The flight from ground level has been destroyed, but the flight giving access to the second floor remains. At this level are six further rooms approached from a central corridor aligned north-south. Four are heated, the central two on either side of the corridor are the only unheated rooms in the house, and these probably served as store-rooms. Part of the central room on the eastern side is partitioned off to serve as a linen cupboard.

51

The Cellar

Access to the cellar is from a door at the rear of the hall, below the second flight of the stairs. The cellar occupies the space below the hall area and the northern wing. It is entirely brick-built, vaulted and divided into compartments, the central compartment retaining evidence of a hoist.

The Garden

Nothing remains of the original garden lay-out, and three large iron sheds occupy the space. These have been attributed to the supermarket era,[3] but in fact were installed c.1913 when W.H. Smith & Co acquired the Mansion House and altered it to accommodate a petrol station and workshops. As Smith's were the leading ironfounders and engineers in north Shropshire and their catalogue specifies such structures, it is reasonable to conclude that they date from that time.[4]

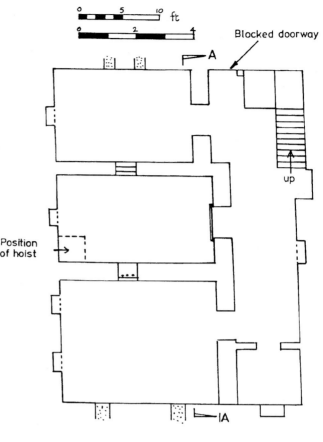

Plan of the cellar

Social History[5]

Nothing is known of the early history of the building, but a description of it in 1798 is worth quoting in full:[6]

'TO LET - An elegant house in Whitchurch in the part called Dodington, late in the occupation of William Bulkeley Esq., (deceased) consisting of:- A spacious hall, 2 parlours,

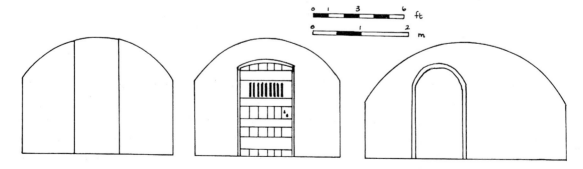

Section A-A through the cellar

a drawing room, kitchen, servants' hall, Butler's pantry and china pantry. Four handsome lodging rooms with a closet to each on 2nd. floor. 5 ditto in attick storey with a nursery and laundry; 3 cellars and 2 wine vaults arched with bricks; a brewhouse, a milkhouse, 4 stall stable, coach-house, granary and feed; pleasure garden, a farmyard, 3 stall stable, a barn containing 4 bays and threshing floor, a cowhouse, Dovehouse and several compact conveniences.' From this it is clear that the Mansion House was also a working farm, and the layout of the buildings and their approach from Rosemary Lane is shown on the 1880 OS Map.

William Bulkeley had insured his property with the Salop Fire Office for £900, with an additional £100 for the adjoining stable, for a period of seven years at a premium of £7, which, with a discount of one guinea totalled £5 19s. After his death in December 1790 his widow, Lucy Bulkeley took over the interest in the property, but in March 1793 the insurance was transferred to his sister, Mrs. Elizabeth Turton.[7] She was the widow of William Turton of Knolton Hall in Flintshire. She died in 1797 and her memorial is in Whitchurch parish church. It records that she left '£1,000 and upwards to be placed at interest for the benefit of such poor widows, poor housekeepers and other poor persons belonging to this parish ...' After her death a sale notice of her effects reads: 'All that elegant household furniture, books and other effects ... consisting of a handsome four-poster bed (mahogoney) with fluted pillars and crimson damask furniture and other good bedding. A table service of Blue and White Nankeen China. An elegant post-chaise and pair of horses; a cabriole, - a harpsichord - an 8-day clock and kitchen furniture. Catalogues will be left in time at the White Lion.'[8] The inclusion of the four-poster bed has a direct bearing on the bed alcove noted in the main bedroom. The Bulkeleys and the Turtons were clearly families of means—the Bulkeleys were apothecaries and owned property in The Bull Ring, and William Turton was steward of the manor for the Duke of Bridgwater.

The next recorded occupants are William Wycherley Brookes and his wife Theodosia (née Lee), a descendant of Philip Henry. They were married in Malpas on August 10th 1812 and are said by a descendant to have 'occupied that comfortable Georgian house in Dodington next to the church, later a school, now, alas, turned into a garage.'[9] W.W. Brookes, a solicitor and member of a prosperous family with local connections traceable to the late 16th century, was the great-grandfather of the late H.W. Brookes Richards, a recent benefactor of the town.

Theodosia died in 1835, pre-deceasing her husband, and it is possible that he left the Mansion House soon afterwards as George Downward, clerk, with his wife, six children, their governess and five servants are recorded as occupants in 1841.[10] The Misses Martha and Mary Turner, sisters of the Whitchurch architect Samuel Turner, followed the Downward family from 1842-9.[11]

Directories and census returns show that the house then had a rapid turnover of tenants until about 1900 when it was taken over by Miss Ada Keitley for her private school for young ladies, offering more extensive boarding facilities than Ellesmere House, opposite, where Miss Keitley had run a similar establishment. In 1904 her school was bought by Shropshire County Council and became Whitchurch Girls' High School, remaining at the Mansion House with Miss Keitley as headmistress before moving to new premises in Salisbury Road in 1912.[12]

This was a turning-point in the fortunes of the house. From that point its decline was consistent. Bought by W.H. Smith & Co, ironfounders and engineers, it became a petrol station, garage and workshops, the first in Whitchurch. Petrol pumps were installed on the pavement,[13] the ground floor was converted to offices and stores and, as mentioned above, three large corrugated iron sheds were erected in the gardens. These served as the workshops, and the south wing was gutted to provide an entrance into them. An inspection pit was installed in the north wing and it is probable that both wings were converted to single-storey units at this time. What remained of the gardens and the farm was later sold to Whitchurch Urban District Council who, in 1928, built council houses fronting onto Rosemary Lane.

In 1961 the garage closed and, after standing empty for a time, the complex was taken over by Kwiksave and converted into a supermarket. At this time the ground floor windows were replaced with the present large commercial ones.

The Mansion House has recently been restored by a local builder who has converted the building into three flats and restored the ground-floor fenestration. This offers hope that the years of neglect, indifference and sheer bad planning decisions are over and that 'The most ambitious house in Whitchurch' will once more have a semblance of its former dignity.

7 Dodington (The Olde House)

As shown on the OS map of 1880 the Olde House is built around three sides of a court-yard, with the entrance from a passageway on the south side. However, this is a misleading impression as both ranges which enclose the courtyard are later extensions and the street-facing range is a self-contained unit with access directly from the street. The main block consists of a simple two-storied range, with the roof space fully used and lit by two dormer windows. Only this part has been recorded, and while it is possible that the courtyard buildings perpetuate an earlier lay-out, they have not been included in the present account as they are structurally later.

The Olde House was recorded for two main reasons: firstly it provides a good example of what is a rare phenomenon in modern times—a relatively unspoilt mid-17th century box-framed town house of modest proportions, and secondly its social history is closely linked with the nonconformist movement and with the Henry family, one-time residents of Dodington House.

7 Dodington,
the south and east elevations

The Timber-Framing

The pattern of timbering on the exterior consists of small rectangles on the front and square framing on the side wall. However, only part of the tie-beam on the side wall is an original timber, the remainder are facsimile timbers of cement rendered to imitate weathered timbers and later painted black. With the peg-holes also repre-sented and the surface painted black and white, the effect of weathered timbers is remarkably accurate.[1] At the Olde House the fake timbers appear to perpetuate the design of the original box-framing. The rear eleva-tion displays genuine square framing, and is exposed internally on the northern wall. The same pattern is visible internally on the southern wall.

55

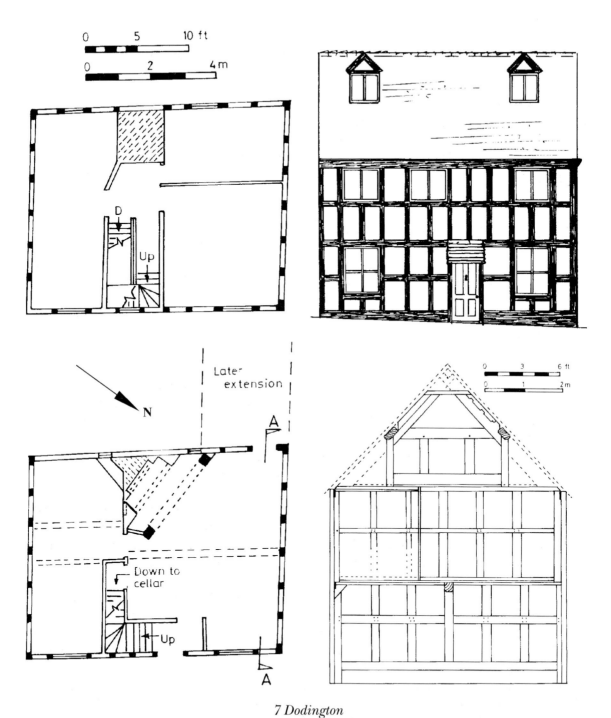

7 Dodington
Plans of the ground floor (lower left), first floor (top left) and a drawing of the east elevation
(top right) all to the scale top left, and of the section A - A (lower right) to its own scale

The Plan

The plan of the Olde House is a simple arrangement of two rooms at each floor level. The staircase, which appears to be unaltered, is immediately to the left of the entrance; and the chimneystack which forms a prominent feature on the rear elevation provides corner fire-places for each of the ground-floor rooms and two lateral ones above. The attic rooms are unheated and are lit by dormer windows high in the roof.

At ground-floor level the northern room, the larger of the two, was originally a 'house-place', that is, the main living room where cooking was also done. In this room the corner fireplace has had two extensions and now contains a deep inglenook. This is in contrast to the parlour fireplace in the southern room which retains its original proportions. Below the parlour is a cellar, a later addition, access to which is from the doorway to the left of the inglenook.

The Social History[2]

Among the deeds of the house is an 1848 Abstract of Title, which refers to an Indenture dated 25th and 26th September 1762. In this the owner is given as Francis Egerton, Duke of Bridgwater and, among other things, lord of the manor of Dodington. His copyhold tenant in 1762 was Thomas Yate and by the Indenture an outright sale of the property to Yate is effected for £78 13s 5d, the duke relinquishing all his manorial rights. The document specifies 'All that copyhold or Customary messuage or dwelling house with the chapel or meeting house standing near the same situate ... then in the occupation of the said Thomas Yate ...' The 'chapel or meeting house' is the erstwhile Presbyterian chapel which is located behind the Olde House and outside its present curtilage, and it is possible that the Yate family gave up part of their holding to enable the chapel to be built. A shared interest in Presbyterianism formed a link between the Henry family at Dodington House and the Yates at the Olde House, and this was further strengthened when Dr. Samuel Bennion, who succeeded Philip Henry, married Grace Yate, a daughter of Thomas Yate of Dearnford in 1703. Samuel had lived with the Henrys in 1691, 'teaching some Gentlemens' sons'.[3]

The congregation founded by Philip Henry at Broad Oak built the first dissenters' chapel in Dodington.[4] This was for Presbyterians and was opened for worship on 13th September 1707. In July 1715 the building was destroyed by High Church rioters, and in 1717 the present building was erected on the same site at government expense. It continued to be used for worship until 1844, but before then there had been a splinter movement which had set up a Congregational church on the opposite side of the road. The Presbyterian label had become 'Unitarian' in 1798.[5] The Dodington Presbyterians were an extremely wealthy and important society. In about 1720 the congregation numbered 300, of whom 30 were county voters, six were gentlemen, 30 were tradesmen, 44 were farmers and 20 were yeomen.[6]

After 1844 the history of the chapel building behind the Olde House was at times bizarre. First a British School, it became a private school for boys until it was sold for £161 in 1891.[7] Since then it has been a builders' store, a ballroom, a music hall, a forces' canteen and a furniture repository. Stripped of all its ecclesiastical fittings it has a forlorn appearance which ill befits the oldest nonconformist chapel in the town.

Thomas Yate died in October 1765, aged 93. He was, therefore, in his 30s when the chapel was built. In the documents he is referred to as 'Thomas Yate of Dodington' to distinguish him from his cousin Thomas Yate of Dearnford Hall on the Tilstock road.

Twenty-three brasses were installed in the chapel. They have since been removed to the Congregational (United Reformed) Church. Included in the collection are those of Thomas Yate and his wife Lydia, their son John and his wife Constance, and their grand-daughters, Constance Mary and Anna.[8]

Among the deeds of the Olde House are some which reflect the comparative wealth and social standing of the Yate family, and others which raise more questions than they answer. Encompassing both categories is the will of John Yate (Thomas's son) who died in 1775. He left all his property including the house in Dodington and his 'two pews in the north aisle of the parish church in Whitchurch marked no. 3 and no. 28' to his wife Constance, with other bequests to his daughter Lydia, her son Thomas Yate Keay and her two daughters Lydia and Katherine. He also left one guinea apiece to 21 relatives 'for a ring' and £5 each to four near relatives 'for mourning'. Though the pews were in the parish church, and not the chapel, they would have been attached to the property and so had a value.

In February 1803 John's grand-daughters were involved in the sale of the house to Elizabeth Jenkins, a widow, for £400. But the deed states that 'The property had been occupied as 3 dwelling houses by John Holt, Thomas Allinson, and Thomas Burrows and was then occupied [at the time of sale] by Mary Jenkins, the Rev. Thos. Jenkins and Robt. Porah.' It is difficult to imagine the Olde House divided into three dwellings, but perhaps the wording is describing a succession of tenants. Thomas Jenkins may have been a minister at the chapel.

Mary Jenkins was clearly a lady of substance. In 1803 she left her four dwelling houses, four stables and three gardens in Dodington to her late husband's daughter, Betty Banks. Presumably Betty was her step-daughter.

In 1804 more numbered pews in the parish church are mentioned when the 'two sitting or kneeling positions in the parish church of Whitchurch in the third pew from the front in the Organ Gallery, then or late in the holding of Mary Jenkins' were sold for 5 guineas.

Before her marriage to Richard Thomas, a baker, but 'with his consent and approbation' Betty Banks sold two of the houses in Dodington to W. Batho, a shoemaker, and Joseph Everall, a grocer. Included in the sale were the two places in the organ gallery of the church. However, this document, dated 1st and 3rd January 1825, is puzzling. The only sum mentioned is 10s, and the property seems to have remained with Betty Thomas, passing later to her husband.

In 1843 Richard Thomas mortgaged three properties to John Barlow, a cabinet maker, paying him a peppercorn rent for the privilege, and in 1846 he sold the Olde House to Daniel Sumner. The indenture included the right of William Smith, a builder, to half use of the well pump on the property. William Smith was the founder of the well-known Whitchurch firm of ironfounders, W.H. Smith & Co.

Thereafter the Olde House's fortunes declined until modern times when sympathetic owners have made it into a most attractive home, at the same time respecting its age, history and structural form.

6, 8 and 10 Dodington

These three cottages, on the eastern side of Dodington as it approaches Watergate, have a continuous eaves level which is lower than that of the adjoining property to the north. No. 6 has a brick front, but nos. 8 and 10 have facsimile timbers (consisting of cement rendered to imitate weathered timbers and later painted black) on the front giving the appearance of a square-framed 17th century range. However, internal inspection revealed that the entire block is basically timber-framed. In 1978 the row was in a dilapidated state and its future was uncertain. However, it was discovered that no. 6 contained a complete cruck truss and the possible remains of three others, and it was, perhaps, this feature which ensured the survival of the block. The decision to retain it was a complete reversal of the ruthless 'slum clearance' policy which had destroyed many other cruck cottages in Whitchurch in the immediate post World War Two period, and, on this account, some relief was felt. In 1992, when no. 8 came on the market, the opportunity was taken to record the block in detail, and it was found that the cruck truss had since been plastered over in no. 6 but was exposed in no. 8. Unfortunately, the stylobate, noted in 1978, had either been removed or is concealed behind false walling.

It was hoped that, by taking a comprehensive look at the block, a plan would emerge, either of a complete medieval house or of a terrace of single-cell cruck dwellings, similar to that in Barrow Street, Much Wenlock.[1] But this was not to be. Truss 'A' was the only cruck truss in the block to survive in anything approaching a complete form. It appeared to have had a matching truss *c*.16ft. to the south of it, now forming the partition between nos. 8 and 10 and largely obscured by the chimneystack. In two further trusses, those shown as part-section B - B and that which relates to the partition behind the chimneystack in

Nos. 6, 8 and 10 Dodington

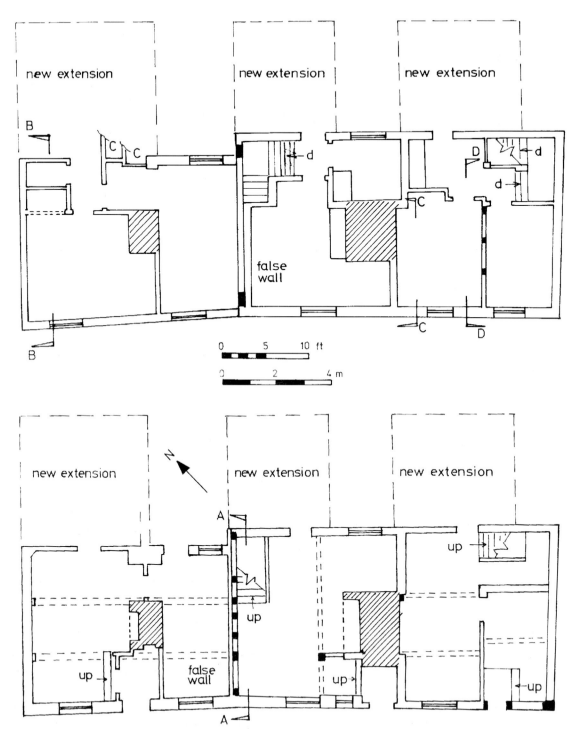

new extension

new extension

new extension

B

C C

d

D d

d

false
wall

C

C

D

0 5 10 ft

0 2 4 m

B

N

new extension

new extension

new extension

A

up

up

up

false
wall

up

up

A

Nos. 6, 8 and 10 Dodington
Lower: Ground floor plans. Top: First floor plans

no. 6, the principals taper towards the top and carry a cruck-type apex, although this is different from the type noted on A - A.[2] There were no indications of cruck construction in no. 10. The disposition of the internal trusses does not easily relate to a traditional plan-form, and while it seems probable that the cruck elements survive from an earlier building on the site, this is by no means certain, and the whole block may be the result of a speculator putting up a row of cottages using whatever second-hand timber was to hand.

Nevertheless, the block has some interesting features and, as far as is known, truss 'A' is the only full cruck truss to survive within the town. There can be no doubt that it was a closed truss. The studs below the tie-beam are all properly morticed, tenoned and pegged, and in 1978 it was noticed that the panels above the tie-beam were filled with wattle and daub and plastered over, as are those in the matching truss. No smoke-blackening was present on either truss.

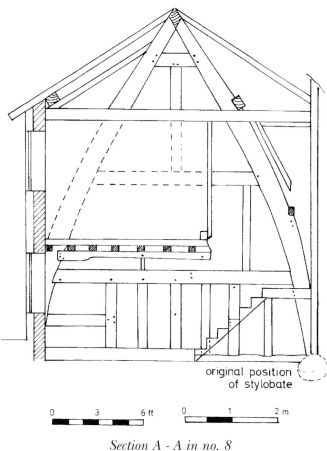

Section A - A in no. 8

The angle of the roof does not follow the backs of the cruck blades, and neither does it follow that of the principals in the end frames. As the photograph shows, the front wall of the block has been raised in order to accommodate an upper storey. This is common practice, especially in towns.

As mentioned above, the frontages of nos. 8 and 10 are misleading. They appear to display 17th century square-framing, five panels high, but the wall itself is of brick and the 'timbers' are fake. The 'weathering' effect to the cement was given by means of a block of wood through which uneven rows of nails were driven and a leather strap attached for the hand. When dragged along the cement base, the nails created the effect of weathered wood graining. The result is realistic and there are several examples of the technique in Whitchurch and in north Shropshire generally.[3]

Stylobates or padstones, the stone blocks supporting the feet of crucks or main posts and into which they were sometimes tenoned, are not common in timber-framing in Shropshire. It is more usual to find the timbers tenoned into a sill-beam. But they have been noted at Ash Wood, and one may be present in Manor Cottage, Prees, both the subject of chapters in this book. They seem to be a feature associated with crucks in Lancashire and Cheshire, the most spectacular examples being those in the Hall Barn at Rivington in Lancashire. Perhaps those in north Shropshire may be seen as a continuation of a trend which stopped at the river Severn.

In no. 10 the seemingly haphazard form of the framing in the trusses at upper floor level tends to support the theory that there is much re-used timber here, and the 'slumped' appearance of section C - C has nothing to do with subsidence but is the result of opportunism and the availability of redundant timbers. The inglenook fireplace in no.8 is an attractive feature, though brick-built and of no great age.

In conclusion, it was thought that nos. 6-10, Dodington was most likely to represent the remodelling of a cruck-framed range of some kind to provide three cottages, though at what date is uncertain. On balance, the consensus of opinion was that truss 'A', the cruck truss, represented a remnant from an on-site structure and was retained because it was in good condition, and that no. 10 was added as a complete dwelling, utilising redundant timbers. The cruck-like apexes in no. 6 are more problematical and may simply represent further re-cycling of material. The raising of

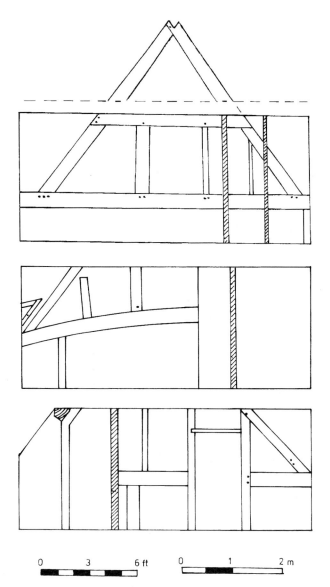

Top: Part section B - B in no. 6
Centre: Part section C - C in no. 10
Bottom: Part section D - D in no. 10

the roof at the front may have been part of the initial remodelling. Although the non-emergence of a comprehensible medieval building was disappointing, the exercise was useful in establishing later building practices, particularly that of re-cycling timbers, and for the modern fetish of having 'black-and-white at any price'.

Barkhill House, 28 Barkhill

Barkhill is a short street, off the west side of Dodington and connecting with Rosemary Lane. Barkhill House is at the south-western end of the street.

The Exterior

The house is basically three-bayed and two-storied, but full use is made of the attic space which contains three bedrooms, each lit by a dormer window. Two of the dormers are identical; the third is larger. The front elevation has a rough-cast cladding, but underneath it is timber-framed. The rear elevation is also timber-framed, but both gable walls are brick-built and contain integral chimneystacks. The front entrance is protected by a porch in which the canopy is supported by two thin reeded pilaster strips on the wall and two attenuated cast-iron columns of barley-twist form. Each of the casement windows on the front elevation has a wooden concave hood and is mullioned and transomed with two or three lights.

At first glance the front elevation appears to present a symmetrical appearance, but there are two elements which upset the balance. One is the enlarged dormer window at the north-eastern end and the other is the enclosure and extension of the space to the north-west of the outbuilt chimneystack. This extension rises to the full height of the house, and the front slope of the roof is designed to accommodate it. The moulded cornice is a continuous feature on the front. From internal evidence, it seems that the extension was an original feature.

The rear elevation is dominated by a large extension which was constructed in two phases, providing a modern kitchen and bedroom accommodation above. There is a rear entrance porch

Barkhill House

which has a small upper room with a cast-iron framed window. The room is supported on two cast-iron pillars. A modern conservatory to the south-west of the extension is a replacement for an older one. It is built around old vine roots. One corner of the extension has the angle rounded off in all-header bond brickwork to first storey height where an elaborate scroll-stop returns the brickwork to a right-angle. Clearly done to enhance the ambience of the conservatory, this detail is reminiscent of the improvements done at street corners under 19th century Street Improvement Acts.

The Interior

The plan of Barkhill House comprises a central entrance hall flanked by one large room on one side and two smaller rooms on the other. As such it is very similar to that of Ellesmere House in Dodington, with which it also shares other similarities. At Barkhill House corner fireplaces serve the two rooms on the north-eastern side. The smaller (front)

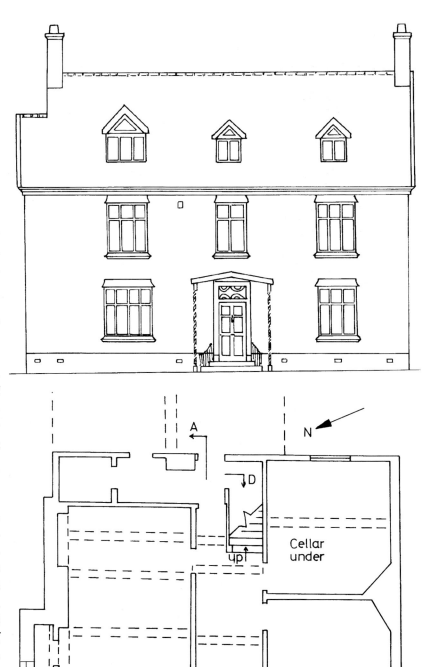

Barkhill House
Top: West elevation; below: Ground floor plan; both to the same scale as the cellar plan, at the top of the following page

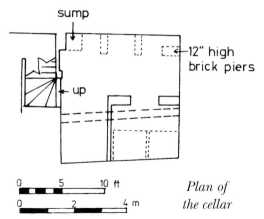

sump

←—12" high brick piers

up

0 5 10 ft

0 2 4 m

Plan of the cellar

room is a parlour, while the rear room, currently in use as a dining room, may always have served that purpose. It was clearly an important room, panelled through out in oak panelling to full room height and with a moulded cornice. Carpenters' mitres occur only on the top corners of the panels and there is a wheat-ear frieze. The overmantel has a large central panel flanked by two smaller panels, all raised and fielded and with bolection moulding. In contrast to the richness of the panelling the spine-beams are totally plain and have no chamfer-stops. The oak floorboards are, on average, 1ft. wide.

The large room on the south-western side may have served as the original kitchen, as was the case at Ellesmere House, although the fireplace at Barkhill House is smaller. To the south of the fireplace is the extension which contains a closet and causes the asymmetrical appearance of the front elevation. The spine-beams in the room are all boxed in, but they are not evenly spaced and one extends into the closet. This suggests that the extension is an original feature, as does the comparative thickness of the outer wall. A similar closet is provided in the room above, and both closets have a small window.

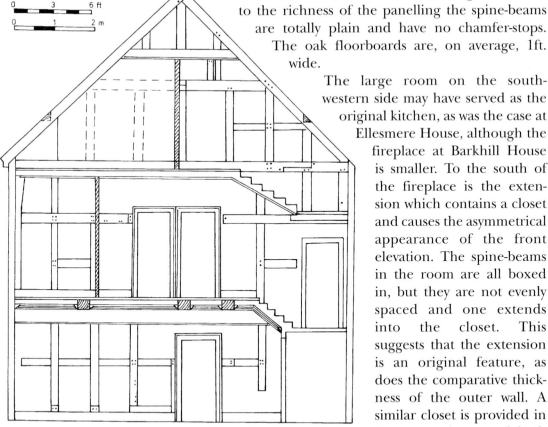

0 3 6 ft

0 1 2 m

Section A - A

The Staircase

Perhaps the outstanding feature of Barkhill House is the staircase. Of dog-leg form with winders and half-landings, it rises through two stories in a consistent fashion, having double-twisted open barley-sugar designed balusters between the string and the moulded hand-rail. The newel-posts are square and have moulded caps.

Other Features

All the internal partitions in Barkhill House are timber-framed and there is evidence that much of the framing is reused. Some of the carpenters' marks are of the crescent type, some are straightforward Roman numerals and others may best be described as idiosyncratic. A scarf-joint in the tie-beam visible from the half-landing on the top floor is edge-halved with two edge-pegs. The corner fireplace in the room above the panelled dining room

Corner fireplace in the south-east room on the ground floor

has an eared surround and appears to be an original fixture. The roof structure is unremarkable, but the use of a sturdy king-strut between the tie-beam and the apex of the principal rafters is interesting. It may be seen to compensate for the single pegging at the apex. There is no evidence of an earlier roof form. One enigmatic feature appears to the west of the doorway which gives access to the ground floor rear extension. Here, on what was originally the rear wall of the house the rail immediately below the level of the ceiling joins a timber set diagonally. The joint is reinforced with a crude iron strap and one peg is visible. Another may be concealed by the strap. The feature is strongly reminiscent of cruck construction, but it is the only indication that the house may incorporate the remains of an earlier structure on the site.

Summary, Discussion and Dating

Barkhill House and Ellesmere House are very similar in their form, size and construction. Both have front and rear walls and internal partitions of timber-framing while employing brick for the gable walls. The similarities even extend to the

Details of staircase

Left: the cellar stairs. Right: storage bins in the cellar

large rear extensions designed to house a kitchen with accommodation above. In each case the plan is similar, full use is made of the roof space and a cellar is located on the right-hand side of the plan. The main differences seem to lie in the use of corner fire-places, the superior quality of the staircase and in the provision of closets by the side of the fireplaces on the south-western side of Barkhill House. This raises the question of the purpose of the closets. From the exterior the extension is reminiscent of a garderobe in an earlier house-type, and it is possible that the closets served a similar purpose, each perhaps housing a close-stool with a removable pot.[1]

A quirk of design occurs in the staircases of both houses and has been noticed in other Whitchurch examples. One baluster is set upside down. In Barkhill House the deviation occurs in both the middle and the upper flight. The frequency of this feature in Whitchurch suggests that it was done deliberately, perhaps as a superstitious charm to bring good fortune to the house.

Both houses are dated to within the early decades of the 18th century, each representative of the transitional period between timber-framing and brick construction.

The Documentary Evidence[2]

The title deeds of Barkhill House consist of 32 documents dated between 1762 and 1915. They can be divided into three groups:

1. Those relating to the house.
2. Those relating to land, gardens, barns, buildings and a malt kiln.
3. A lawsuit relating to the recovery of an inheritance. This document, dated 1st July 1789, bears a royal seal.

1. The House

A deed dated 24th September 1762 records that the Duke of Bridgwater sold 'All that copyhold messuage or dwelling-house in a certain street called the Bark Hill and now in the holding of William Turton, gent., to Thomas Jenks, gent., for the sum of £33. 17s. 10d.' William Turton is described in the deed as the deputy steward of the manor of Dodington and later became the steward. His widow, Elizabeth Turton, later inherited 'The Mansion House' from her brother William Bulkely.[3] The lord of the manor in 1762 was 'the most noble ffrancis Duke of Bridgwater Marquis of Brackley, Baron Ellesmere.'

Thomas Jenks bought the freehold of the property in 1769 by a deed of enfranchisement for £45 16s 8d, but six years later sold it to Richard Payne, a cheese factor, for £400. Payne had first leased the house for a year, before which it was occupied by William Lovell Brookes, a member of a prominent Dodington family of mercers and solicitors. Following Payne's death in 1778 the house was sold for £370 to Robert Clay, the proprietor of the 'White Lion' in Watergate.[4] The house was let to tenants, one of whom was Major Charles Shirreff, the officer in charge of French prisoners of war who were quartered in Whitchurch during the Napoleonic wars of 1800-15. A later occupant of the house wrote 'One if not more was quartered in Bark Hill House and a pair of jack-boots and I think, a hat, were found in a forgotten cupboard 60 or 70 years later. Some died here and were buried in the churchyard.'[5] Major Shirreff, a colourful character, was primarily responsible for introducing freemasonry to Whitchurch. In this he was aided by the Rector, the Rev. Lord Francis Henry Egerton. The Lodge met at the 'White Lion' in Watergate, and when Shirreff died in 1807 a stone bearing masonic symbols and traditionally carved by French prisoners of war was placed on his grave. In 1974, when the present rectory was built in the churchyard, the stone was was placed in the North Shropshire Masonic Temple, Castle Hill.[6]

Robert Clay sold Barkhill House as investment property to Mrs. Elizabeth Mayow in 1818. A notable tenant was Mrs. Clay Finch, a local historian and widow of the vicar of Ash. She lived there until 1915 when Major R.S.L. Mayow sold the house to Percy Williams, a Whitchurch builder. He and his wife were the first owner-occupiers of the property. It was he who applied the rendering to the timber-framed walls and re-fenestrated the front elevation while his wife, helped by her maid, stripped the panelling in the dining room of layers of paint to reveal the nature of the oak.[7] The next owner was Dr. Lee Abbot who took over c.1920. He adapted part of the premises as a surgery and waiting room. In 1927 he found a number of copper coins under an attic floor, one of which was dated 1698, the others between 1740 and 1752. There was also a token with an anvil and furnace on one side and 'WILKINSON IRONMASTER' on the other.[8] He was a keen orchid grower and it was he who built the original heated conservatory on the south and west sides. He also installed a generator to provide electric light in the house, several years before mains electricity came to Whitchurch.[9]

When Dr. Abbot retired in 1939 the house was bought by Dr. Gerard Rogerson and his wife, Dr. Evelyn Rogerson. While her husband was on active service during the war, Dr. Evelyn carried on the practice with the help of her sister, Dr. Williams. On their retirement in 1988 their son Mr. Martin Rogerson, a solicitor, and his wife Felicity took over the house.

2. Other Deeds

A group of documents in the collection relates to lands and buildings adjacent to the house, and date from 1762 when John Benson, a prosperous Whitchurch innholder, whose will is included in the collection, first leased and then bought them from the Duke of Bridgwater. His daughter, Elizabeth Spencer, inherited these properties, but in a deed of 1789 some were made over to the use of Robert Rider of Fetter Lane, London and his heirs. This seems to be the cause of the Suit of Recovery of an Inheritance which reached the Law Courts at Westminster, and it is the correlative document which bears the royal seal.

In 1790 John Knight, gent. of Dodington bought various parcels of land in Dodington from Elizabeth Spencer, by then a widow, and her son Daniel. They included the orchard opposite Barkhill House on which the Telephone Exchange now stands.[10] John Knight was a wealthy lawyer in Whitchurch.[11] A deed of 1823 records the purchase of a farmyard, buildings and a garden near Barkhill by Mrs. Elizabeth Mayow from Mr. and Mrs. John Knight. By this transaction the house and surrounding lands came under single ownership for the first time.

A malt kiln is mentioned several times in the deeds from 1797 to 1820, the last being an insurance certificate from the Birmingham Fire Office. The firemark is still visible on no. 26 Barkhill, currently the premises of Wm. C. Smith, builders.[12]

3. Recovery Précis

1st July 1789, 29th year of George III.

Demand for recovery between Thomas Williams and Robert Rider, held in St. Stephen's Hall, Westminster. Thomas Williams demanded possession of one garden, 40 acres of land, 30 acres of meadow, 20 acres of pasture for cattle with appurtenances in Dodington as his right and inheritance, saying that Robert Rider did not have entry as Hugh Hunt unjustly maintained. Robert Rider defended his right to the property and summoned Daniel Spencer as his witness, who in turn called Richard Smith as a witness.

Richard Smith called Thomas Francis Martin who said that he (Robert Rider) was seised of the tenement of his demesne as of fee and right and said that Hugh Hunt did not disseise the said Thomas of the tenements and of this he put himself upon the country.

Thomas Williams came again to court 'and the said Thomas Francis (Martin) although solemnly called cameth not again but departed in contempt of the court and maketh default. Therefore it is considered that the said Thomas doth recover his seisin against the said Robert of the tenements etc. and that the said Robert have of the land of Daniel to the value ...'

The document concludes with: 'All and singular which Premises at the request of the said Thomas by the tenor of these presents we have commanded to be exemplified in testimony whereof we have caused our seal appointed for sealing writs in the Bench afores'd to be fixed to these presents.'

Witness Alexander Lord Loughborough at Westminster the first day of July in the 29th year of the King's Reign.

The Royal Seal

The seal is that used to authenticate an Exemption of Recovery through the Court of Common Pleas. Such seals were a variant of the Great Seals, the main difference being their smaller size. It is not in good condition, but, by comparing it with others and with reference to published material, it has been possible to reproduce both sides, and these are shown on the drawings. The obverse shows the king, George III, enthroned, crowned, wearing the robes, collar and badge of the Garter, holding the orb and sceptre, and surrounded by figures which include Piety, Justice, Minerva, Hercules, Brittania and Plenty. In front of the throne is a lion lying with one paw resting on the other. The reverse is consistent with the King's Great Seal and shows the Royal Arms, ensigned with the crown and supported by dragon and greyhound, figures which were introduced during the reign of Elizabeth I. The Royal Arms, which were in use until 1801, includes quarterly England impaling Scotland, France, Ireland and Hanover. The Hanoverian symbols include three lions, hearts, a white horse and the golden crown of Charlemagne.[13]

The Royal Seal, 1789
Left: obverse, right: reverse

The Old Eagles Inn, Watergate

'The Old Eagles' in Watergate, has a modest two-bayed, two-storied front elevation with 19th century Flemish-bonded brickwork. The four windows are each six-light sashes and the entrance into the public room from the street is through a typical Victorian door-frame which has pilasters, a flat lintel and a flat projecting canopy. There is a dentilled eaves course and the roof space is lit by two small roof lights. Access to the rear of the property from Watergate is via a communal passageway between the public house and no. 11 Watergate, though contained wholly within the curtilage of no. 11. There is independent rear access to 'The Old Eagles' from Mill Street.

The only external clues that 'The Old Eagles' is historically older than the small Victorian public house suggested by its appearance, comes in the off-centre positioning of the doorway and in the general asymmetrical disposition of the openings.

Internally the most striking feature is the line of heavy floor joists, laid flat and exposed to view. Though irregular in size and disposition they average 7ins. in width, 5ins. in depth below ceiling level and are spaced at intervals of 1ft. 4ins. It is clear by their size and spacing that they relate to a late medieval building.

The 'Old Eagles'

No other early features survive at ground-floor level, although at the head of the cellar steps there is a post which has the remains of a lateral diagonal brace connected to it. It is difficult to relate this post to either the medieval structure or to the 19th century building.

The attic area has an inserted floor, and it is at this level that the surviving features of the historic building are apparent. Two cruck-like blades rise on either side to support a cambered collar-beam. At floor level there are spur-ties which form part of the assembly

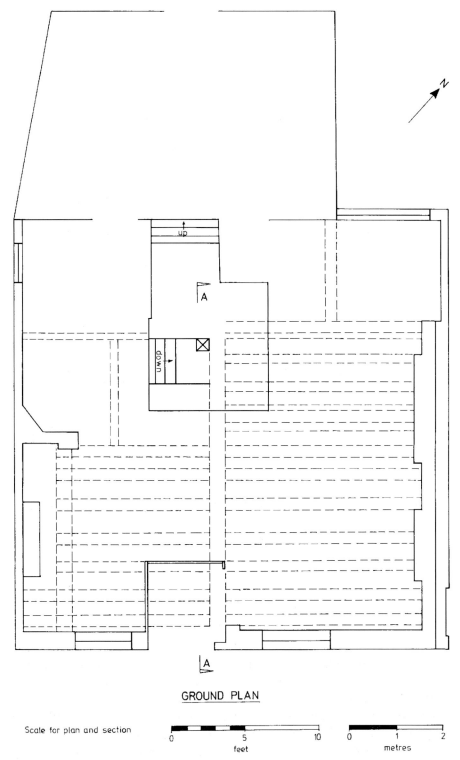

up

A

down

N

GROUND PLAN

Scale for plan and section

0   5   10
         feet

0   1   2
        metres

Ground floor plan, and section A - A opposite

72

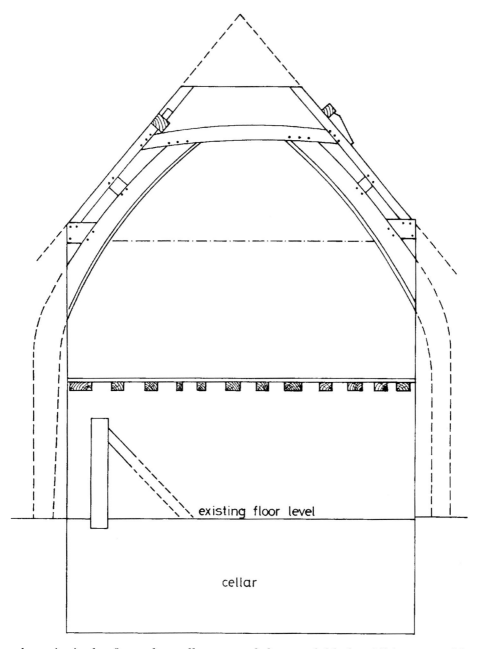

existing floor level

cellar

between the principal rafters, the wall-posts and the cruck blades. Mid-way on either side, between the spurs and the collar, there is a connecting strut between the cruck blade and the principal rafter. All the joints are morticed, tenoned and pegged, the heaviest timbers being triple-pegged. It seems reasonable to conclude that this truss acted as the central truss of the structure as the face of the cruck is hollow-moulded on either side; the moulding being visible along the whole of the exposed surface.

Above the collar-beam the roof is ceiled and plastered and it is impossible to establish whether any of the original superstructure survives or what form it took.

The discovery of the medieval features at 'The Old Eagles' raises three main questions: what form did the cruck truss originally take, in what type of building was it used and what is its approximate date?

The Cruck Truss

It is clear that the crucks support the collar-beam and do not meet at the apex. Historically this puts the truss into the category of 'Base-cruck', but the standard base-cruck usually functions as an open truss in the centre of an open hall whose end sections take a box-framed or an aisled form. At 'The Old Eagles', however, a heavily joisted floor about 7ft. 6ins. from the ground appears to be an integral part of the frame, suggesting that the truss was open only from first-floor level. Although the proportions of the truss are fairly consistent with the average dimensions of other base-crucks, it is possible that the crucks rose from first-floor level and had supporting posts or even stone walls below, in which case they would be classed as hybrid crucks of the 'raised' or 'upper base-cruck' variety.

It is difficult to determine the position of the original wall-plates. The existing spurs would normally indicate that the wall-plates were supported at that level, but in this case it seems likely that the spurs provide additional tie-backs and that the wall-plates were located at a level mid-way between the original first floor and the later inserted floor. The crucks have been cut back when the building was narrowed at a later date. A street map of Whitchuch dated 1761 shows the property projecting into Watergate by approximately 2ft.

The Building Type

The quality of the carpentry and the moulding on the crucks indicate that 'The Old Eagles' had its origins in a high-class building requiring a lofty open upper hall, and a ground floor room fulfilling a secondary purpose. The most likely explanation is that it was a medieval guild hall of some kind. Its form and size suggest a corporate rather than a domestic use. It was set parallel to Watergate and probably extended further on each side than the present boundaries.

Dating

The base-cruck truss has none of the features normally associated with classic base-crucks: double tie-beams, aisled features, deep arch-bracing and purlins set square like arcade plates. Nevertheless, the crucks support the collar-beam in an uncompromising fashion, and if they originally reached ground level, their purpose would be to get unrestricted floor space in the hall area and to avoid the use of arcade posts which would restrict movement at ground level. Some of the components such as the connecting struts and the triple pegs suggest an early date, but the general lightness of the frame relates more comfortably to advanced techniques. Perhaps a date of *c.*1400 would represent a reasonable compromise. Certainly it is the earliest framed building known in Whitchurch.

17 - 23 Watergate

Nos. 17 - 23, Watergate consist of a block of four shops with a frontage measuring 82ft. The shops have rooms above and there is a high cart-entry in the centre. For many years 17 and 19, the premises on the northern side of the cart-entry, were empty, their structural deterioration causing much concern, and they were placed on the 'Buildings at Risk' register by North Shropshire District Council. In the autumn of 1995 the Whitchurch Buildings Recording Group obtained permission to record them. It was immediately apparent that these were only part of a cohesive block which incorporated 21 and 23 and, in order to present a comprehensive record and to make a reasoned assessment of the structure and plan, the whole block would need to be taken into account.[1]

Externally the block presents a two-storied façade with modern shop-fronts and is plastered over. Mock timbers are painted onto the plaster in similar fashion to that which occurs elsewhere in the town.[2] However, due to the neglect, much of the original timber-framing is now fully exposed internally in nos. 17 and 19. While it is impossible to work out the design of the ground-floor framing, that of the upper storey consists of close-studding divided by a rail set somewhat lower than mid-way. Similar framework occurs on the rear wall, though here the uprights are a little more widely spaced. There is no evidence that the building was jettied.

Viewed from the street the shallow pitch of the roof suggests that the front slope was raised at some time, a common practice in Whitchurch,[3] but it is indeed original. Several other interesting features were found but perhaps the most significant discovery was that the chambers above 17 and 19 contain fragments of wall-paintings. As these are the only freehand paintings yet found in Whitchurch considerable time was spent in recording them.[4]

17 - 23 Watergate (the old Raven Inn)

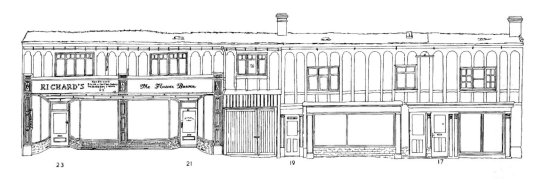

17 - 23 Watergate

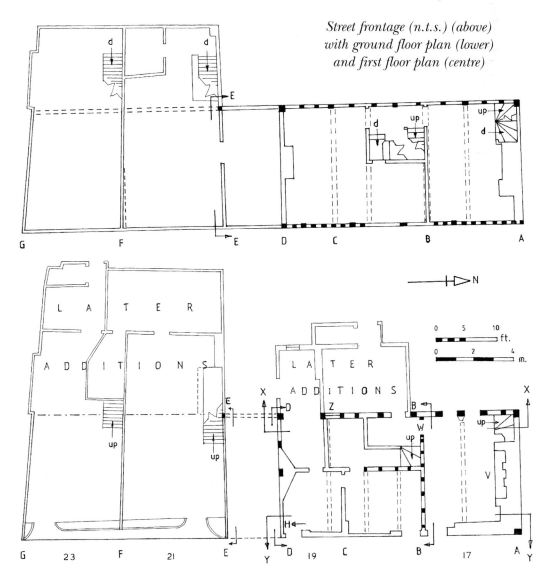

Street frontage (n.t.s.) (above)
with ground floor plan (lower)
and first floor plan (centre)

76

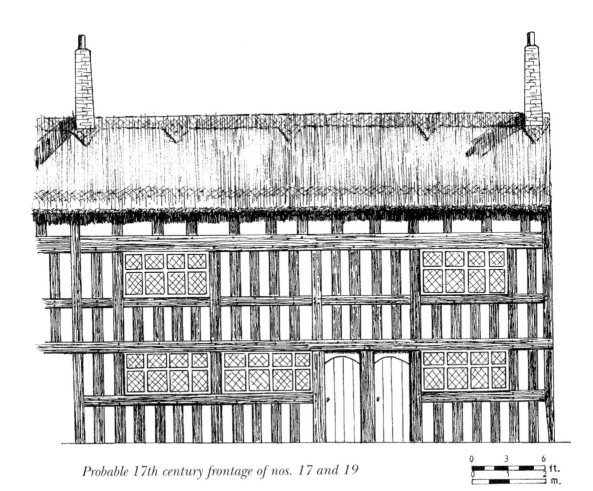

Probable 17th century frontage of nos. 17 and 19

Interpretation of the block led to much discussion. On the OS map the yard at the rear is shown as 'Raven Yard'. The cottages which at one time occupied the yard were demolished during the early years of the Second World War, but there are documentary references to an inn called the 'Raven' in Watergate and the block has proved to be this long-lost hostelry and not a town house as such. Dendrochronological dating has established a felling date of 1625 for the timbers.[5]

The Plan

As the measured drawing opposite shows, the block consists of six bays, three of them 16ft., the cart-entry is 8ft., but the two bays which comprise 19 are of unequal size. The larger is 12ft. and the smaller is 9ft. It is clear that all the attached buildings at the rear are later additions, though of differing times and

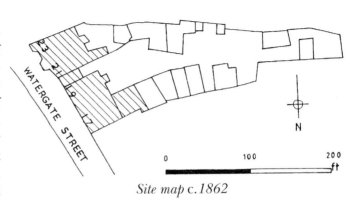

Site map c.1862

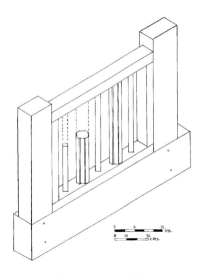

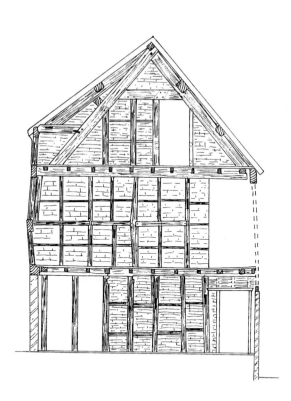

Section B - B (top right).
Section E - E (bottom right).
Detail of window at Z (refer to section X - X opposite) (top left).
Chamfer stops in no. 17 (below). The top one is the lintel at V (refer to ground floor plan), the bottom ones on a beam

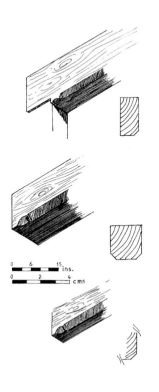

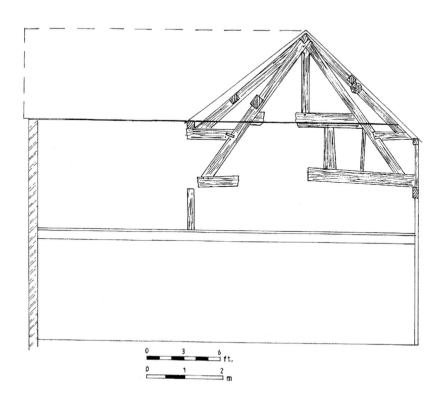

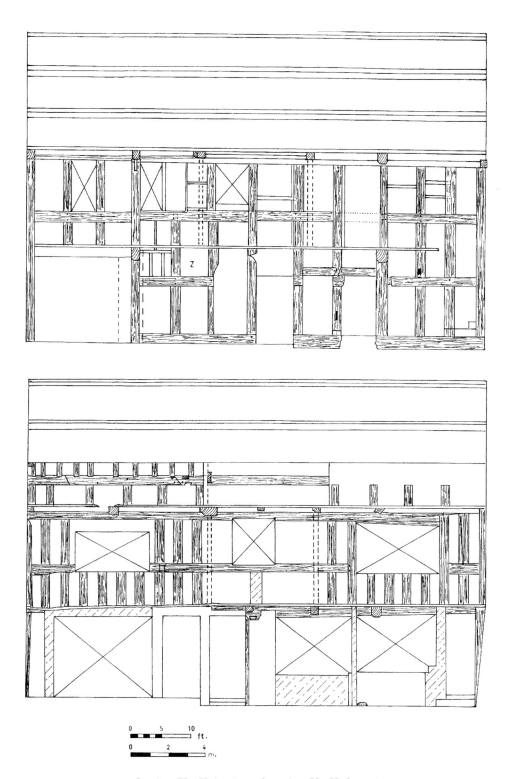

Section X - X (top) and section Y - Y (lower)

qualities. The central bay of nos. 17 - 19 is occupied by the main staircase, and while the structural timbers of the stairwell appear to be either original or from an early remodelling, much of the secondary fabric represents renewal work of a later date. It is clear that the chimneystack at the southern end of no. 19, that which backs onto the cart-entry, is a later insertion. It serves two corner fireplaces at ground level and one lateral fireplace at first floor level. Here distortion has resulted in it standing proud of the wall and wall-paintings can be discerned at the back of it. At the northern end of no. 17 the chimneystack serves lateral fireplaces at each floor level, and its funnel-shaped form with small bricks measuring 9ins. x 2ins. x 4ins. suggests that it is either an original feature or an early insertion.

Although no early fittings remain, the hearth at ground level in no. 17 is large enough for cooking, and the mantel beam has a narrow chamfer and stops, similar although not quite identical in form to those on the transverse beam in the same room. On the rear (west) wall the beam is supported by a post which is clearly additional to the wall-post at that point. This raises the question of whether the bay was originally open to the roof and the upper floor inserted at a later date and, therefore, how the original building functioned. While the beam-support could be interpreted as a structural necessity that arose from on-site problems during building or shortly afterwards, there is evidence that the floors at both levels are insertions. The attic floors are supported from plates attached to the main frame, and the first storey floors have no corresponding supports in the main frame. It appears, therefore, that nos. 17 and 19 began life as a large open structure before its conversion to an inn. Its purpose at this time is unknown, even difficult to suggest in an area of the town which, though not the main High Street, was a primary approach to the town. It must have been more than a utilitarian barn or such-like, because the quality of the framing and the proportions of the frontage, so clearly a factor, distinguish it from those designed for simple storage. It may be a fanciful suggestion but the thought occurs that it is an early example of speculative systems building where, as now, basic construction takes place in 'shell' form and the client's requirements are added later. On the opposite side of the street are the remains of a similar block with an identical pattern of framing suggesting that this too was 17th century speculative building in what was a 'boom' period.

The bays beyond the cart-entry, though clearly defined, contain nothing to suggest that they functioned in any other way than chambers at first floor level with rooms below.

Overall the plan in its second phase cannot be made to fit the concept of a private house. Features such as a hall, open or floored, solar or parlour, screens passage with or without a spere-truss, and service rooms cannot be detected. No chamber or bay differs much in size from its neighbour and no difference in function can be discerned. On the other hand the size, layout, provision of a cart-entry, central stairwell and kitchen at one end would accord with the planning of an inn, and it is suggested that this is how the building functioned in its second phase of development. The point is pursued later.

The Cart-entry

It was first necessary to establish whether the cart-entry was an original feature or had been driven through at a later date. At some time the height was raised, and the boarding of the ceiling is relatively modern, but the four corner posts which define the outline stand slightly proud of the walling and have no features such as empty mortices which would indicate a continuation of the front and rear walls. The lateral wall on the southern side is bricked over and, although timbers remain exposed on the northern side, they are comparatively featureless. Roof trusses also demarcate the cart-entry and it seems reasonable to conclude that it was part of the original concept.

The Roof

The roof trusses are consistent throughout the block, their positions marking the bay divisions. The only inconsistency is the presence of an intermediate truss between E and F and this has every appearance of being a later insertion which was probably introduced when the rear range was added to no. 21. Section B - B may be taken as typical of the original trusses and is seen to consist of a straightforward assembly of tie-and-collar-beam with principal rafters coupled to provide support for the ridge purlin. On the eastern side spurs supporting blocking-pieces are provided to accommodate the raised angle of the roof and if the line of the principal rafter is continued downwards it will by-pass the original position of the wall-plate. When this is seen in conjunction with the fact that the side-purlin is housed on the blocking-piece and was never intended to make contact with the principal rafter it is evident that the shallow pitch of the roof on the street side is an original feature. It must have been designed to get more light into the upper reaches and is a faint echo of the galleried form of some medieval inns. Another feature of the roof which is worth noting is the absence of any provision for wind-bracing. This was probably seen as an opportunity to cut costs, adding support to the theory that the building was a commercial enterprise, but increasing its vulnerablity regarding structural stability. Another indication of cost-cutting is that most of the joints, even the main ones, are single-pegged. While single-pegging is often found as a feature in early buildings, it is unusual to find it used in the early 17th century.

All except one of the spurs are joined to the principal rafter with a mortice-and-tenon joint. The exception occurs on the northern truss (E - E) in no. 21, that which is on the southern side of the cart-entry. Here a bare-faced half-lapped dovetail makes the connection. This joint has a long history and its use here must represent a late example of the genre.

The Wall-paintings

As mentioned above, the paintings are the only freehand painted decoration yet found in Whitchurch. They occur in the upper rooms in both no. 17 and 19, but are fragmentary and in very poor condition (see reproduction on the cover). In no. 19 small portions can be discerned on the front wall, but a section in slightly better condition survives on the southern wall to the east of the inserted chimneystack. Here on one stud in particular there is a zig-zag pattern of framework with sprays of flowers and leaves. The flowers include a stylistic open five-petalled dog-rose, mulberries carefully depicted and showing the natural hang of the fruit, clove-pinks, otherwise gillyflowers, and borage. All had culinary and/or medicinal usages. Mulberries and gillyflowers were widely used in the late 16th and 17th centuries. In addition to their numerous uses as a fruit, mulberries provided dyes and sweetening for the sour wines imported from France and Spain. Gillyflowers were

*The design of the wall-paintings in no. 17, showing the use of classical arches,
columns and gillyflowers*

not the familiar modern wall-flowers, but correctly clove-pinks which, as the name implies, gave a flavouring of cloves in cookery and also to wine. They were also used medicinally and were a favourite motif in embroidery.[6]

There are probably more flower motifs, but those described above are the best preserved. The paintings are carried out in the appropriate colours, mostly pink, blue and orange against a dark background. On the stud in question the design appears to join a horizontal frieze which probably encompassed the room, but the frieze is barely discernible.

In the equivalent room in no. 17 the paintings are even more fragmentary, but a section is evident on the front wall. Here the paintings occur on the studs and on the plaster of the interstices. It is clear that the interstices received a later coating of plaster which was left plain and, later still, a covering of wall-paper. A different design is used in this room, one which includes classical arches and columns, but the occasional gillyflower still makes an appearance and is indistinguishable from its counterpart in no. 19.

That both first floor chambers were skillfully and lavishly decorated in this way suggests that they had equal importance. The better chambers in inns were often called by the main motif of the decoration, and it can be speculated that such was the case in this Watergate property.[7]

The Ovolo-moulded Window
Only one early window was found, and this was largely obscured with plaster. Its position is marked at Z on the plan and the three-light form is shown in detail. Originally it would have been located on the external wall, and indeed the outward facing surfaces of the framing, mullions and diamond bars are weathered, whereas the inner faces are crisp. The mullions have ovolo-moulding on both faces, a feature noted in houses in south Wales though not the north, but which is general in Shropshire.[8] The simplicity of the window framing makes it possible that it was applied to the framework as a later insertion, but it could equally be an original feature.

The window had no provision for glazing, but there may have been an internal shutter arrangement. When it was blocked, lumps of peat were used, but these disintegrated when removed. Peat was also found as blocking material in other parts of the house.

The Hinged Door
As so few of the early fittings remain, this four-planked door, whose position is marked on the plan, is noticeable, particularly on account of its iron pintles and hinges with the straps across three of the planks. One of the hinges from the door marked at W on the plans is shown below (n.t.s.). The presentation side of the door is on the northern side.

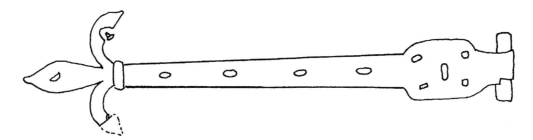

The Carpenters' Marks
Few carpenters' assembly marks are visible at present, but they may become more apparent when the timbers are stripped. In no. 21 there is a set on the southern roof truss where the tie-beam and principal rafters join and in the same plane where two verticals occur. They are punched on with the tip of a chisel but, unfortunately, they are not properly sequenced, the double digits appearing twice.

Rat-trap Brickwork
Much of the later partitioning in nos. 17 and 19 is carried out with rat-trap style brickwork (where the bricks are laid on edge), and this forms a distinctive feature. It occurs particularly on the measured section B - B and on the partition wall on the eastern side of the stair-well. As only one leaf of brickwork occurs in each case, it cannot be considered as

bonded, but the bricks are laid on their narrow edges, in the style of rat-trap bond, instead of being laid flat. Thus savings in material and weight are effected and a wall with insulating properties of a thickness not exceeding the timber framework enclosing it is obtained. It is one of only two examples of rat-trap brickwork noted in Whitchurch although several instances of its use in bonded form occur elsewhere in Shropshire, usually in outer walls.

Rear Doorstep

The rear entrance to no. 17 has a door-step made from a composite material, very hard and durable and closely resembling that found at Ashwood, a farmhouse situated a few miles to the south-east of Whitchurch. The latter has the initial 'B' from the Blockley works imprinted on the soffit. R.P. Blockley was a Victorian entrepreneur who set up a tilery and brickworks on the Shropshire coalfield at New Hadley, specialising in blue and red bricks. Doorsteps must have been a by-product. Blockley's products are still in demand, and indeed the firm is one of Europe's major manufacturers of facing bricks and clay paviors.[9]

Assessment and Dating

As mentioned above, the property does not comply with the accepted layout of a domestic range, neither does it appear to have been adapted from such a form. Little evidence of early usage remains at ground level, as is usually the case with town properties, and there is a possibility that its first conversion was to shops at ground level and living quarters above. However, if such was the case, questions arise regarding how the individual units functioned, how they were lighted and heated and where the stairs were positioned. Furthermore why was such a wide cart-entry needed and who used it? None of these questions can be answered satisfactorily and the most likely explanation remains that nos. 17 and 19 at least were first built as a large open unit, unfloored and unheated, which was later fitted out to serve as an inn. If this is accepted, perhaps it is not impertinent to refer to it by the name that occurs in the documents, the Raven. The next question concerns its type. Medieval inns were usually of two plan-forms, the courtyard type or the block/gatehouse type. Although timber-framed inns were usually of the courtyard type, the Raven's plan most closely resembles that of the George Inn at Stamford, a gatehouse type.[10]

If various factors are considered, the Raven fits neatly into the pre-requisites of an inn. It is located on the main approach road into the town, and has a wide cart-entry. It is close to the town centre and has a choice of accommodation to suit different pockets. Stabling would, doubtless, be available at the rear, and stables are mentioned in the deeds. All factors point to its early conversion to an inn, and indeed, despite the peculiar method of floor insertion, there is a possibility that it was built as such. As the documentary evidence shows, the block had been in use as 'The Raven' for some time when first mentioned in 1667.

Historical Evidence[11]

As mentioned above, the yard behind nos. 17 and 19 is still known as 'The Raven Yard', and that the four properties, 17, 19, 21 and 23, were originally 'The sign of the Raven' is made clear in the deeds of nos. 17 and 19: '... And that messuage or shop and dwelling house thereto belonging ... and at one time part of a dwelling house called the Raven Inn in Watergate Street, Whitchurch and now occupied by John Newbrook.'[12]

The first mention of the sign of the Raven is in the 1667 survey of the manor by the steward, John Eddows: 'Arthur Cooper for a house, the Sign of the Raven'. His father held a three- life lease on the property from Ralph Brereton, Grocott and Edwards. At that time the rent was 1s 3d.[13]

There are several copyhold surrenders which refer to the Raven; that of 1712 mentions a kiln door and a quince tree.[14] The quince tree seems to have been a distinctive feature, other surrenders mention it and spaces are described with it as a focal point. Quince trees were important in the domestic economy of the 16th and 17th centuries, the fruit was used in the production of pickles, creams, pastes, wine, jellies and a preserve, the modern equivalent of which is marmalade.[15] But the quince preserve had a consistency almost of fudge and was cut in strips and eaten with bread. It is still made and consumed in that manner in Portugal. Indeed, Portuguese quinces were called *marmelo* and the term *marmalade* was coined to describe the preserve most commonly made from them.[16]

A surrender of 1725, in addition to mentioning the quince tree twice, includes the name of Edward Deaves, gent. There is reason to think that the Deaves family were early licensees of the Raven. This point will be pursued later. The same document mentions 'the new building' at the rear which must refer to one or more of the brick-built extensions, the most likely being those on nos. 21 and 23.[17]

By 1778 the Raven was divided into two dwellings, although it is clear that half of it, that is the present nos. 17 and 19, continued in use as an inn.[18] The last reference to it being held by a victualler is in 1790, when the licensee was Joseph Chester.[19] It probably carried on as an inn for some time after that, but then was occupied by various tradesmen.

By 1809 the block was divided into four tenements. The surrender of the time states '... all that messuage formerly in two parts and now in four dwelling houses ... formerly commonly known by the name of "The sign of the Raven".' Joseph Chester, the last licensee, is mentioned in the deed, and was, presumably, still alive.[20]

The first reference to cottages built in the Raven yard occurs in 1835. Four cottages, brick-built and with slate roofs, were offered for renting at £17 per annum each. Each had a garden and a pig-sty. They are described as having 'only been built a few years' and with the benefit of a 'never- failing spring well called the Raven Well.'[21] The well is marked on the 1888 OS map. They survived until the 1940s when they were condemned by the local council as unfit for human habitation and demolished.

In 1862 the block, or at least most of it, had a narrow escape from demolition when it stood in the path of the proposed railway which was intended to run from Newcastle-under-Lyme through Market Drayton and Whitchurch to join the Shrewsbury and Chester railway near Pulford in Cheshire. There was to be a connection with the Shrewsbury and Crewe railway at Whitchurch.[22] Known as 'The Potteries Junction Railway' it never left the drawing-board. On the plan for its passage through Whitchurch the plots 124, 125 and 126 correspond to the present 19, 21 and 23. Also shown is plot 132, the stables in the old Raven Inn yard, then owned by Ann Ackers and leased to John Marten, a general dealer.

Kelly's Directories between 1868 and 1875 give a clear picture of the types of tradesmen who ran businesses from the four shops. They include a general dealer, hairdresser, plumber and glazier, fishmonger and poulterer, saddler, milliner, bootmaker, confectioner, fried fish supplier, optician, and master tailor. There are no references to no. 17 as a separate establishment in the directories between 1868 and 1905 when Maud Newbrook, daughter of John Newbrook the fishmonger at 19, is listed there as a milliner. It seems likely that 17 and 19 were used as one and that Maud was allowed to use the front room of 17 as her shop. This is borne out by an advertisement in 1875 for the sale of 17 which gives details of 'a parlour or front shop, cellar, and several bedrooms.'[23]

There is a copious archive on the Newbrook family of fishmongers from 1885 to 1972.[24] All the Whitchurch directories until 1913 show Richard Newbrook as the proprietor, but recent correspondence with his great grandson points towards John, Richard's son, first setting up the business in c.1887. At that time John was only 19 and would be considered 'under age'. It seems likely that Richard rented the premises in his own name and the billhead 'R. Newbrook and Sons' bears this out. The bill also gives an idea of some of the hazards in the life of a fishmonger a century ago. Short weight and unsaleable fish having to be buried being but two.

In 1909 Mrs. Sarah Ashley became the tenant of no. 21. Her son George has vivid memories of his childhood there, including as many as 19 convalescent soldiers from the army camp at Prees Heath being billeted at a time during the First World War. Presumably the soldiers slept on mattresses on the floor. But his abiding memory is of the rats which came 'out of the woodwork' at night and devoured any food available. So bold were the vermin that they would scamper round the table legs while the children were eating their supper.[25] George Ashley also remembers the Newbrook family of fishmongers next door and his recollections are contained in the archive.

Soon after the Ashleys left, that is c.1921, the block was sold. George Edge, a builder, bought no. 21 and it was he who re-fronted the whole range with pseudo-framing. He also altered the doors and windows, and, with a partner, set up an electrical business, 'Edge and Davies'. At the same time no. 23 was renovated, tiled throughout with white tiles and opened as the 'Wirswell Dairy' by Vickerman Mainprize. The dairy was named after the farm where the milk was produced.[26] His son and daughters continued to run the dairy until c.1970 when the premises became first an antique shop and, more recently, Richards' Drapers and Haberdashers.

In 1921 John Newbrook bought nos. 17 and 19 at a special Court Baron for the manor of Whitchurch when Earl Brownlow sold the remainder of his copyhold properties. It is clear that the block was still in single ownership at that time and, as mentioned above, nos. 17 and 19 are referred to as 'part of a dwelling house called the Raven Inn.'[27] The Newbrooks carried on the fish business until 1971, clocking up an unbroken 84 years of trading, although the family no longer lived 'over the shop' but had moved to a new house at The Chemistry, an area on the western side of Whitchurch the name of which is thought to have derived from an oak acid processing plant once there, built by John Newbrook c.1916.[28] After 1971 nos. 17 and 19 passed through various hands, deteriorating all the time. At present the premises are in a state of dereliction, although those on the other side of the cart-entry, 21 and 23, are in good repair and house viable businesses.

Inventory of Richard Deaves[29]

As mentioned above, there is circumstantial evidence to link Richard Deaves with the Raven Inn, and an Edward Deaves features in a surrender of 1725. While Richard Deaves' inventory does not describe him as an innkeeper, his will does, and his inventory shows all the characteristics of an inn with the large quantities of bedding, napery, brass, pewter, treen ware and beer. All the other known inns of Whitchurch were in the High Street, and it is likely that the area of the Pool Dam was being redeveloped in the early 17th century. Clearly Richard Deaves (or Deave as he is sometimes mentioned) was relatively wealthy and the size of the property, the quality of the wall-paintings, the provision for stabling and other features, described above, support the thesis that his inn was the Raven. He had his own riding horse, always a sign of wealth, and it appears that the establishment was reasonably self-sufficient regarding provisions. The large amount of corn, both growing and in the house suggests that he was engaged in selective farming, but the location of his cornfield is not known. The following is a transcript of his Inventory:

RICHARD DEAVES

A trew and perfect Inventorie of all the goodes Cattell and Chattells of Richard Deaves of Whitchurch deceased taken the seacond day of September Anno dm 1634 Priced by us whose names are subscribed

Imp. Corne upon the ground and in the house		13.06.08
It.	Hey	5.00.00
It.	Two ironbound Cartes with other implements of husbandrie	3.06.08
It.	Implementes of Huswiverie with yarne	1.00.00
It.	Two horses	4.00.00
It.	Three kyne	6.00.00
It.	Swyne	3.06.08
It.	ffewell of all sortes	4.00.00
It.	Mucke	1.00.00
It.	One mare	2.00.00
It.	Brasse	5.00.00
It.	Pewter	2.13.04
It.	Iron ware of all sortes	1.06.08
It.	Bacon & beefe in the howse	0.13.04
It.	Treene ware of all sortes	3.06.08
It.	Butter and cheese	0.14.04
It.	Bedding of all sortes	30.00.00
It.	Bedsteedes	6.00.00
It.	Naperie ware of all sortes	13.06.08
It.	Curtaines carpettes & Cushins	2.10.00
It.	Silver plate	5.00.00
It.	Coffers and trunkes	1.10.00
It.	Cheares and stooles	1.10.00

It.	Cuppboardes	1.00.00
It.	Tables and formes	3.00.00
It.	Beere in the howse	2.13.08
It.	One peese & a Crosbow with some other trifling thinges	0.13.08
It.	His Saddle bridle and wearing apparrell	5.00.00
	Sum totall	128.17.04

Lawrence Ricofte
Thomas Broughall
William Gregory
George Whittingham

38 & 42 Watergate

No. 38 Watergate was examined in 1983 before it underwent a thorough refurbishment. At that time the Recording Group had not been formed and so it was not until 1993 that it was measured and drawn in detail. Richard Hughes, a member of the group, was responsible for the refurbishment, and his notes made at the time have proved a valuable source of information. The following report seeks to synthesise the evidence presented in 1983 with what was learned from the stripping out and the present state of the property. There is a ' swings and roundabouts' situation in that, for example, the roof space, inaccessible in 1983, has been opened, but the flat joists over the northern bay have been removed, leaving only their witness marks on truss A - A. However, Mr Hughes's first-hand account of the alterations means a reasoned statement can be presented even though some of the original problems of interpretation remain.

The main problem concerns the original southern extent of no. 38. Was the through passage between nos. 38 and 40 an early right of way between the houses, or did it represent space acquired from the truncation of a third bay originally belonging to no. 38, or was it space which technically belongs to no. 40. The upper storey above the passage belongs to no. 40 and in 1983 it housed the only toilet in the building, then a nine-roomed house. It was converted to a walk-in wardrobe during alterations. The truss on the northern side of the passage (B - B) is a closed truss and, as far as can be determined, is identical to truss A - A. However, it is probably wise to take nos. 38, 40 and 42 into consideration as not only were the three dwellings at one time in single ownership, but 40 and 42 incorporate communicating doors, now blocked, at upper and lower levels, and similar doors are shown on truss B - B, linking nos. 38 and 40.

38 Watergate

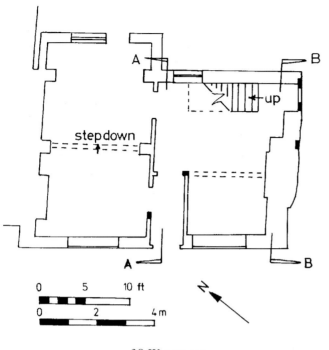

38 Watergate

Above: Ground floor plan.
Below: Section A - A (left) and B - B (right).
Right: Sketch of side passage (n.t.s.)

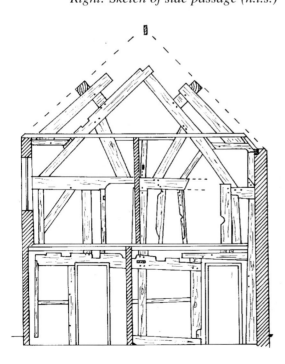

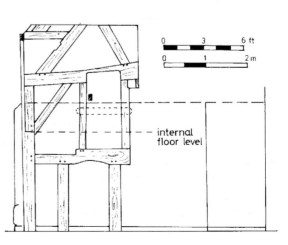

Description

In 1983 no. 38 was assessed as a box-framed two-bayed property of two stories, set parallel to the street and encased in later brickwork. The original steep (50 degree) pitch of the roof suggested that it had been thatched. Its height has not been increased in modern times, but the line of the original principal rafters, revealed when the roof space was opened, shows how at some time the roof has been raised by 3ft. This, coupled with the inserted floor and chimneystack in the southern bay, tends to support the view, formed in 1983, that originally this was a 'croglofft' cottage, with the sleeping-platform or 'croglofft' above the flat joists of the northern bay approached via a ladder from the open southern bay. The presence of two doorways in the upper part of the central frame suggests that this was a superior kind of croglofft, with properly partitioned rooms, but, of course, the door-ways may be later insertions.

The open bay was probably heated by a fire against the gable wall. Smoke was extracted by means of a 'fumbrell' or wattle and daub hood which simply drew the smoke upwards. In themselves they were a fire hazard and there was evidence in this bay that a severe conflagration had taken place at some time. However, such smoke-hoods occasionally survive, and the fragment of timber which, in 1983, was visible at the rear of no. 38, between the older and newer brick chimneys on the south gable, may have represented the remains of the original smoke-hood. This feature is no longer visible as the older chimney has been removed. The fire would have effectively heated the whole house, the only chilly room would have been that under the croglofft, and this may not have been intended for family use but have housed the family cow. The cottage is very similar in form to 'The Old Shop' on Haughmond Hill near Shrewsbury where investigation revealed a similar evolution.[1]

Modernisation, probably in the 18th or 19th century, was simple. The roof line was raised by *c.*3ft., a floor was inserted into the southern bay, the old smoke-hood replaced with a brick chimneystack, and another stack built in the gable wall to serve the northern rooms, by then a parlour and a bedroom. To insert this stack the end truss was mutilated and the stack was positioned so that part of it was outbuilt, leaving a gap, now bridged, between nos. 36 and 38. In effect the three-roomed cottage had become a two (or three)-up and two-down.

Details

Some of the details in no. 38 are interesting. Four different types of infilling for the timber-frame were encountered, but some may relate to later repairs and alterations. One area had split ash staves placed horizontally with a vertical basket-work of hazel twigs, a type noted elsewhere in Whitchurch; in other

Sketch of rear of no. 38 (n.t.s.)

91

places the staves were of wider split timber and split ash was used vertically; in the third case the basket-work was of split oak and the fourth had oak pegs driven into diagonally drilled holes in the framework and a basket-work of hazel twigs. The daub was made with long grass or hay, not with chopped straw as with other Whitchurch examples, but it was not possible to determine what had been used as the binding and spreading agent. It did not have the appearance of the usual cow dung.

There were a few windows which had an early appearance and may have been original. These had wrought-iron blacksmith-made frames with a small planted strip of oak carrying the rebate for the glass. The catches consisted of a rotatable ring which carried a tongue to engage with a slot in the frame, and these opening lights were hung on pin-and-thimble hinges, similar to but smaller than those used on farm gates. Such windows have been noted elsewhere in Whitchurch and they occur also at Alkington Hall.

Rush-taper marks from the pre-electric lighting system were found on the timbers in the north-east bedroom.

Dating

Dating the building has to be done on stylistic evidence. The timbers are substantial but features such as the extended tie-beams, straight windbraces, thin infil timbers and sharply cut-back heads to the posts (now obscured) suggest a date in the second half of the 17th century. Croglofft cottages, by their nature, rarely survive in a recognisable form, especially in towns. Therefore, if the interpretation is correct, no. 38 Watergate represents an example of a house-type which, though common in the 17th century, is rarely found today.[2]

Inter-relationship of 38 - 42 Watergate

There remains the question of how far a two-bay croglofft cottage can be reconciled with nos. 40 and 42, and how the through passage related to the plots. No. 40 appears to have been thoroughly redeveloped in at least two major phases, first in the early-to-mid 18th century when 38 was altered, and later extended to the rear when drained land became available after 1811. At present it stretches back some 50ft. from the street, but has a frontage of only 13ft. The bulk of the roof-line runs gable-end on to the street, but until 1983 the frontage bay had a 4ft. parapet with a stone coping, disguising the fact that the parallel roof-line effectively covered only half of the street-facing bay. Behind the parapet was a gutter and a dormer window. The parapet wall was badly frost-damaged and was demolished as part of the 1983 refurbishment programme, the roof extended and a Velux roof light fitted. Clearly, no. 40 occupies a 'contrived' plot. It is a nine-roomed house with three rooms on each of the

42 Watergate

three stories and a stairwell and hall between the front and rear bays. Entrance to the property is from the passage, but stripping-out revealed that at one time the front elevation had a central doorway flanked by two flat-headed windows with brick voussoirs. These were balanced by two similar windows at first-floor level which, with the parapet roof, would have given a symmetrical appearance to the frontage, essential in a Georgian concept.

No. 42 has a frontage of 22ft. It is a two-bay three-storied property, roughcast on the front elevation and with a modern shop-window and entrance door at ground level. A passage to the north of the shop is contained within the building and gives access to the rear. Basically the structure is one room deep, but it has a two-storied wing forming an extension to the rear and four further single-storied brick-built additions, some of them relating to the bakery business carried on by the Grace family of master bakers for many years. At first floor level timbers relating to an earlier roof-line are visible, and it is clear that the third storey is an addition, probably part of the 'Georgianisation' programme which included the four sash windows on the front elevation. These windows have been squared up, but in 1983 they presented a slumped appearance, probably due to a combination of their insertion into an already warped timber-frame and the risk factor of adding a third storey to a structure with inadequate foundations on unstable land. A large chimneystack built at the rear had sunk dramatically causing further warping of the framework and emphasising the ground conditions. The rear elevation of the street-facing block has flimsy square-framing, seven panels high, with brick infilling, but internally some of the framing of the original rear wall is visible and this is much more substantial. At first floor level some of the later partitioning and framing has infilling of peat blocks layered with a fine-textured mud.[3]

As with nos. 38 and 40, the boundary of 42 is not clear-cut. The front elevation shows brick quoins which relate to the northern limit of the property, but similar quoins at the southern end relate to the adjoining building, no. 44 Watergate. This raises the question of whether no. 42 was once part of a much larger building.

Conclusions

In Ludlow, a Shropshire town which has had extensive historical research, the standard burgage plot measures 33ft. in width, that is, two statute perches. In Shrewsbury recent research has shown many plot sizes conforming with measurements based on multiples of the perch.[4] It is not known how far the application of the perch applies to the Whitchurch burgage plots although the 16½ft. denominator seems to feature in many properties. But if, as seems likely, it was standard practice to employ perch-based measurements it means that, allowing for some small adjustments, the range of properties which comprise nos. 38 - 42 Watergate could be contained within two burgage plots. There is, therefore, a possibility that two croglofft cottages once occupied the site. As mentioned above, no. 42 was largely rebuilt, no. 40 occupies a contrived plot and the only really questionable item is the through passage and what part it played in the development. The measurements show that it could be contained within the burgage plot of no. 38, and there would be sufficient space for the other house to have its own through passage. But it may, of course represent an ancient right of way, giving access to the rear of several Watergate properties and, until it was drained, to the mill pool.

Historical Note[5]

According to the deeds of the house the occupant(s) of no. 38 Watergate have the right to moor a boat on the mill pool and to fish therein.[6] This clause, of course, relates to the time when the mill and its pool were prominent features of this part of the town. On the oldest surviving town map of 1761 the mill is shown on the western side of the road at the junction of what is now Mill Street and Watergate, and the pool occupied a large area, later known as the White Lion Meadow. The mill was demolished in 1811 so that the Ellesmere Canal could be brought into the town, and was largely rebuilt as the 'Lord Hill' public house. The pool was drained and the area used for refuse. In 1983 peat deposits were found to a depth of *c.*10ft. immediately at the rear of nos. 38 - 42, Watergate and in these the upper layers were interspersed with driftwood. This meant that plans to build an outside staircase to serve the flats into which no. 40 was to be converted had to be abandoned, although the unstable ground had not deterred earlier builders from constructing a nine-roomed house, 50ft. deep (no. 40), between the two older framed houses, or from adding a third storey to no. 42.

It has only been possible to trace occupancy of no. 38 from 1841 when the premises were tenanted by the Botwood family.[7] William Botwood was a hairdresser and was still there in 1862 when documents associated with the ill-fated 'Potts' railway make it clear that nos. 38, 40 and 42 Watergate were owned by the Rev. J. Colley, curate of St. Alkmund's church.[8] No. 38 was still in use as a hairdresser's in 1888, but by 1891 a general labourer, Joseph Langford, his wife, four children and a boarder occupied the house.[9] It had a brief spell as an agency for the Singer Sewing Machine Co. between 1916 and 1922, but was used again as a hairdressing saloon at least until 1937.[10] By 1941 Robert Grace, a well-known baker and confectioner owned the block and ran no. 42 as a bakery. The Wilkinson family were tenants of no. 38. John ('Jack') Wilkinson was a market trader in footwear and used the northern bay for storage. His mother lived on the premises, as did his sister Gertie who managed the stock. But during the war he changed to selling china and pottery, because, in his own words 'there was less bother with foot sizes'. He opened a shop in Green End leaving his sister to run no. 38.[11] By 1975 the Haller family owned and occupied nos. 38 and 40. At present all three properties are in separate ownership.

21 - 23 High Street ('Walker's')

There is no great display of genuine timber-framing in Whitchurch High Street. Mostly, where it survives at all, it is hidden behind later brick or stuccoed façades. But an exception is 21 - 23, currently known as 'Walker's', sometimes called 'Ye Olde Shoppe' but referred to as 'The Old Cooperage' about 1870 from the type of business carried on there. For many years it has been a restaurant, bakery and food supply outlet. An old photograph shows the frontage as it appeared about 1870 and is included on p.97 so that a comparison may be made with its present form. The main changes relate to the differences in the ground floor fenestration, the removal of the dormer window, the chimney, the pentice roofs, and the lowering of the steps. Aesthetically these are sad losses, although they do not affect the basic structure or the interpretation of the plan. The change most deplored by Whitchurchians is the removal of the two porterages: external shelves at waist height upon which porters could rest sacks of flour, corn and similar goods while loading or unloading. These survived until *c.*1970, serving as external display areas, and were the only known

ones in Shropshire.[1] There are some changes in the pattern of the framing. Most noticeable is the disappearance of the mid-rail in the upper storey of the southern unit and the alterations in the gable end. Here, the St. Andrew's cross shown in the sketch of the frontage as it was in 1992 (p.97) was painted on, although a painting done in 1923 shows an identical cross in genuine timbers in exactly the same position.[2]

An alleyway known as 'Bluegates' is located immediately to the south of 'Walker's'—the chamber over the entry being part of the adjoining property. From the front there is a clear division and this is emphasised by a break

21 - 23 High Street, or 'Walker's'

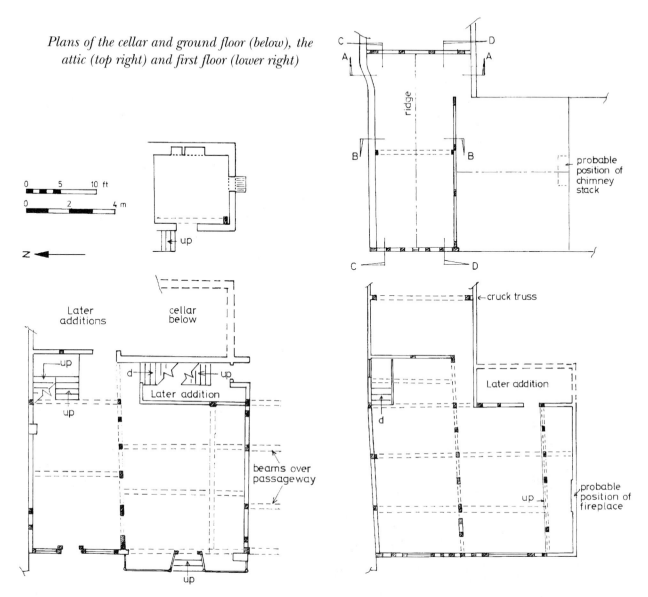

Plans of the cellar and ground floor (below), the attic (top right) and first floor (lower right)

The Plan

Basically, the property is L-shaped and consists of two main units, a crosswing to the north (no. 23) and a 'hall' range at right-angles to it (no. 21). As shown on section D - D (p.99) the hall roof is taller than the crosswing. It is fully two-storied and the presence of a dormer window in the 1870 photograph suggests that the roof space was used for accommodation. Most probably the hall range was rebuilt in the late 16th or early 17th century. As the whole of the ground floor and first floor are in commercial use it is difficult to determine whether there are any abnormalities in the lay-out of the interior, but nothing significant is apparent. The most striking feature is the irregular shape, a feature noted in almost all the town properties surveyed.

The crosswing has a later continuation eastwards, the full extent of which is not shown on the plans, but at first floor level part of a cruck truss is visible about half-way along its length. The blades are thin and stilted and appear to be late in date. It is possible that the crosswing was extended when the hall was rebuilt.

The Crosswing

Externally the crosswing displays decorative work, some of which would not have been visible when the pentice roofs were in place. The tie-beam of the jettied gable and the fascia-board which masks the top-plate of the upper storey each have a band of carving which may be described as a type of guilloche design. The fascia board breaks in the middle to accommodate the window of the upper floor. On the 1870 photograph this window is seen to have its own hood board, echoing the form of the pentice roofs at the lower level, but it is possible that originally the break in the fascia board was to accommodate a projecting oriel window. There are no obvious signs of supporting brackets on the studs, but the timbers have received so much remedial treatment that it is difficult to be certain.

Top: The east elevation sketched in 1992.
Below: The 'Old Cooperage' in 1870
from a photo by J.R. Crosse

The guilloche carving is badly weathered, but that on the soffit of the first-floor jetty is crisp, protected as it was for many years by the lower pentice roof and by its natural position. Here the motifs are paired daggers with trefoil heads, reminiscent of the Decorated style of English tracery, curiously archaic in their context. On the bressumer and flush with the surface are small rectangular features which, at first glance, look like the ends of floor joists but are more likely to represent the infilling of the housings for the timbers of the pentice roof.

97

Details of patterning (starting from the top) in no. 23 on: a tie beam; the top plate; a bressumer; and soffit of the lower jetty

The Crosswing Roof

The external details suggest that the unit originally functioned as a solar crosswing, perhaps with a shop below. The 'solar' concept is supported by the nature of the central truss in the upper chamber, at present located above an inserted ceiling. As shown on section B - B the collar-beam, supported by arch-braces, indicates that this was an open truss, intended to be seen from first-floor level. Chamfering on both sides and the inclusion of a decorative boss in the middle confirms this judgment. Unfortunately the soffit of the boss was too badly mutilated to allow reconstruction. The drawing shows how the truss has slumped northwards without any fractures occurring in the timbers, although joints have opened to a certain extent. Remedial braces are not shown. There was no evidence of smoke-blackening, nor of a chimneystack, therefore it is unlikely that the chamber was ever heated, unless by a portable charcoal-burning brazier.

The post marked 'X' is carpentered to provide an original integration of the two units, and, as the longitudinal sections C - C and D - D show, the crosswing has cusped wind-braces only on the northern side, with just one token straight windbrace on the southern side. These features suggest that the original hall was single-storied and had a roof-line lower than that of the crosswing which was floored at first-floor level.

Local residents remember that until the 1950s there was a long pole with a metal hook on the end which rested on brackets on the wall in the Bluegates entry. This was thought to be an implement for pulling burning thatch from roofs, a left-over from another era. There was dismay when the pole disappeared. However, it seems to have found a resting-place in the roof of the crosswing, but, sadly, the metal hook has been removed.

The Social History[3]

It is unusual to be able to relate a probate inventory to a standing building, but, bearing in mind the Burghall family connection with the property, it seems a reasonable exercise in the case of George 'Borghall'.[4] The inventory was taken in 1562 and is doubly valuable because it names the rooms. It also confirms that the chamber over the Bluegates entry was part of the property, that the extension to the crosswing had not been built and that the hall had an upper floor. What is not clear is whether the hall range had been rebuilt by then. The rooms listed are: 'Hawle, parler, chamber over the hawle, chamber over the gate, shop, chamber over the shop, chamber over the parler.' The value of the contents was £8 5s 10d.

A later inventory, that relating to Thomas Burghall[5] was taken in December 1641, and it also names the rooms. From this it is clear that the extension to the crosswing was in

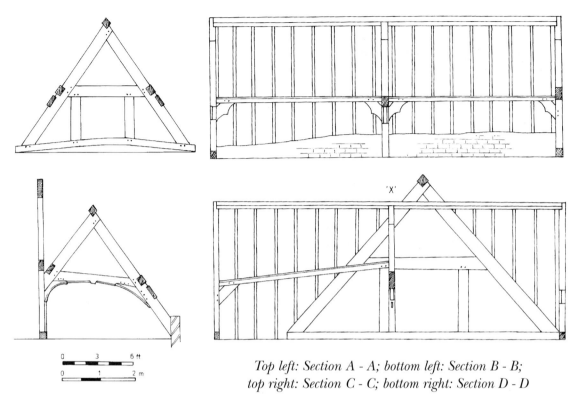

Top left: Section A - A; bottom left: Section B - B;
top right: Section C - C; bottom right: Section D - D

place, and it is likely that the hall range had been rebuilt by that time. The rooms listed are: 'Hall, Parlour, New Chamber, Chamber over ye Hall, Chamber over ye Gates, Chamber over the parlour, Darke Chamber, The further chamber, Chamber over ye Shop, Ye Buttery, Ye Kitchen.' Different permutations can be made for the disposition of the rooms, particularly those at first-floor level, but the overall size of the property seems to have been much as it is at present, apart from the chamber over Bluegates which is now in separate occupation.

The property is recorded as an inn, 'The Swan', during the 17th and early 18th centuries, and its location is made clear by the reference to 'a certain way or passage called the Swan Inn Yard or Bluegates.'[6] It should not be confused with another of the same name on the opposite side of the High Street, nor with yet another 'Swan' in Watergate.

A series of 14 copyhold surrenders to the Court Baron of the Manor of Whitchurch traces the transfer of tenancies between 1648 and 1774.[7] They all refer to the property as 'The Swan Inn' or 'formerly known as the Swan'. The first, dated 1647/8 states that 'Mary Burgall, widow, and John Meare and Margery his wife do surrender 1 shoppe in the occupation of Ralph Bradock butcher (being part of one messuage containing $2\frac{1}{2}$ burgages more or less) being part of the Swan to the use of J. Meare and his wife. It is not known when the 'Swan' was delicensed, but a surrender of 1758 refers to 'some of the estate of Geo Paule, formerly known as The Swan Inne.'

From the number of tenants mentioned in each surrender from the early 18th century onwards, it seems that only part of the complex was in use as an inn, and that the premises were divided into at least two and sometimes as many as four tenements which stretched eastwards along Bluegates. The preamble to the 1774 surrender states 'To this Court cometh Mary Clarke, widdow, to surrender all that customary messuage or burgage now divided into four dwellings together with all shops, buildings, cellars in High Street in several occupation of Mary Clarke, J. Roles, Will Morrey and Will Wickstead and some of their undertenants.'

In 1799 the property was insured with the Salop Fire Office by Thomas Sadler, Huckster and Toyseller and 'his other dwelling house situate nearby' was also insured. Both premises are described as of 'brick, timber, lath, plaister, slate and tile' and it seems clear that it is nos. 21 and 23 that are being referred to. By this time the complex had been divided into two tenements. On the frontage there is still one firemark on each unit.[8] A notice of sale makes it clear that the division had certainly been done by 1819 and that the block comprised two shops, the southern unit, no. 21, being the huckster's shop, and the cross-wing, no. 23, a cooper's shop. The entry reads 'High Street, two messuages with Coopers' and Hucksters' shops thereto belonging ... and held by James and Ed. Barlow; also dwelling house adjacent used as warehouse ...'[9] James Barlow had been a cooper in the town since at least 1790, but by 1825 John Cook had taken over the business.[10] After his death c.1845 his widow, Mary, ran the cooperage for several years until her death at the age of 69 in 1859.[11] Her three sons and three living-in apprentices made the pails, tubs, cheese moulds, dolly-pegs and other artifacts which can be seen in the photograph of c.1870. At this time Thomas Caldicote used the southern unit as a Provision Warehouse. He is recorded as a provision dealer and his wife Elizabeth as a lodging-house keeper. She had two lodgers, a cooper and an upholsterer.[12]

George Cook, Mary's eldest son, managed the cooperage after his mother's death with one living-in apprentice, but ten years later his nephew Frederick was his only assistant. George died in 1887 and Frederick carried on the business for several more years with his Aunt Elizabeth as housekeeper.[13] From this it is clear that no. 23 was a cooperage for most of the 19th century, and was known in the town as 'The Old Cooperage' until well into the 1930s.

No. 21, the southern unit, had more varied occupants during this period and it is difficult to separate the tenants of no. 21 from those living in Bluegates, but by 1879 Thomas Ankers was established there as a baker.[14] In 1885 John Walker came to Whitchurch from Mansfield and took over the bakery from Ankers. He established a successful business and took an active part in local affairs.[15] When he died in 1905 one of his six sons, Richard, took over the bakery which continued to trade as 'J. Walker'. The family controlled the business after Richard's death in 1930 until 1960 when it was bought by J.W. Absolon. A master baker, Absolon converted the first-floor storerooms into a café, and with the help of his wife, three daughters, ten assistants in the shop and bakery and two roundsmen for daily bread deliveries the business flourished.

No. 23, the old cooperage, was used by Arthur L. Wood as an antique shop from c.1937, but c.1970 the whole block returned to single ownership when it was acquired by the Absolon family. It was at this time that the porterages and the thatching rake were removed.

After the Absolon family retired in 1978 the shop, still known as 'Walker's', was bought by T.O. Williams of Wem who removed the infill from the timber frame partition between the two shops at ground level and re-sited the staircase. Later owners, the Finneys continued to trade under the 'Walker's' name as do the current owners, the Tiptons who have the distinction of being the last of the old established bakers and confectioners in the town.

34 - 42 High Street

This group of buildings were not fully recorded, but contain details of architectural interest.

34 High Street
Situated at the junction of High Street and Pepper Street, this is a fine three-storied Georgian building with a four-bayed frontage, raised quoins, a modillion cornice, parapet and kneelers. The windows are flat-headed and have keystones and sill-brackets. If the original multi-paned glazing could be restored, this would be one of the most stylish properties in the High Street. It is thought to have been the town house of the Bridgwater family, one-time lords of the manor.[1]

34 High Street

36 & 38 High Street
A three-storied structure with a complicated roofline. The ground floor is in commercial use. At first floor level the northern room has a bolection-moulded fireplace in the west wall, while that in the southern room has Jacobean-type carving. Roundels are incorporated in the frieze, and on the jambs are two carved heads, one of which bears a distinct resemblance to Van Dyck's portrayals of Charles I. At second floor level the main rooms have ovolo-moulded spine-beams with cyma stops. The extremely fine dog-leg staircase is illustrated over-leaf. A section of the roof space where the axis is at right-angles to the High Street appears to incorporate a former agricultural building. The roof truss

36 and 38 High Street, the top of the fireplace in the southern room

36 and 38 High Street. Left: The staircase. Right the front

has a king-post rising from the tie-beam and there are two lateral struts from the king-post to the principal rafters. In the east wall of this roof section are two stone triangular ornamental pieces which mask the ends of beams from another section of the building. They have an ecclesiastic appearance and incorporate a type of roll-and-hollow moulding. Possibly they came from one of the churches. The staircase and the fireplace details suggest a date of *c*.1670-80.

40 & 42 High Street

In 1904 the famous clock-making firm of Joyce vacated this site which had housed the factory since the 1780s. The site was redeveloped by Mr. Caleb Birchall for his ironmongery retail business, and he commissioned a Whitchurch architect, William Webb of Bargates, to design the striking cast-iron frontage which was cast in modular form by McFarlane's of Glasgow.

40 - 42 High Street, the striking cast-iron frontage

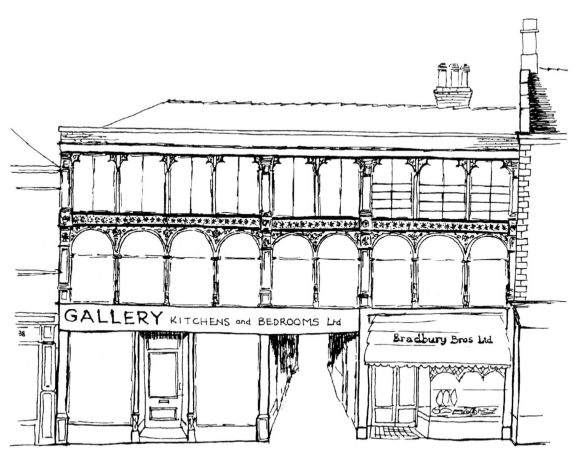

40 - 42 High Street, a sketch of the shop front bringing out the detail of the ironwork

Commercial rivalry was probably behind this action. Whitchurch was the home of a famous firm of iron founders, W.H. Smith, at the time. There is nothing comparable with this façade in any other Shropshire town.[2]

35 & 37 High Street

This pair of buildings were not fully recorded, but contain details of architectural interest.

35 High Street
At one time this building was the 'Ring of Bells' inn. The street frontage incorporates a fine set of cast-iron pillars made *c.*1900 by W.H. Smith of Whitchurch.[1]

37 High Street
A timber-framed three-bayed, three-storied building. The roof is plain and has side purlins. There is a rear wing at right-angles to the main axis. The wing appears to incorporate former agricultural units and there is a hoist to what was perhaps a granary. The main feature of interest is a surviving portion of a Jacobean staircase. Only the flight to the attic remains but it displays, on a smaller scale, the features noted in no. 38 High Street. It may be the work of the same carpenter.

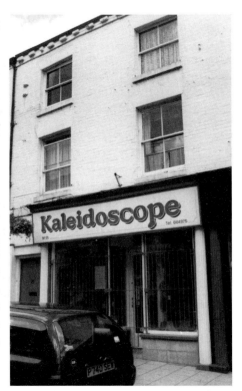

35 High Street

41 - 45 High Street

41 High Street
This property forms the beginning of a homogeneous group of three properties on the eastern side of the High Street that ends with no. 45. As shown on the photograph, the street frontage has decorative timber-work, but this is pseudo-framing applied to the genuine framing which forms the line of the street encroachment.

The plan is very simple. As with no. 45 there are two rooms at each floor level, the staircase is against the northern wall and a large

41 - 45 High Street

lateral chimneystack on the southern wall provides fireplaces at the three levels. The entrance position is at the southern end of the front elevation, that is, in the opposite position to that at no. 45, but likewise appears to be original.

No. 41 has more early 17th century framing remaining in the front and rear walls internally than the other properties in the block, and the later 17th century work is distinguished by the sharply cut-back heads to the posts, also noted in nos. 43 and 45.

No original fenestration remains on any of the properties, and the mixture of designs appears to emphasise the desire for individuality that characterics each of the units in the block.

43 High Street
Although mostly rebuilt in the late 17th century the property is clearly part of the block of nos. 41 - 45 which represents encroachment into the High Street. The roof timbers in the attic have chiselled carpenters' marks and straight windbraces, but there are earlier scribed marks on the framing in the second storey.

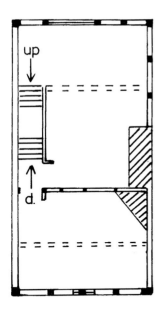
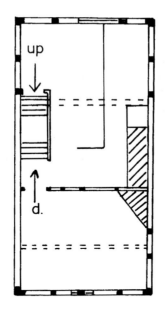
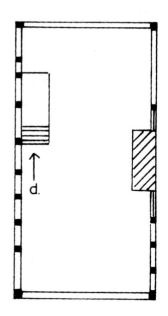

Plans of 41 High Street.

Below: High Street frontage of no. 41 (n.t.s.)

*The cellar (bottom left),
the ground floor (bottom right),
the first floor (top left),
second floor (top centre),
and attic (top right)*

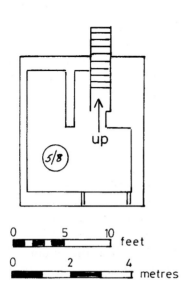

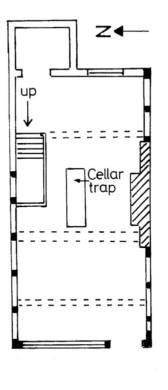

No. 41

0   5   10 feet

0   2   4 metres

45 High Street

The commercial premises on the eastern side of the High Street terminate at Church Street, and between the church and no. 45, at present known as 'Shirley's Plaice' and in use as a wet fish shop, are only the 'Black Bear' public house and a small bookshop (no. 47 High Street), itself a flat-roofed forward extension from the recessed part of the 'Black Bear'. It is the front of this recessed area which demarcates an earlier building line. The OS map of 1880 shows no. 45 as occupying the northernmost of three plots of equal size. The plots form a regular rectangle, the buildings are each three-storied and have a continuous eaves level, suggesting that part of their building history has a common theme although the design of the timberwork on the front elevations varies slightly. No. 45 is the least altered, and the pattern of small rectangular framing, four panels high above the shop front, is genuinely timber-framed, whereas on the other two frontages the timbers are applied. Original framing is also retained on the rear elevation of no. 45 where it is three panels high. Clearly this was an economy measure, the more expensive

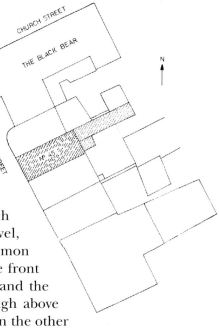

Site plan based on OS map 1880 (n.t.s.)

framing used where it would be seen to best advantage, that is, from the High Street.

In each building the plan is very simple, two rooms in depth with the staircase against the northern wall, provision for a corner fireplace in the shop and a lateral fireplace in the living room behind the shop. No original fenestration survives on any of the properties, but the entrance positions appear to be unchanged. In each building the main posts have the heads sharply cut back. In no. 45 this shows as a feature on the exterior and is also present internally on the truss which divides it from no. 43.

Section A - A shows how the block forms an encroachment into the High Street from an earlier building line, and this is repeated on the northern side of Section B - B. There can be little doubt that the earlier phase had a lower roofline, was two storeys high and remains encapsulated within the enlarged building. As mentioned above, the only

East elevation (n.t.s.)

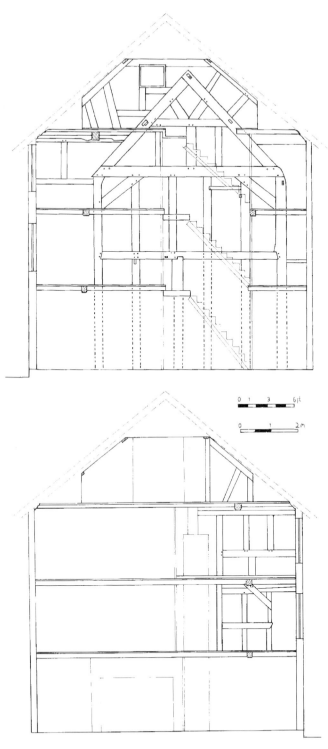

external evidence of the earlier building line is seen in the front wall of the recessed area of the 'Black Bear', whilst the narrow frame now forms part of the end frame of no. 45. Early and late 17th century dates are suggested for the two phases.

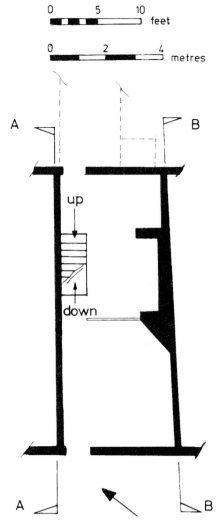

Above: Ground plan of 45 High Street

Top: Section A - A showing street encroachment from earlier building.
Bottom: Section B - B

50 - 54 High Street

50 & 52 High Street

Recently uncovered on the fascia board below a bay window at first floor level are two elaborate and prominent marks, one is a monogram, JHR (John Henry Read), a tailor, and the other is the date 1878 (see below). Businesses had a permanence in Victorian times, not envisaged today.

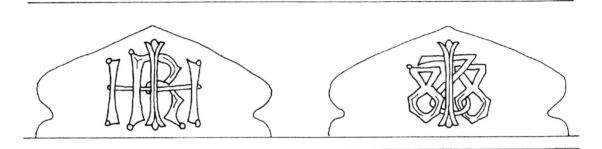

54 High Street

The domestic quarters of this property are approached from a side passage and a rear hall which contains an 18th century dog-leg staircase. It has square newel posts, chamfered on all four arrises and finished with cyma stops. The finials are chunky and rounded, the handrail fairly wide, and each tread supports two balusters which are not turned but are tapered and moulded. A quatrefoil is carved on each tread-end, but may be decoration added later. The dado is panelled, the panels following a parallel plane with the rise. Those relating to the upper flight have carpenters' mitres, while the lower run has masons' mitres. The soffit of the upper flight is also panelled. There is

The panelled dado at no. 54 (n.t.s.)

no evidence that the staircase is a reused feature, and is likely to be another example of the elegant staircases favoured in Whitchurch.

54 High Street.
Details of the staircase (n.t.s.)

60 High Street

60 High Street is on the western side of the street and occupies slightly less than half of the plot of land between Jones's Yard and Barlow's Yard. The larger portion is occupied by no. 58 which extends over Jones's Yard. Each property presents a three-storied frontage to the High Street and has a combined commercial and residential use. Above the shop windows the plain brick façade contains four sash windows at each level. These are flat-headed and recessed, with 16 lights in each of the first floor set and twelve lights in the second floor; but two windows are blocked, and it is in the middle of these that the property division occurs. Until the late 19th century the plot was in single occupation and probably represents the site of a substantial medieval holding. No. 60 contains timbers which have a medieval appearance, but it was not possible to examine the interior of no. 58. However, it was noted that both properties share a large chimneystack in the front units—its position in no. 60 being marked on section D - D.

The Plan and the Stencilled Wall Decoration

Measurements were taken on both the ground floor and the first floor to ascertain whether the bay divisions coincided. While there was a discrepancy in the front bay, the main truss lines matched perfectly and it is clear that the property consists of three bays running back from the street. The first bay represents street encroachment, probably of 18th century date, and has its roof line parallel

58 and 60 High Street, once a combined property. 'Something Else' (no. 60) is now 'Tolchards'

111

The High Street frontage (n.t.s.)

with the street, while the other two bays are timber-framed, have their origin in medieval times and are set gable-end on to the street. The encroachment bay is entirely brick-built, is three storied and contains a cellar in which part of the base of the shared stack is set

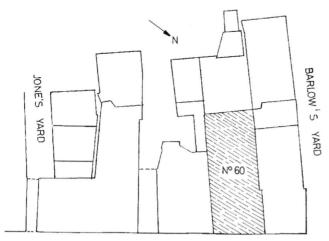

Site plan based on OS Map 1880 (n.t.s.).
The High Street frontage is at the foot of the plan

diagonally. In the attic room are sections of stencilled wall decoration in a repetitive pattern of leaves and petals contained within swirling arabesques. The colouring is a medium blue and black on a yellow ochre background. As such it is very similar to that found recently at 12 Friar Street, Worcester which is described as a 'pre-neoclassical floral design copying wood-block printed wallpaper.' The suggested date is 1740-50. If allowance is made for a slight

Detail of the wall painting in the attic of no. 60
(drawn by K. Priddy and M. Dutton)

time-lag for fashionable trends to reach Whitchurch it implies that the wall-painting at no. 60 is contemporary with the building of the encroachment bay.[1]

The Earlier Range

Trusses A, B and C enclose two bays of a timber-framed building. A single tier of threaded purlins was originally continuous in each bay, but they have been largely replaced.

The visible parts of truss A, shown as section A - A on the drawings, are evident from the east. Beyond it is an entirely modern extension which has obscured the western face

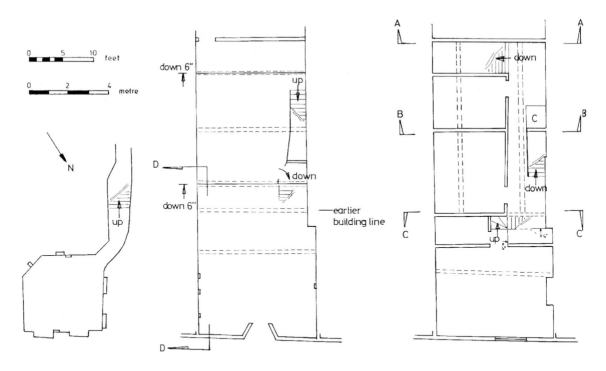

Above: Plans of 60 High Street's cellar (left), ground floor (centre) and first floor (right)
Below: Section A - A (left) and B - B (right) (both drawn to same scale as sections opposite)

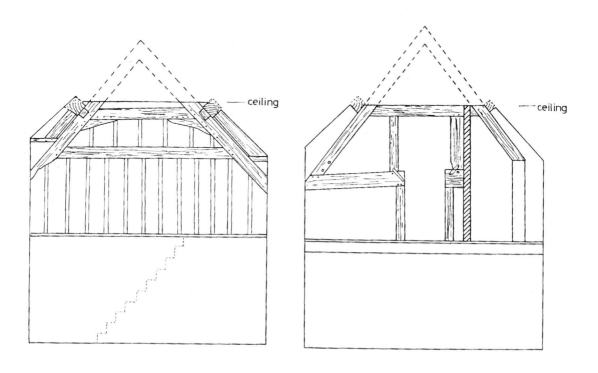

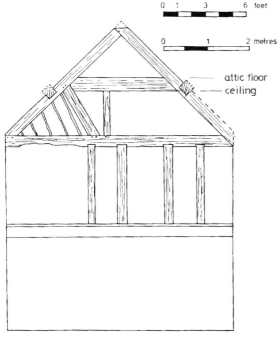

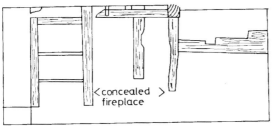

Top: Section C - C
Bottom: Section D - D

of the truss. However, judicious probing revealed that there was chamfering on both sides of the principal rafter and also on both faces of the collar-beam and the arch-braces. This suggests that the truss functioned as the open central truss of a two-bay unit in much the same way as was noted at the High Street Garage. Unlike the Garage, however, there is a horizontal beam only four feet below the collar-beam. This unusual feature must have been included to give added rigidity to the truss; it cannot represent a later insertion as it is properly morticed, tenoned and pegged at either end into the principal rafters. Even so, it should be secondary and could have been morticed in, perhaps when this became the end wall.

Truss B is of queen-post construction and is currently filled with wattle and daub. It appears always to have been a closed truss. On its eastern face some of the joints are distinguished by paired crescent carpenters' marks and it also bears rush taper marks. If truss A has been interpreted correctly, truss B would demarcate the eastern end of the open unit.

Truss C is drawn from the western side and includes a row of inserted vertical timbers in addition to a doorhead at the northern end. The doorway was probably made to give access to the street encroachment bay. The eastern side of the truss has weathering upon it and there are indications that it was a jettied frame, although now largely plastered over. These features provide the evidence that this truss demarcates the earlier building line, and it appears that there was a floored bay (between B and C) in addition to and in front of the two open bays.

Conclusions

In the late 19th century nos. 58 and 60 High Street were one property, but as no access could be gained to no. 58 an important part of the structural history cannot, as yet, be determined. However, there are strong similarities between no. 60, nos. 21 and 23 High Street and the High Street Garage, only a very short distance away. On the latter site it is argued that what remains was the solar wing to a medieval open hall that had been demolished. It has some idiosyncratic aspects which are not present in no. 60, but the carpentry details, particularly those in the open trusses, are almost identical. It is suggested, therefore, that no. 60 represents the solar wing to an open hall which was located on the site of no. 58, but, if this is correct, it was a spacious two-bayed solar with an open central truss with, in addition, it had a floored bay nearest the street. On the other hand it could be argued that, as no. 60 clearly continued westwards, more than just one bay is missing and perhaps its plot accommodated a whole medieval in-line house set gable-end on to a narrow frontage, with the open bays relating to a two-bayed hall open from ground level, the floored bay representing a small solar and the missing service end located beyond the hall. On balance, however, the solar wing hypothesis is that which is favoured.

It is suggested that the encroachment bay dates from *c.*1760. Dendrochronological sampling was carried out on the earlier phase in 1993, but gave only a date range of 1563 - 1597. A date of post-1552 was obtained from a tie-beam, but on this the sapwood was missing. While it could relate to an earlier building phase, it is more likely to belong to the date range given. With the other two High Street properties taken into consideration, it seems that in Whitchurch the medieval house-plan, with variations, persisted into the latter part of the 16th century.[2]

Historical Note[3]
Various Shropshire directories make it clear that nos. 58 and 60 High Street were one property at least in the early 19th century. In 1823 Sarah Venables was described as a baker and flour dealer in High Street, but by 1828-9 Venables and Son are listed in Bargates.[4] The family seems to have had more than one business outlet and members were not only bakers and confectioners but smiths, mercers, grocers and ironmongers.[5] From the regularity of its position in the directories it has been deduced that the property in the High Street was no. 58, and this is confirmed in 1868.[6] The family continued to live and work there throughout the rest of the 19th century. In 1903 E.J. Bailey bought the property and the business and by 1909 had divided the property into two units. He continued to use the northern half (no. 60) as a bakery, while no. 58 was leased to Alfred Hendrick, a watchmaker and jeweller.[7] No. 58 is still occupied by the widow of another jeweller, Mr. R.A. Edwards, who took over in 1937 but no. 60 ceased to be a bakery in 1985. Both units were sold in 1983, resold in 1985, and are now in separate ownership. No. 60 was run for several years as a bookshop/antiques called 'Something Else' by the owner/occupiers Mr. and Mrs. R. Forster, and is now called 'Tolchards'.[8]

The High Street Garage & 2 Bargates

The property known as the High Street Garage at Whitchurch is situated at the northern end of the High Street on the western side, facing the church. This area at present effectively terminates the commercial premises in the High Street, and beyond the Garage the road takes a wide sweep into Yardington. But until 1976 the western side of Bargates, as this part of the town is known, remained a built up area. A public house—the 'Lamb Hotel'—adjoined the Garage on the northern side and there were houses beyond the 'Lamb'.

The Garage now stands in isolation for the properties on its southern side have also been demolished. This is regrettable on two counts. Firstly it gives a gap-toothed effect to the most important area of the town and secondly it has removed an integral part of the Garage property, namely the late medieval hall relating to the surviving solar wing. It must be admitted that the description of the missing unit as a 'hall' is supposition; nothing was recorded prior to its demolition in the 1920s, but a 19th century watercolour shows the building as twin-gabled and having a further unit with a lower roof line.[1] The property stood structurally detached from its neighbours on either side, and so it is possible that when complete it represented a fully developed three-part plan late medieval house with

a service end, hall and solar cross-wing. It was probably T-shaped, but at some time the hall was remodelled and given a gable-end to match that of the solar. The chimney stack that marked the division of the twin gables remains as a disused facility on the long southern wall of the Garage and the space previously occupied by the hall and service bay is now the Garage forecourt. Whatever shape the house took, all that remains of the medieval complex are two bays, basically timber-framed but with much modern brickwork. These have

The High Street Garage

117

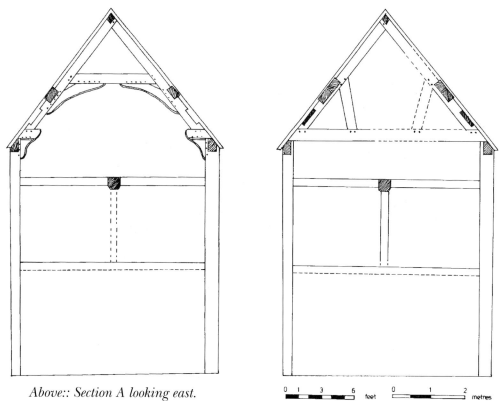

Above:: Section A looking east.
Right: Section B looking west.
Below: Longitudinal section looking north

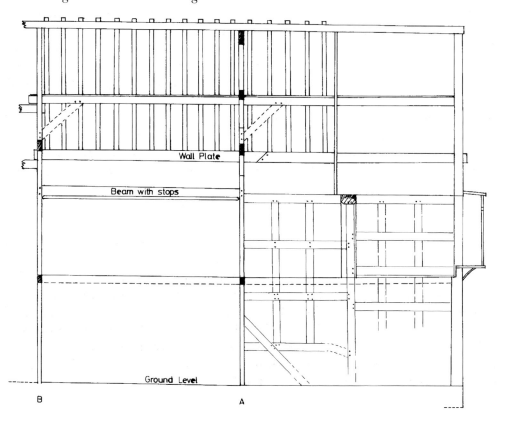

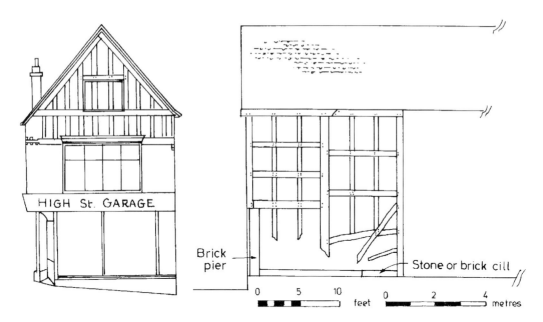

East (left) and north (right) elevations of the High Street Garage

had brick extensions built along the plot to the west and the whole premises are in commercial use, the supposed solar as storage for motor parts.

The Solar Wing

It must be emphasised that in assigning the role of the surviving unit to that of a solar crosswing a certain amount of guesswork has been employed, but the question that should be asked is what is its function otherwise? Even if the hall and service end were part of a complete 'gable end-on plan' running back along a burgage plot the architectural evidence points to the solar end overlooking the street and having an unrivalled view of the church. External timber-framing survives only on part of the long northern wall where it is mostly in the form of square and rectangular panels. Much has been replaced with brickwork but the square-framing seems to have been six panels high, the mark of a superior building. A continuous post at the western end of the framing represents the open central truss of the solar and another, mid-way between it and the end post demarcates a half-bay and divides the rectangular framing from the square framing. Though a small point, it is significant that the regular square framing is used for the half-bay nearest to the street. Even though it is unlikely that the whole wall would be exposed to view originally the builders took care to put the more expensive framing towards the better end and thus emphasise the superior end of the solar.

The whole bays are of equal width, each measuring 17ft. 2ins. x 16ft. 6ins., and it seems likely that they constituted the whole of that particular part of the house. The truss at the western end— 'B'—was clearly a closed truss. It has been badly mutilated and any evidence of early continuation that it may have had to the west before the present brick extension was built has been removed as the western side of the truss appears to have no signs of weathering. At some time a chimney was inserted into the frame; its removal has left a gap, shown by the broken lines on the section drawing.

The Central Truss

There can be no doubt that section 'A' was an open truss located mid-way along the length of the solar. It has a collar-beam supported by arch-braces so fashioned that small spandrels occur in the angles between the two. At tie-beam level there are two stub tie-beams or 'spurs' which support the principal rafters and are in turn supported by angle-brackets. The latter are not integral with the post-heads but are triple-pegged into them and into the stub tie-beams. That this assembly was considered an important and decorative feature is evident from the half-ogee curved form resulting from the rounding off on the ends of the stub tie-beam and the hollowing out of the bracket. The ogee in a wider spread is repeated above by the arch-braces to the collar-beam. Chamfering is present on both sides of the arch-braces, the stub-ties and the brackets, but not on the collar-beam itself. An impression is gained of an aesthetic appeal deliberately contrived and subtly effective.

Windbraces and other features

On the southern slope of the roof two straight windbraces remain *in situ*. They are tenoned into the purlin and seated on the backs of the principal rafters. The matching members have been removed from the northern slope but the longitudinal section shows where they were positioned on that side. It is curious that only one pair was used in each bay, but it is quite clear that no more were intended, as neither mortices nor peg-holes for them are present. The rafters are mostly modern although a few older ones remain.

On the wall-plate, to the east of the central truss, there is a failed splayed and bridled scarf with two edge-pegs. The splay is continuous and the joint is a very simple one which accounts in part for its failure.

Only four joists relating to the second floor are visible at present. They appear on the southern side of the spine-beam, described below. They measure 5ins. x 4ins., are placed at intervals of 1ft. 6ins. and have 4in. bare-faced soffit-tenons; but these are not secured with pegs which probably accounts for some structural failure at this point with the joists becoming partially dislodged from their housing.[2]

Fixed to the purlin on the southern slope of the roof is a steel-yard which is shown as a detail on the drawings. Its presence suggests that at some time the solar was used for measuring and storing a commodity, the nature of which remains unknown.

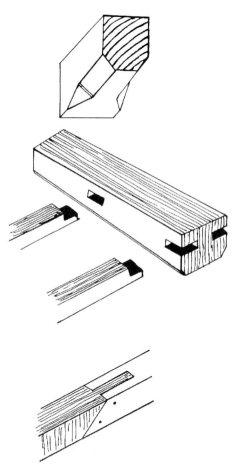

Top: Straight cut stop.
Centre: Spine beam joints
with bare faced soffit-tenon.
Bottom: Scarf joint on wall plate
showing splayed and bridled scarf
with two edge pegs

120

During the Second World War a temporary dormer window was inserted into the southern slope of the roof for A.R.P. fire-watching purposes. In the course of enquiries several local residents mentioned this, and traces remain of the arrangement.

It is the floor levels which represent the area of most concern regarding the interpretation of the building. A substantial spine-beam measuring 1ft. square and with a 3in. chamfer and straight-cut stops at each end supports the upper floor between trusses 'A' and 'B'. It appears to be properly tenoned into central vertical posts on each truss. The evidence is very

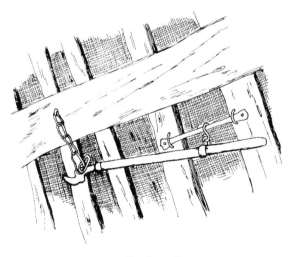

Steel-yard

clear on section 'B' and although on section 'A' the framing is boarded and wall-papered over, the mutilated stop on the chamfer remains and the tenon may be discerned by probing. It is clear that the spine beam does not extend into the northern bay. Here a different beam runs transversely and is supported on brick pillars built out from the walls, indicating that the floor is a later insertion. If the longitudinal beam is an original feature, as it appears to be, it means that only one bay of the solar was floored at the second level, the other designed to be open from first floor level. In other words there was a 'croglofft' arrangement. Such Welsh influence was common in the Whitchurch area and, during the course of enquiries, many old people recalled using crogloffts for sleeping space. But these were invariably in cottages.[3] It is unusual to encounter the practice in the solar of a superior house and it means that the elaborate central truss could never be seen in its entirety. From the croglofft the stub tie-beams would appear at 3ft. above the floor level while from the open bay they would be 10ft. 3ins. above floor level.

The matter is further complicated by the fact that there is a window, now blocked, but probably an original feature, in the gable of the street-facing elevation. Though simply consisting of three gaps between the studs it has a proper lintel tenoned and pegged into mortices in the flanking studs; and although the blocking studs are modern the window frame is chamfered and the tie-beam is reduced in thickness where the frame occurs. It would have been impossible to reach the window from the floor of the open bay without a long ladder and, if permanently unshuttered, would have kept both bays of the solar at unacceptably low temperatures. A possible explanation is that the gaps were provided for the escape of smoke, a true 'wind-eye'. But any heating must have been provided by a portable brazier, probably peat-burning. Although there appears to be fugitive blackening on the timbers of the central truss as though from the smoke of an open fire, this is associated with a flaking whitewash now dirt-encrusted.

There is, however, an alternative and perhaps a more acceptable explanation for the anomaly of the floor levels and that is to regard the brick pillars in the easternmost bay as later supports for the replacement of an original spine beam which bridged the bay in a north-south plane. This would mean that the joists could extend beyond the front wall face and support a jetty. At present there is no firm evidence of a jetty, but the modern shop front may represent the infilling of an earlier jettied elevation. This reasoning still leaves unexplained the fact that the stub-tie details would appear at only 3ft. above floor level. The only possibly counter to that is to regard the stub-ties as interrupted tie-beams, a means of allowing head-room in the solar.

Conclusions and Dating

Nothing is known about the social history of the building, and, as stated above, its description as a solar has to be a tentative one as most of the original building is missing. However, certain conclusions may be drawn from the style of the framing, some of which have already been mentioned. Clearly the form of the central truss was of primary importance. Often stub tie-beams are associated with deep-swinging arch-braces which reach well below wall-plate level. On the whole Shropshire's box-framed houses tend to terminate the arch-braces on the principal rafters, although there are some notable exceptions.[4] In the case of the Garage it is possible that the carpenter was striving for the effect of a hammer-beam truss without the complications and expense normally associated with such a roof-form.

Compared with the central truss some of the other carpentry details are very simple and it is suggested that in some instances archaic forms are employed. The spine-beam, though of large scantling, has only a plain chamfer and straight-cut stops; the windbraces are plain and straight and a minimum number are used; the joists, though strong, lack pegging and have the simplest form of jointing, and the scarf-joint on the wall-plate is so basic that it finds no place in the text-books.

Given these factors and in the absence of documentary evidence a date of between 1450 and 1500 is suggested, although there is no reason why it should not be a product of the 16th century.

2 Bargates

This is a two-bayed, timber-framed structure which has acquired a brick 'skin' on the front. As in many Whitchurch properties, the roof has been raised and angled out to create a two-storied property from an original one-and-a-half stories. On the north side the exposed gable exhibits typical 17th century box-framing with a cross-rail at first storey height, tie-beam and collar-beam with two queen-struts. Below the tie-beam three studs divide the area into four panels, and there are two straight tension-braces from the posts to the sill. A fine set of chiselled carpenters' marks are exposed on the gable. There is a gap between 2 Bargates and the High Street Garage which was once occupied by the supposed hall range of the latter property.

2 Bargates

St. Mary's Cottage, St. Mary's Street

Occupying the corner of Church Street and St. Mary's Street, St. Mary's Cottage is a pretty, 'gothicised' house with twin gables facing the street and a flight of steps from street level to the main entrance. Property boundaries hereabouts, as elsewhere in Whitchurch, are curiously interlocked and an attempt to unravel the plans and boundaries of adjoining premises, instead of throwing light on the corner property, merely resulted in more confusion. On the lower ground floor, the room currently in use as the kitchen is front-facing but partly underground and is served by a large chimneystack, designed as an outbuilt feature but later incorporated at two levels into a lean-to extension to the north-west. The walls of the semi-underground storey are thicker than those of the upper stories, suggesting that they are stone-built. There is no evidence of external or internal timber-framing; the only timber-work is in the roof-space at the apexes of the two trusses. Neither is smoke-blackened, and, although they are substantial timbers, of 10in. scantling, they appear to be re-used. The ridge-purlin which they support is also a later introduction.

The Windows

Striking features of the property are the 'gothick' windows on the front elevation. The room to the left of the entrance is not at present part of St. Mary's Cottage and this has the only un-gothicised window apart from the kitchen window. As shown on section D - D, so determined were the 'improvers' to gothicise most of the fenestration that floor and ceiling levels were disregarded. Particularly incongruous is the arrangement of the

St Mary's Cottage

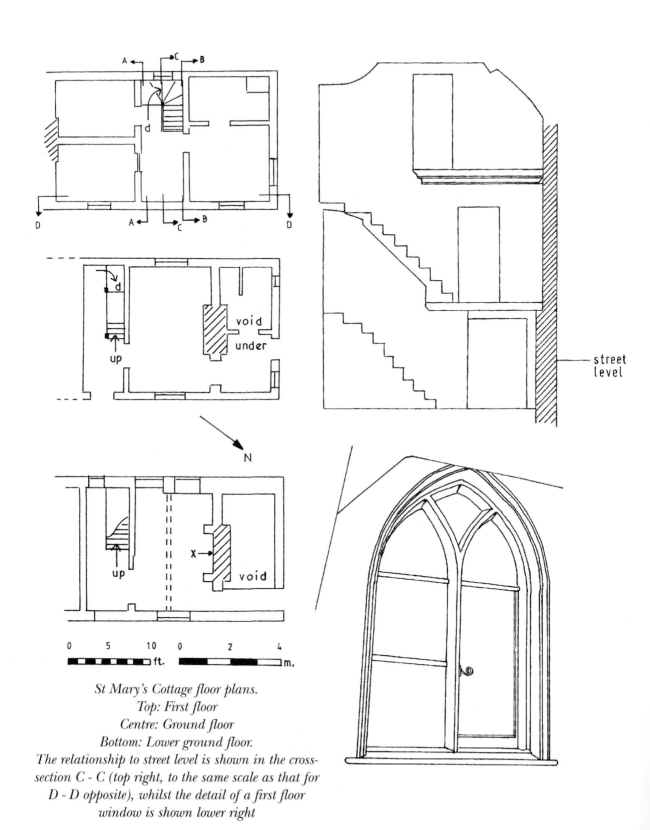

St Mary's Cottage floor plans.
Top: First floor
Centre: Ground floor
Bottom: Lower ground floor.
The relationship to street level is shown in the cross-section C - C (top right, to the same scale as that for D - D opposite), whilst the detail of a first floor window is shown lower right

Section D - D

window immediately above the entrance, the internal effect of which is shown on the three-dimensional drawing on the next page.

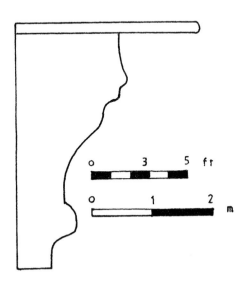

Lintel moulding

The Kitchen Fireplace Lintel

Clearly designed for cooking, the fireplace itself is unremarkable, but it has a wooden lintel which is cut from a longer length and is embellished with what appears to be a 14th century moulding. The provenance of the lintel is not known, but it is obvious that in its original incarnation its function was a different one. The moulding cannot easily be linked to any obvious classic variety, but it gives the impression of having an ecclesiastical background, and is a truly gothic feature of the house as opposed to the 'gothick' windows.

Summary

A number of questions are raised by the proximity of the property to the church, the simplicity of the plan, the flight of steps, the semi-underground kitchen and the void below the north-eastern

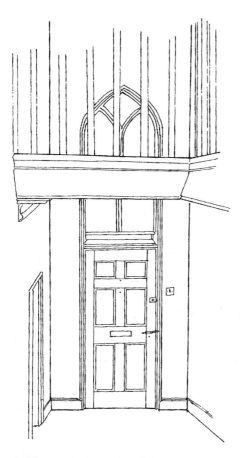

Entrance area viewed from interior
(n.t.s)

portion of the extension. It was hoped that recording work would answer at least some of these questions, but so complete was the remodelling that at the end of the exercise the only acceptable conclusions were that the house presents as many difficulties of interpretation as it did before investigations began. The distance between the roof trusses is 5ft. 4ins., the average width of a medieval screens passage, and the space relates directly to the present entrance position, but this is not sufficient evidence on which to base a medieval first-floor hall-house, tempting though such a postulation might be.

9 & 17 St Mary's Street

The following two properties are ones which, for various reasons, were not fully recorded but which contain details of architectural interest.

9 St. Mary's Street

This appears to consist of one bay of a larger structure. It contains the remains of one transverse timber-framed truss with a tie-beam, collar-beam, principal rafters, one visible queen-strut and a trenched purlin. Later the roof was angled out with blocking-pieces, and new purlins were introduced. In the ground floor room is a spine-beam with ovolo-moulding upon it, but the end stops are concealed within the later brick walls. A suggested date for the earlier work is *c.*1620-40.

9 St. Mary's Street—'Firefly'

17 St. Mary's Street

In the course of conversion to flats in 1977/8, a fine mid-17th century staircase was removed. It had a string, twisted balusters, a moulded newel-post with a ball finial, a moulded hand-rail and decorative work on the risers. At first floor level there is a plank-and-muntin partition, the only example of its kind known in Whitchurch and not common in Shropshire. At the rear of the property is a timber-framed barn.

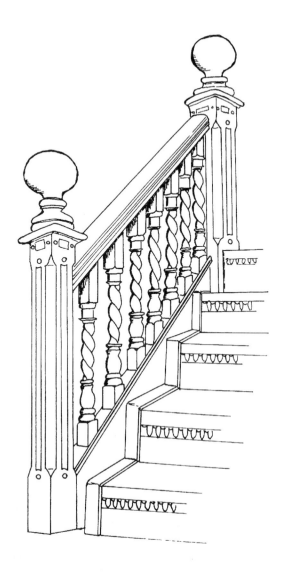

Above: 17 St. Mary's Street.
Right: Detail of the staircase, now demol-
ished, from 17 St. Mary's Street as traced
from a photograph

17 Green End

'Green End' in Whitchurch branches eastwards from the southern end of the High Street, and no. 17 is on the northern side of the street, a short distance from The Bull Ring.

The Exterior

No. 17 is a brick-built house in Flemish bond. It has been suggested that it dates from *c*.1700,[1] but current investigations point towards a later date, nearer *c*.1740, and to associations with the Shrewsbury architect, Thomas Farnolls Pritchard (1723-77). It is three bays wide, two full stories in height and has two dormer windows wholly contained in the roof which is of gabled form. The gable walls extend beyond the roof and are finished with coping stones and kneelers. The dressings are of stone, and these include quoins, a plat-band, and keystones over the flat-headed sash windows. There is a decorated modillion eaves cornice and a frieze at eaves' level which has a band of egg-and-leaf ornament surmounted by a band containing trygliphs. The entrance, centrally placed, is reached via a flight of stone steps and the panelled door is surmounted by a plain fanlight above which is a semi-circular hood. Although deep enough to have had a scallop-shell interior, it is now plain, and may always have been so.

The house is set back from the street and originally there were four decorative piers on the boundary. Two of these were placed at the corners and two were gate-piers at the entrance. Brick-built and plastered over to give a panelled effect, each had a moulded stone cap and was surmounted by a ball finial. Two remain, and the cap and finial of another was reused for decoration when the

15 and 17 Green End

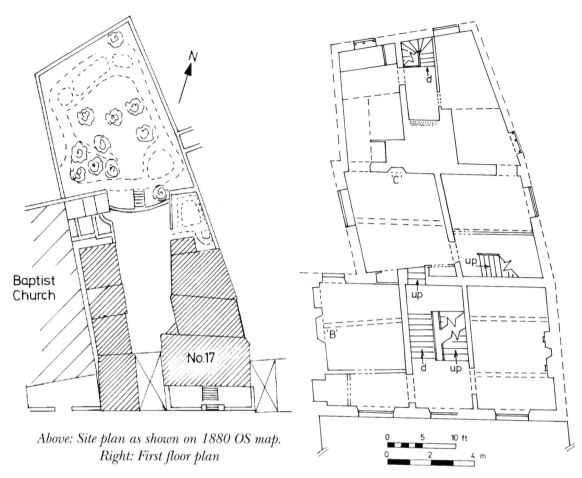

Above: Site plan as shown on 1880 OS map.
Right: First floor plan

ground floor of the western bay of the house was partitioned off, altered and extended forwards to provide commercial premises.

The 1880 OS map shows that the property boundary included the adjoining building on the western side, the range of stabling behind it, the wide carriageway entry contained within the street-facing range, ancillary buildings and extensive gardens at the rear. It is a matter of some debate regarding whether the adjoining building is contemporary with the house. Built of a similar, though not identical, type of brick, finished with similar stone quoins, and containing the carriage entry, it is possible that this is so; and internally at upper floor level there is a feature, described later, which supports this theory. Also, the roof line at the rear is continuous with that of the house, and there is a dentilated eaves cornice. But, viewed from the street, its size, proportions and alignment result in it over-shadowing the house. It is two bays wide, fully two-storied, and the eaves level is the same as that of the house. But it projects forwards from the building line of the house onto the boundary and has a parapet roof, features which give it an overpowering effect. There are further differences: the windows have eared surrounds and projecting sills with brackets, and the modillion eaves cornice is smaller, plainer and without the egg-and-leaf frieze. A possible explanation is that it and the extension to the western bay of the house represent

South elevation before c.1885, shown without garden wall and gate posts

a remodelling of the 1880s when the block was owned by a wholesale and retail grocer, William Ledsham. The ground floor bay to the west of the carriage entry is at present a modern shop and the whole unit is in separate occupation.

The Interior

Apart from the mutilation of the western bay to provide shop premises, the interior of 17 Green End has suffered comparatively little from modernisation, and several original features remain. Some of the details of the staircase may be compared with those at the Mansion House. The carving on the tread-ends is very similar, but in other respects the treatment reflects the difference in the size of the two houses, 17 Green End having only two balusters to each tread and the flight terminating with an in-line square newel-post instead of sweeping round in a grand manner.

The ground-floor reception room on the eastern side has raised and fielded dado panelling which may be original but has the appearance of a later insertion. It is surmounted by a narrow frieze of lozenge-within-lozenge design. In the same room there is an open-fronted display cupboard with shaped shelves.

A corridor at first-floor level spans the entire width of the house at the front. From it access is gained to the room on the eastern side which has a classical door surround. At the stairhead there is a decorative archway. Another classical door surround, this time with

131

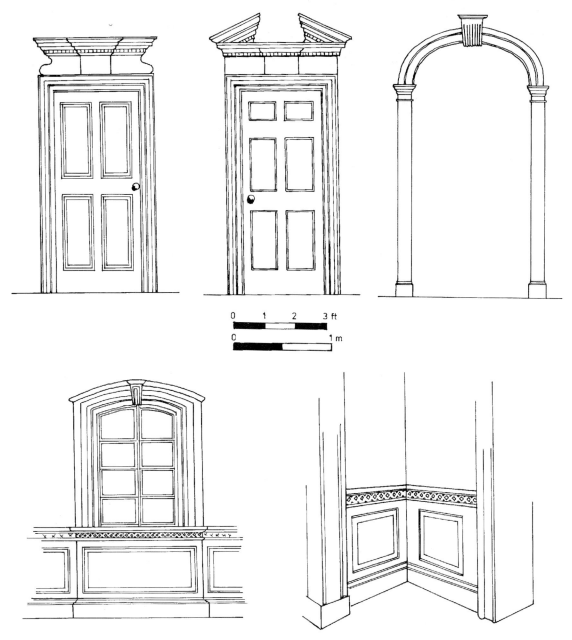

Top left: Doorway to first floor front bedroom.
Top centre: Doorway to first floor rear bedroom.
Top right: Archway on first floor landing.
Bottom left: China cupboard in easternmost front room on the ground floor.
Bottom right: Panelling in easternmost front room on the ground floor

Exterior details (n.t.s.).
Left: Gatepost. Top right: Cornice.
Bottom right: Moulding on hood bracket

a broken pediment, gives access to the western bedroom. At the end of the corridor a third doorway gives access to a toilet at present. It is at this point that the relationship with the adjoining building is called into question. There can be no doubt that the doorway has been moved and the most likely time for this is when the toilet was installed. The doorcase is tightly up against the window frame on one side and the doorway with the broken pediment on the other. It overshadows the latter, being taller and having an unbroken triangular pediment. Its most logical position would be in the end wall, where it would have given access to the adjoining block. Indeed there is some slight evidence of a blocked opening behind the toilet, but until such time that the wall is stripped out this must remain a tentative suggestion. Another explanation for a doorway in this position is as a dummy feature, creating the impression of a much larger house.

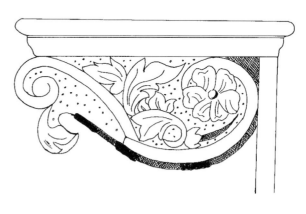

Staircase details (n.t.s.).
Left: Balusters.
Above: Tread-end

Left: Fireplace B, first floor, rear westernmost room. Right: Fireplace A, ground floor, front easternmost room

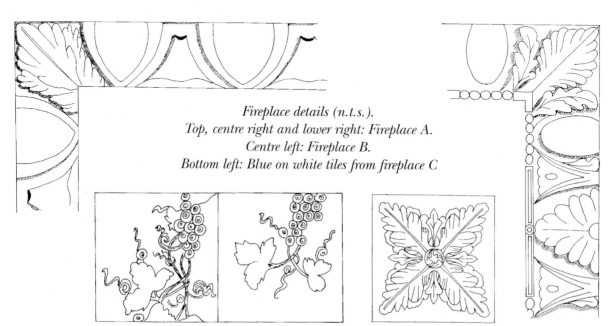

Fireplace details (n.t.s.).
Top, centre right and lower right: Fireplace A.
Centre left: Fireplace B.
Bottom left: Blue on white tiles from fireplace C

The Fireplaces

Three particularly interesting fireplaces remain. That marked 'A' on the drawings is in the eastern ground-floor room, and though smaller and less decorative, is very similar to that in the dining room at Hatton Grange near Shifnal which is probably Pritchard's only complete surviving country house. At Hatton Grange the lintel of the fireplace has a central vase flanked by swirling deeply undercut acanthus-leaf fronds. This is surmounted by a band of egg-and-leaf ornament and another containing trygliphs. At 17 Green End the lintel design echoes that of the grander Shifnal house, and has a surround of egg-and-leaf ornament. Each has an inner surround of white marble, but while the Hatton Grange fireplace remains unaltered, that at Green End acquired tiled cheeks and a cast-iron grate in Victorian times. The common denominator of the motifs which appear on the exterior of 17 Green End and on the fireplaces in both houses suggest that Pritchard was involved with 17 Green End, and in addition to the stylistic link there is another, admittedly tenuous link, which is mentioned below under 'Historical Notes'.

At first-floor level the room off the corridor on the western side has a fireplace with a surround of egg-and-leaf moulding which matches exactly the design of the frieze below the modillion eaves cornice on the external front wall. A narrow band of the same ornament is incorporated into the moulded mantel-beam. This seems to provide further indication of Pritchard's connection with the house. This fireplace is marked 'B' on the drawings.

Fireplace 'C' is in the rear room off the half-landing. It has a moulded mantel-shelf, a deeply recessed eared surround and an inner surround of blue and white tiles which may be English Delft ware. They have the appearance of having been reused from some larger and grander design.

A fourth fireplace in the front bedroom on the eastern side is entirely Victorian, but has a charm of its own.

Summary

17 Green End is, at present, in a dilapidated state, and the shop premises on the front are an accretion which adds to the general debasement and run-down appearance of the block. However, it is basically a very fine eighteenth-century town house, tastefully fitted out and with rooms of a manageable size. The carriage entry, stabling and gardens suggest occupation by a family of means, but without pretensions. If the Pritchard connection is accepted, its importance increases greatly, and perhaps goes some way towards filling in the gaps in Pritchard's career. It could represent an early example of his genre.

Details of ceiling rose and mouldings from the front easternmost ground floor room (n.t.s.)

135

Historical Notes[2]

At present nothing is known of the origins and early history of the house. For the greater part of the nineteenth century it was occupied by the Corser family. Richard Corser, a wealthy grocer and ironmonger, bought the house in the mid-1820s from Mrs. Mary Elizabeth Murhall (or Morhall) Griffiths when he retired from business at 9 High Street, leaving his son Henry to carry on the business there.[3] 'Morhall' is a name which features frequently in documents relating to Whitchurch; the family appears to have been prosperous in the 18th century. There may be a connection with Thomas Farnolls Pritchard's architectural practice as there is a monument, signed by him, in St. Mary's church, Shrewsbury to a Mary Morhall who died in 1765. Additionally, there are architectural features linking Pritchard with this house and with one of his known works, Hatton Grange, near Shifnal.

An entry written in December 1828 in Richard Corser's personal memorandum book refers to a transaction concerning the house in the previous century when 'On the 23rd April 1793 Mr Knight paid the expenses at the Wt Lion Wchch on the sale of the house in the Green End to Mr Rowland of the Crimps - which Richard Corser now inhabits.'[4]

On his retirement Richard, with his wife Amelia and their five unmarried daughters, Margaret, Mary, Amelia, Emma and Eliza moved to what must have seemed elegant and spacious accommodation after living over the shop since 1789. This was the year of their marriage and the year in which he took over the business from his aunt Mrs. Ann Brookes.[5] A member of a well-known and prosperous Whitchurch family, Richard Corser was a much respected figure in the town. He was appointed Feoffee (the equivalent of a modern day governor) of the Grammar School in 1806 and by 1822 was treasurer of the Union Society (a local friendly, or welfare, society) and agent for the Sun Fire Office.[6] A fire insurance plaque remains above the keystone of the central window in the upper storey of the house, which shows the three leopards' heads of the Salop Fire Office before it amalgamated with the Sun. Unfortunately the policy number cannot be deciphered. Corser's memorandum book frequently refers to his duties as church treasurer in dispensing money to the poor from various charities. It also shows that he invested both his and the church's money wisely, both in his nephew's bank, Corser, Naylor and Hassell, and in land.[7] He died in 1836, leaving his widow and four spinster daughters well provided for.[8] They continued to live in the Green End House. Mary had married William Sprent, a Chester grocer, in 1828 and had a dowry of £1,000. Another daughter, Anne, had married her cousin John Corser, a Shrewsbury solicitor in 1817.[9] Two of their descendants still live in Whitchurch. Two years after her father's death, Amelia died in Shrewsbury.[10]

The 1841 census records that Mrs. Amelia Corser with her daughters Emma and Eliza and two female servants were living in premises situated between the Baptist chapel (now the Ritts Night Club) and the Wheatsheaf Inn. This, of course, accurately describes the location of 17 Green End. Mrs. Corser died in June 1843 and in her will she left property in Chetwynd, near Newport, Shropshire to her elder son Robert who was grocer and tea merchant in Leadenhall Street, London.[11] She also left £500 each to her younger son Henry and her married daughter Anne. She left the use of all her household goods to her daughters Margaret, Emma, Anne and Eliza with the proviso that if any daughter married her interest in the estate should cease absolutely, 'as if she had died'.[12] Margaret, Emma and Eliza continued to live in the house which by 1870 was known by the number 13;[13] it has since been re-numbered. They are each listed as 'annuitant' in the census returns and continued to employ two servants.[14] They all achieved a life-span of over 80 years.[15]

After Eliza Corser's death in April 1883, the property was sold to William Ledsham, a grocer who had started business at 19 High Street on the south side of Bluegates.[16] In 1885 he is recorded as a 'wholesale and family grocer and provision stores' at 13 Green End.[17] He and his wife and young family occupied the house, but he used the stables and other outbuildings as storage space for his wholesale trade which also included that of a corn factor. As mentioned earlier, it is possible that the shop which so disfigures the present frontage was built at this time to serve the retail side of the business and that the adjoining unit to the west of the carriage entry was remodelled to accommodate the wholesale enterprise. A description of the business in 1891 bears this out. It reads:

> W. Ledsham, Wholesale and Family Grocer, Provision Merchant and Corn Factor, 13 Green End, Whitchurch. Just about twenty years ago Mr W. Ledsham commenced in business in High Street and removed about five years ago to more commodious premises at 13 Green End, as a wholesale family grocer, provision merchant and corn factor, and he has every reason to be pleased with the success he has achieved. At the present time he is doing a valuable trade in the town and surrounding districts, having gained a reputation for supplying the best quality goods at lowest consistent prices. The premises in occupation at the address named are large and commodious; they possess a good shop and warehouse frontage of considerable length, and extend well to the rear, being very conveniently arranged to suit all requirements. In each department Mr Ledsham holds a splendid stock of goods, including all kinds of groceries, teas, coffees, spices, provisions, tinned goods, also linseed and cotton cakes, meal, bran, flour, corn, oats, beans etc., all of which he obtains direct from the best sources of supply. He employs an adequate staff of assistants and keeps horses and conveyances to deliver orders in town or country. Mr Ledsham is much respected by all who know him.[18]

Mrs. Ledsham died c.1890, as in 1891 William is described as a widower, aged 46, employing a housekeeper, and with four young children. A 20-year old assistant, Robert Williams, also 'lived in'.[19]

Two changes had occurred by 1905. Wilfred Horton had become a partner in the firm which was then known as Ledsham and Horton, and the property was re-numbered, becoming no. 17. This probably followed the building of the Oddfellows Hall in 1901 when old property on the site was demolished.[20] By 1909 Horton was the sole proprietor of the grocery business. He and his family lived in the house for several years, but by 1926 had moved to The Firs in Chester Road, a house since demolished.[21] He let part of the premises to Alexander Ayton, a dentist, who used the eastern room on the ground floor as his surgery under the address of 17a Green End.[22] Mr Ayton retired c.1960, after which the rooms were used as offices for the grocery business.[23] This continued as a wholesale concern until 1980, trading as W. Horton Ltd, but was then purchased by Mr. Michael White, a tobacco wholesaler who still owns the premises although the business has moved to a new estate.

The last use of the shop was as a fast-food outlet, 'Megabites' which is, perhaps, indicative of the cultural level to which the property had fallen. Parts of the block are used intermittently, but the main house is in a state of disrepair and presents a forlorn aspect to Green End.

18 Green End

Once part of a larger structure, 18 Green End is a small two-storied dwelling which incorporates a shop at ground level. The shop front dates from the early 20th century and has a fascia above which is 6ins. x 6ins. dentil moulding in timber. On either side of the large shop window is a Ruabon brick moulded pilaster with a terracotta panel. Similar brickwork also occurs at the rear where the upper windows and one lower window have moulded lintels and cills, while the other has an elaborate moulded brick framework. On the front, two panels of simple rectangular timber-framing occur between the shop window and the eaves line, and a dormer window is contained wholly within the roof. A similar dormer window is situated over the wide passageway to the east of the shop. As the title deeds indicate, this is a remnant of the dwelling which was taken down to create a cart entry for timber wagons *c.*1831. The entry is shown on the OS map of 1880.

The property is basically box-framed and has 2in. x 9in. brick infilling, presumably replacing the original wattle and daub panels. The walls of the upper front (north elevation) and the side wall adjacent to no. 16 (C - C) retain their original framing, although a deep concrete plinth now supports the framing. The rear frame has at some time been replaced with a 9in. brick wall, but the gable end retains some timber-framing visible on the south elevation.

The side wall adjacent to the passageway is of inferior timber-framing and incorporates rat-trap bonded brickwork, similar in construction to the partitions in the upper floor. It includes a blocked door which has the remains of an architrave around it. This would have connected with that part of the complex which was demolished.

18 Green End

139

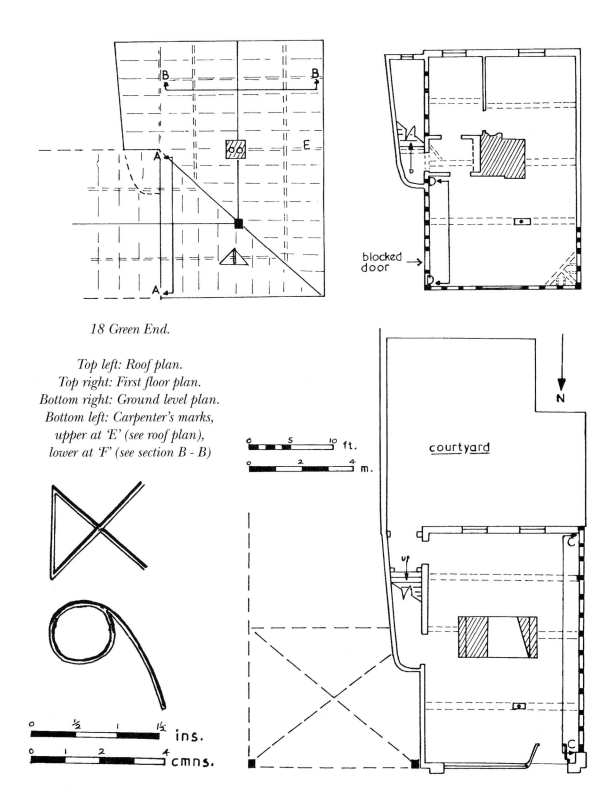

18 Green End.

Top left: Roof plan.
Top right: First floor plan.
Bottom right: Ground level plan.
Bottom left: Carpenter's marks,
upper at 'E' (see roof plan),
lower at 'F' (see section B - B)

blocked
door →

courtyard

N

0   5   10 ft.

0   2   4   m.

0   ½   1   1½ ins.

0   1   2   4   cmns.

South elevation

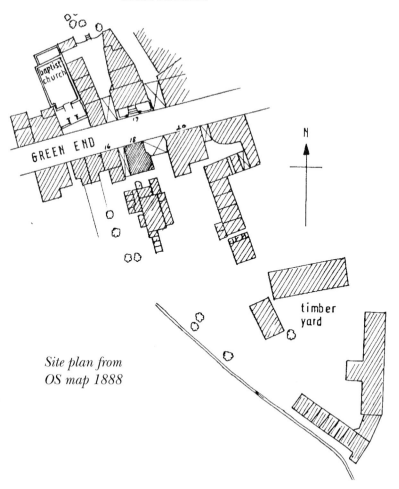

*Site plan from
OS map 1888*

It was probably at the time when this demolition took place, (*c.*1831), that the staircase on the passage side of no. 18 was made. Typically the space between the chimneystack and the eastern side wall would contain a staircase of some kind, perhaps a winding stair, and there is some evidence that this was the case at no. 18. The stack itself is brick-built, very large, and serves two fireplaces on each floor.

The L-shaped roof which is hipped at the western end on the front is of one building phase but contains much re-used timber, as does the interior of the house. The ridges of the front and rear wings meet at right-angles with a 12ins. x 12ins. x 24ins. baulk of timber which does not appear ever to have been supported, and, as a result of sagging, the adjacent purlin is now supported by a timber prop in the roof and by 2in. diameter iron pillars in both the ground and first floors. There are no ridge purlins; the rafters are joined with rather crude half-laps. Between the house and the passageway, there is a truss of king-post construction with V-shaped lateral braces (A - A), and in the rear wing there is a simple collar-beam truss (B - B). This

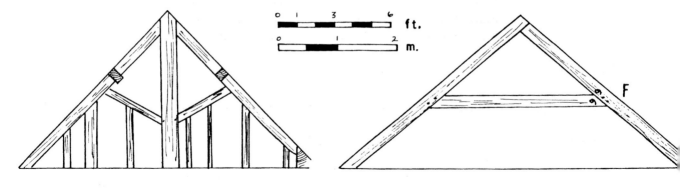

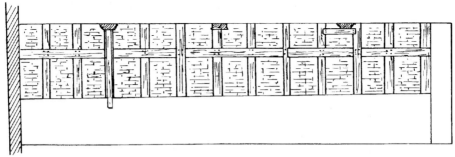

Section A - A (top left)
Section B - B (top right)
Section C - C (above)
Section D - D (right)

has a carpenter's mark shown at 'F' and at 'E' (refer to the roof plan) is a different type of mark.

The present owners uncovered a layer of peat in the back yard which indicates that the town pool, now the White Lion Meadow, originally extended to this area. Also uncovered was a brick tank with a tap and provision for heating. It was below the level of the yard, and its use unclear.

It seems likely that the original block was built as a pair of box-framed town houses in the second half of the 17th century. Traditional techniques and patterns were still used, but much of the framing was done with re-used timbers.

Precis of Deeds relating to 18 Green End

1676 13th April   Court Baron, Manor of Whitchurch, for the Earl of Bridgwater: William Cotton Esq. and Dorothy his wife surrendered all their customary houses land and tenements within the manor to Abigail

Cotton, widow and heir of Ralph Cotton, Gent, deceased, son and heir of William Cotton for life. To Rowland Cotton son and heir of Ralph Cotton, Gent. deceased, and Abigail, in Tail. Abigail Cotton was admitted tenant (of all the Cotton properties).

1723 23rd April	Rowland Cotton, son and heir of Ralph, admitted tenant.
1754 20th April	William Cotton, son and heir of Rowland, admitted tenant.
1762 24th/25th all Sept.	Deed of Enfranchisement: William Cotton purchased the freehold of the property held by him on a copyhold lease from the Duke of Bridgwater in consideration of £216 15s 4d. The property included Alkington Hall estate and two dwelling houses in Green End.
1776 5th July	The Cotton property in Whitchurch and Dodington was transferred to Joseph Green of Birmingham and his wife Rebecca, née Cotton, daughter of William Cotton, who paid Rebecca Cotton, widow of William £800, and £500 for the freehold.
1793 16th Dec.	The Rev. L.D. Cokburne and Mary Teresa his wife (née Cotton) and her brother the Rev. Evelyn Rowland Cotton bought the estate in Whitchurch and Dodington paying £500 for the freehold.
1795 8th June	Will of Rev. E.R. Cotton: The estates in Alkington & Whitchurch together with other lands in Derbyshire & Staffs were left to his nephew Richard Rowland Ward who was to pay £100 p.a. to his aunt, Mrs. Cokburne.
1795 20th Oct.	Indenture between Rev. E.R. Cotton, Rev. C.S. Hope of Derby and James Marshall of Bridgnorth, gent. Sold Alkington Hall, farm & those dwelling houses in Whitchurch now in the tenure of Mr. Turner, Attorney, and his undertenants.
1800 30th Jan.	The Rev. R.R. Ward sold for £1,020 two messuages or dwelling houses in The Green late in the holding of William Turner or his undertenants to Samuel Turner.
1800 4th Feb.	Samuel Turner redeemed for £1 11s 10½d charged upon a dwelling house with garden buildings & appurtenances part of which was formerly a Bowling Green in Green End the property of William Turner & also several shops, dwelling houses gardens & timber yard in or near Green End in the occupation of Joseph Beddowes, Olivia

Harper, Thomas Blackhurst, Mary Doe, William Turner or their undertenants.

1810 1st Dec.	Samuel Turner died, a bachelor & intestate.

1815 15th Jan.   William Turner declared bankrupt.

1815 20th June   William Turner, architect, brother & heir of Samuel Turner inherited the lease of two dwelling houses in Green End.

1820 22nd & 26th Sept.   The estate of William Turner, bankrupt (architect, dealer & chapman) conveyed two houses & premises in Green End to Thomas Bennion on payment of one peppercorn lawfully demanded.

1826 8th April   Thomas Bennion, carpenter, mortgaged two houses in Green End to Robert Phillips, bricklayer, £130.

1830 12th Nov.   Death of Robert Phillips.

1831 29th Jan.   Ellen Phillips, widow & administrix of Robert Phillips received from Thomas Whittingham, timber merchant, the sum of £80 for part of the property sold by Thomas Bennion to Thomas Whittingham who has had possession, which £80 is part of the principal sum of £130.

18th April   Will of Thomas Bennion. He left all his property to his wife, Amelia & then to his daughter Elizabeth including his freehold dwelling house in Green End.

1837 8th Sept.   Charles Phillips sold to William Brookes, Solicitor, all that dwelling house & appurtenances which have not been sold to Thomas Whittingham, timber merchant.

1864 25th May   Elizabeth Fowles, widow, (daughter & heir of Thomas Bennion) mortgaged the dwelling house in Green End (in her occupation) to John Martin, photographic artist of Watergate, for the sum of £70 with interest of 5% p.a.

1868 2nd April   Mortgage transferred to the Whitchurch Union Society, Treasurer: Edward Lea.

1876 21st Nov.   Elizabeth Fowles died. Freehold house & garden in Green End inherited by her son John Weston Fowles in occupation of Thomas Spencer, rent: £10 p.a. Still a mortgage of £100 & interest 5% p.a.

1882 7th Dec.	John Fowles paid off £100 mortgage to Edward Lea, & John Martin paid £42 for the purchase of no. 20 Green End. (The numbers have have subsequently altered, no. 20 is now no. 18)
1897 26th March	John Martin sold house, shops & premises at no. 20 Green End to William Henry Smith, ironfounder, for £600.
1901 13th Aug.	William H. Smith, ironfounder, sold premises formerly no.20 but now no. 18 Green End in the occupation of Edward Jones & Co., watchmaker, to Robert Thursfield Smith Jn. Esq., timber merchant, for £508.
1922 25th May	Partnership between Edward Jones, watchmaker, jeweller & optician of no. 18 Green End & George Allman, watchmaker formed to carry on business as 'Jones & Allman'.
1927 13th Apr.	Mr. R.T. Smith sold 18 Green End to Messrs E. Jones & G. Allman for £1,000. N.B. The partners had no right of way through the yard iron door or into the passageway between no. 18 & the former no. 16.
1939 2nd June	George Allman bought no. 18 Green End for £1,000 on the retirement of Edward Jones. Partnership dissolved.
1952 10th Jan.	Death of George Allman. Premises left to his son George Reginald Allman, optician.
1987 31st March	18 Green End sold to A.K. & S.M. Jones.
1997 2nd Dec.	18 Green End sold to Martin & Carol Jones.

Assessment

For such a small property 18 Green End has a surprising amount of detailed history. Not only can its structural development be traced both 'on the ground' and through the documents, but there are some important and locally famous names associated with it. These include the Earl of Bridgwater, who at that time (1676) was John Egerton; the local talented Cotton family who produced a Lord Mayor of London in addition to other illustrious members; and William Turner, described in the deeds simultaneously as 'architect, dealer and chapman.' He seems to have had a chequered career, working with Thomas Telford on the Ellesmere Canal, involved with Cholmondeley Castle and responsible for the old rectory in Whitchurch at one point and declared bankrupt at another.[1] Thomas Bennion had the privilege of paying the picturesque rent of 'one peppercorn' to Turner's estate for the property which at that time consisted of the two dwellings. Also involved were the Whittington family of timber merchants—for whom the cart-entry was made by demolishing the adjoining dwelling—and W.H. Smith & Co, ironfounders and engineers, whose founder in 1837 set out to make 'anything his neighbour might want.' So successful was the enterprise that Smith & Co. became the town's major employers and their products are still in use all over the world.[2] The firm must have bought 18 Green End purely as an investment, for there is no record of the premises being used for engineering purposes.

Gazetteer of other Whitchurch properties

The following brief descriptions are of properties which, for various reasons, were not fully recorded but which contain details of architectural interest.

The Old Rectory

Occupying what is clearly an old moated site, the Old Rectory is a brick-built house of two stories with attics and a basement. It is five bays wide, has a long service range and appears to be all of one mid-18th century build. In spite of an extensive archive of surviving documents, the name of the architect is uncertain. It is thought to have been the work of William Turner, a local man.[1] In 1749 or shortly afterwards, the predecessor to the present building was demolished. This probably had medieval origins. It is possible that the site is that of the Whitchurch manor house, held in the 14th century by the le Strange family, but this assumes that they did not live in the castle. Later it came into the possession of the powerful Egerton family, Earls of Bridgwater and Barons Ellesmere. The ninth earl, Francis Henry Egerton, (b.1756), became Rector of Whitchurch, one of a line of eccentric incumbents. About 1784 an eminent landscape designer,

*The Old Rectory front elevation (upper)
and rear elevation (lower)*

William Emes was commissioned to work at the Rectory and to create a park to improve the setting of the house. Sadly, very little of Emes' work remains.[2]

During the Second World War the Old Rectory had an important role as a 'Y' class tracking station, with staff engaged in tapping German communications, decyphering them and feeding the resultant information to the main headquarters at Bletchley Park.

It is hoped to make a full recording of the house and its history which will be published separately.

1 & 3 Church Street

These are two brick-built cottages, formerly part of a terrace. Stripping-out in January 1991 revealed that the transverse wall dividing the two cottages was timber-framed and of medieval form. Peat 'bricks' were recovered from a framed partition in no.3.

Horse & Jockey Inn, Church Street

A two-storied, two-bay property with external walls of brick. The roof shows four phases of a building sequence, phase three of upper-cruck construction.

12 & 14 Highgate

A pair of 'two-up, two-down' box-framed cottages, each one-and-a-half stories in height, and sharing a central chimneystack. Each has a dormer window front and back, the front dormers wholly in the roof and the rear ones of a simpler raking type. The cottages are bricked over, pebble-dashed at the front and with

Top: 1 and 3 Church Street
Centre: The Horse & Jockey
Lower: 12 - 14 Highgate after restoration

15 Claypit Street before restoration (above left) and after (above right)

'painted-on' timbers on the exposed gable wall, but they seem to be of a late 17th - early 18th century date and to represent a time when good quality accommodation was provided for the journeyman class of worker, before the industrial revolution. Such relatively unaltered examples are rare.

12 - 14 Highgate before restoration, with the pebble-dash still on

15 Claypit Street

A small box-framed two-bayed cottage, originally one-and-a-half storied, but later raised to two full stories. A flattened ogee-headed doorway, the only example of this feature found in Whitchurch, appears to mark the original entrance.

'The Laurels', 29 Alkington Road

This is a long, four bayed, brick built, two-storied house, one room deep and following the curve of the road. It has an unusual and irregular plan which appears to incorporate at least two, possibly three, houses. The two eastern bays are divided by a wide passage, the purpose of which is unknown. There is a bay beyond the central stack which has a decorative plastered ceiling and panelled walls. This bay has a cellar below with access originally from the street, but now only from the inside.

The house defies interpretation. The roof timbers clearly relate to later roof raising and are crude in concept, but the architecture of 'The Laurels' will inevitably always be upstaged by the fact that it was the home of Edward German Jones, better known as the composer, Edward German.

1 Newtown

Newtown was subjected to ruthless 'slum clearance' in pre and post-war periods, and parts of it have a desolate appearance. No. 1 remains on the western side and, with the adjoining dwelling, no. 3, presents the form of a 'hall and crosswing' plan similar to that of 21 and 23 High Street ('Walker's') whose frontage is visible from the Newtown

Top: 'The Laurels', 29 Alkington Road.
Lower: 1 and 3 Newtown

properties. Both 1 and 3 have been drastically modernised, the roof timbers replaced and the exteriors plastered over, but the jettied form of the crosswing in no. 1 is discernible. The range is likely to have 16th century origins.

Ash Wood, Ash

The history of Ash Wood, a farmhouse within the civil parish of Whitchurch Rural, is essentially the history of the Hughes family. It is a family tradition that in the time of King Offa 'we came one day's march out of Wales, squatted in an ash wood, built a turf hut and have been here ever since.'[1] There is, of course, nothing to substantiate the legend, but the present owner has deeds of the property from 1515 onwards which, despite some gaps in the documentary sequence, give a record of unbroken succession from that date forward. At its hey-day in the early 19th century the 90 acres comprising Ash Wood were part of a larger estate which included four town houses in Whitchurch, several houses in the immediate vicinity and some labourers' cottages. But in 1922 the Ash Wood holding was reduced to 50 acres when the estate was divided between nine legatees. Previously the inheritance pattern had usually been that of primogeniture. In 1954, when the present owner inherited the farm, 50 acres were incapable of generating sufficient income for modern needs and therefore the land was leased to a neighbouring farmer, the owner breaking with tradition and becoming the first non-farming Hughes to live at Ash Wood. One of his ancestors was described as a 'husbandman' in 1587, but as he was literate he would be better classed as a 'yeoman', a term which fairly describes this family of farmers. Ash Wood's mixed farming pattern, specializing in cheese production, is typical of this part of north Shropshire.

The Farmhouse

In its present form Ash Wood is a T-shaped building, the bar of the 'T' consisting of a brick-built two-storied front unit with a central entrance and a room on either side. This unit was built by the present owner's grandfather in 1886, the date of his inheritance. It replaced a two-bay unit of a slightly smaller size which, when it was being demolished, yielded a beam

Ash Wood, west and south elevations

151

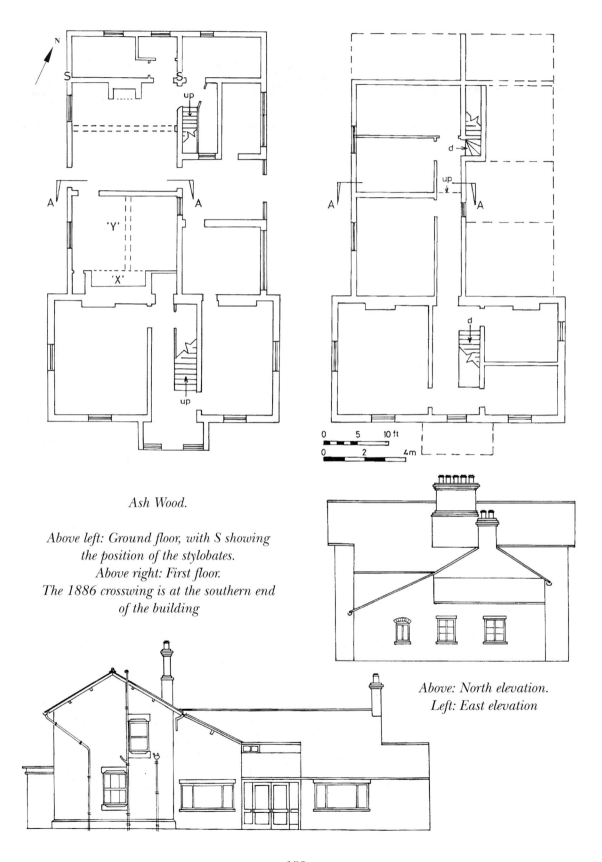

Ash Wood.

Above left: Ground floor, with S showing the position of the stylobates.
Above right: First floor.
The 1886 crosswing is at the southern end of the building

Above: North elevation.
Left: East elevation

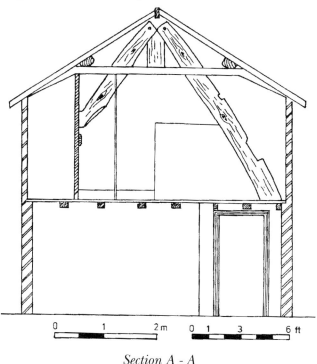

This beam was recovered during demolition of the timber-framed wing.
Both references relate to a Richard Hughes

bearing the inscription '16 R·H 55'. This Richard Hughes was born in 1634 and had married in 1654. An old photograph, taken in 1886 and just before demolition commenced, shows that the outer walls were timber-framed and had been stuccoed over. It was built with two full stories and attics contained within the roof-space. The photograph shows a window high in the gable of the western end, and the eastern gable may have been similarly lighted, although, if the inventory of 1727 has been interpreted correctly and the cheese chamber was located in the crosswing at upper floor level, it need not necessarily have had a floored attic above it. Some of the old bricks taken from the chimneystack and elsewhere have been incorporated into the fireplace of the old kitchen in the rear range. Others were used to floor the shippons of the Victorian farmbuildings which were built in 1887 as models of their kind. The bricks are soft, full of pebbles and measure on average $8^{1}/_{2}$ins. x $4^{1}/_{2}$ins. x $2^{1}/_{4}$ins. Some bear the marks of the rushes on which they were laid to dry, prior to firing.

During demolition four ground-floor levels were found. The existing floor was of partly-glazed tiles, 9ins. square x $1^{1}/_{2}$ins; beneath was a floor of tiles measuring 7ins. square x $1^{1}/_{2}$ins. These were semi-glazed and had a 'pock-marked' surface. The next layer was of unglazed tiles, similar in texture to the early bricks and measuring 7ins. square x $2^{1}/_{2}$ins. and finally a floor of beaten or 'pathered' clay.[2] Samples of each layer have been preserved.

Forming the stem of the 'T' is a range which has had many alterations over the years. The old photograph shows that before the 1886 crosswing was built there was a porch on the western side and a lobby entry which gave access to the then kitchen (formerly the hall) and to the western room of the earlier crosswing, at that time probably a parlour. This entrance was later blocked. Two internal trusses of the rear range are of cruck construction. Section A - A shows that much of one truss remains beneath later plaster

Section A - A

Four faces of cruck remnant taken from A - A (n.t.s.)

and has an apex based on either classification 'G' (where the blades meet on a king-post rising from a collar) or 'F3' (as 'G', but where the collar is lapped across the blades).[3] Unlike either of these groups, in this instance the ridge-purlin is carried in a 'V' cut from the tops of the blades and the top of the king-post, but the crucial area of the collar is obscured and it is impossible to be more specific regarding its group. 'G' is an uncommon group, virtually confined to the west of the Severn and Dee and so the question arises of whether it is an expression of some deeply embedded folk memory that is manifested here. Truss A is a closed truss and shows no signs on either face of weathering or of smoke blackening. It probably represents the end truss of a single-bay open hall which was built with an efficient means of smoke extraction from the start. The truss was cut through in 1856 to provide a passage between two bedrooms and when the lower part of the eastern blade was taken out recently it was found to have the initials R.H. and A.P. and the date 1856 inscribed in the cut area. This suggests that the alteration was carried out by the owner's great-grandfather, another Richard, who had inherited in 1841. Of particular interest is the spur which formed the connection between the blade and the wall-post. On this may be seen the crescent form of the carpenters' assembly marks.

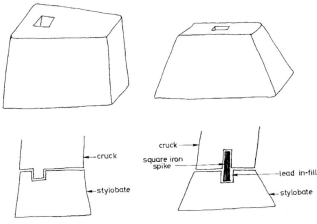

It is interesting that the feet of the two blades on the next truss northwards were supported on stylobates. On one the outer edge was continued to form a tenon which was housed into a mortice cut

Details of two stylobates (n.t.s.)

into the top edge of the stylobate, and on the other a metal spike was let into the stylobate, sealed around with molten lead, and engaging the foot of the blade. The use of stylobates is uncommon in Shropshire and totally absent in the south of the county, but is noted in two other houses in this survey.[4] The practice is more common in Cheshire; perhaps this is an influence percolating into north Shropshire. Ash Wood is under two miles from the Cheshire border.

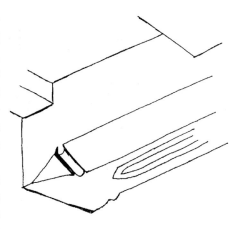

Detail of spine beam soffit (n.t.s.)

The room immediately to the north of the large central stack, originally the hall and later the kitchen, is now a pleasant sitting-room. As late as the present owner's boyhood this room was called the 'haus'.[5] It has a moulded spine-beam and on stylistic grounds a date in the first quarter of the 17th century is suggested for this feature. It is the only spine-beam noted in the survey which has moulding on the soffit and this, coupled with the beautifully carved stop ends, suggests a particularly prosperous time for the family. The inglenook fireplace contains a carved wooden surround executed by the present owner's father, Richard William Hughes. On the jambs he carved the initials and dates of those members of the Hughes family whose inheritance and death can be determined from the deeds, and on the lintel are symbols of rural life. It is a work of great skill, as are other artifacts made by both father and son.

Fireplace at X carved by R.W.H. in 1900, with details of the left side, right side and frieze of overmantel (n.t.s.)

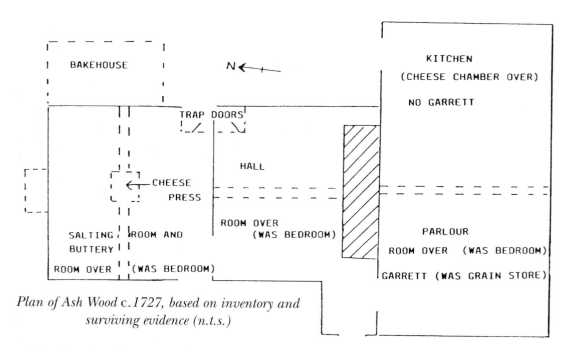

*Plan of Ash Wood c.1727, based on inventory and
surviving evidence (n.t.s.)*

The fireplace is part of the large chimneystack which serves both the crosswing and the southern half of the older range. When the crosswing was rebuilt in 1886 the stack was found to contain a concealed chamber above the inglenook. It was contrived with a loose brick wall so that when necessary a fugitive could enter the chamber and rebuild the wall from the inside. Ventilation was provided by means of small holes in the floor. Whether or not the family has a history of recusancy is not known, but equally the chamber may have served as a refuge from the press gangs in the Napoleonic wars, a view held by the present owner's grandfather. The chamber no longer exists, but there are marks which indicate its position.

To the north of Truss 'A' is the present kitchen, but in the probate inventory dated 1727 this is called 'the salting room and buttery'.[6] In this room the cheese press has left witness marks on the ceiling beam, and the sandstone block is, at present, used as a garden seat. If the inventory has been interpreted correctly, the room above was a bedroom, but the main bedroom was above the hall and there was no communication between the two. Each was approached from a trap-door in the room below, and until 1856, when alterations were made, truss 'A' which formed the partition was completely closed at first floor level. The maturing cheeses were stored in the chamber above the kitchen, which at that time was most likely to have been the larger of the two rooms in the cross-wing. It has been calculated that 4 tons of Cheshire cheese, worth £14,000 by today's standards, were in store in February 1727.

An account exists which is thought to relate to the rebuilding and heightening of the exterior walls of the northern range. In February 1824 £16 was paid for 10,616 bricks from William Beckett, and a bricklayer called Hallmark was paid a total of £5 for laying them. At this time it seems likely that although the wall-framing was removed the purlins

156

were raised and reused and the upper parts of the crucks were left undisturbed as were the stylobates. Many of these bricks are distinguished by a fault in the mould and have been noted elsewhere in north Shropshire and south Cheshire.[7] The bricks for the 1886 crosswing came from a brick-works, no longer in production, at Fenn's Bank, about six miles to the west of Ash Wood.

Richard Hughes, grandfather of the present Richard Hughes and builder of the 1886 cross wing

The Barhill Account Book

In 1798 William Hughes took a lease on Barhill Farm, just over the Cheshire border and about ten miles from Ash Wood. His younger brother Richard carried on farming at Ash Wood, paying rent to William. The move was probably made to take advantage of a larger acreage, 200 as opposed to Ash Wood's 90, and the boom in farming at the time. William's account book for Barhill has survived and is kept at Ash Wood. Although there are breaks in the accounting, the book was in use until 1837. It contains valuable information not only on farming matters but on economic, social and family history. It records that his ingoing was £379 and that he paid his labourers 1s 6d per day. He maintained close ties with Ash Wood and details of the brickwork, noted above, are recorded. He was also engaged in building operations at Barhill, in 1801 paying £9 12s for 48,000 green bricks. The coal for firing them cost £7 15s 3½d, the brick tax £10 16s 7½d, plus an additional levy of 6s when they were fired. An interesting sidelight on these figures is that the tax was more expensive than the bricks.

Dendrochronological Dating[8]

In February 1994 samples were taken for analysis which gave a felling date of 1550 for the cruck timbers of the open hall and 1620 for the inserted ceiling and soffit-moulded spine-beam. Among the deeds of the house is one dated 1557 which seems to indicate that the house was built by by the present owner's ancestor, Henry Hughes, replacing what is described as a 'cottage' and providing a change of site (though not far) for the family. It is possible that the 'pathered' floor in the crosswing, mentioned earlier, is a remnant of this cottage. The acreage at the time is given as the modern equivalent of 9.625. Three fields are named—The Ferney Lees, The Whetefield and the Little Mede. These names are still in use today. The inclusion of a wheatfield implies well cultivated ground in good heart. It has not been possible to relate the 1620 date to a specific member of the family, it being too early for the Richard Hughes who left evidence of his building activities elsewhere, but carrying on events from 1557 the next informative deed is dated 1587 and shows that John Hughes and his wife Ellen were acquiring land in the neighbouring township of Broughall. The deed specifies that the land had been held previously by John's father, Henry and that Henry, described as a husbandman, was still living. John is described as Henry's bastard son. In 1601 his name appears on the Presentment Roll for the Manor of Whitchurch as one of many who were *essoined*, that is, excused for non-appearance in Court.[9]

Conclusion

At vernacular level it is unusual to be able to relate informative documents to a specific house. This makes Ash Wood invaluable as a source of building and social history. Furthermore, because the property has remained in the hands of one family, the provenance of most of the furniture, pictures and ornaments is known. Some of the artifacts form a tangible link with other farms in the area, particularly Grove Farm in Ash Parva and the context is given in that chapter under 'The Richard Jones Connection' and 'The Wedding Feast Annuity'. The head of the Hughes family always was and still is the sole trustee of the latter. The 1557 deed, mentioned above, is the earliest document relating to Ash Wood which specifies land, and a recent hedgerow dating exercise gave a date of 1450.[10] The earliest artifact in the house is a silver penny of 1307, minted in Canterbury and found in the garden. Whether the find indicates occupation of the site at that time is, of course, open to question, but it forms the starting point of a remarkable heritage which, fortunately, will be carried on by the present owner's son who will be about the fourteenth member of the family in direct succession.

Appendix A. Richard Hughes' Will and Inventory, 1727[11]

Richard Hughes, yeoman, died in 1727. His elder son, William, inherited Ash Wood and to his younger son Samuel he bequeathed other properties which he owned in Wem and Whitchurch. There was also a daughter Elisabeth who received £200. Her age is given as under 25 and she may have been his daughter by a late second or even third marriage, as he was first married at the age of 20. His will is simple and straightforward and the accompanying inventory is given in full below. Although Shropshire inventories which name the rooms are not unknown, they tend to be the exception rather than the rule and this example provides a clear picture of Ash Wood before the 1886 wing was built. It is also, in essence, a graphic account of a well-managed farm with stock and cash in hand which provided the means to wait for the best time to sell stock, and to store a year's production of cheese, again to be sold at the best time. His milk herd was clearly the highest valued livestock and this is reflected in the value of the cheese. It has been calculated that about 4 tons of cheese was in store and ready to sell. This would be what is known as Cheshire cheese, the average weight of which is 40lbs. Therefore there would be about 230 cheeses in store, all of which needed to be turned daily to ensure it ripened evenly. The house was well furnished and comfortable and there was six months' supply of bread-flour.

'A true and perfect inventory of all and singular the goods chattels and cattle forming personall estate of Richard Hughes Yeoman late of Ash Wood in the County of Salop Taken and appraised on the twenty sixth day of Ffebruary in the first year of the Raign of our Soverign Lord George the Second now King of Great Brittain anno dom 1727-8 By us hwose names are subscribed

	£	s	d
23 Cows at 3 pounds a peece.............................	69	0	0
3 Two year old heiffers at two pounds a peece...	6	0	0
3 Year old calves at one pound a peece..............	3	0	0
5 Rearing calves at 10s a peece..........................	2	0	0
3 Mares one being infold at £3.6.8 each.............	10	0	0
2 Store piggs at 10s a peece...............................	1	0	0
14 Threshings of wheat.......................................	4	0	0
Oats in the barn..	4	10	0
1 Stack of Hay...	10	0	0
Hay in the Barns...	5	0	0
One cart £4, too tumbrells too harrows and a plough one pound fifteen shillings...................	5	15	0
Chains and all other implements of husbandry..	1	10	0

Goods in the house

In the kitchen
10 pewter dishes, 12 plates, 3 kettles
one furnace, one warming pan, one grate
one fire shovell, 1 pair tongs £4, one table
one forme, 1 saddle, and other goods................. 5 10 0

In the parlor
Two feather beds 10s. Ffurniture thereunto
belonging. Two tables, one form, 1 saddle
and other goods.. 6 5 0

In the Hall
One table one cubort, two forms and other goods..1 10 0

In the room over the Hall
One ffeather bedd 10s, ffurniture thereunto
belonging Six cane chairs and one grate............ 5 3 0

In the room over the Parlor
Two ffeather bedds, ffurniture thereunto belonging,
one coffer, 4 joynt stools and other sundory goods ... 5 18 0

In the Garrett over the Parlor
Wheat twenty measures Six Pounds. Oats 8 bushells
Four pounds. Barley and some other goods....... 11 5 0
In the Cheese Chamber
Cheese to the value of £50. Bacon, beef,
and some other sundory goods £2............................ 52 0 0

In the Chamber over the Buttery
One ffeather bedd, and ffurniture thereunto
belonging. One Coffor and other sundory goods......   2 10 0

In the Salting room and Buttery
One cheese press, two curdmills, three
barrells, one churn and other sundory goods............   2 10 0

In the Bakehouse
Some sundory goods...   0 13 4

All the linnen...   5 0 0

Wearing apparrell and money in his purse................ 60 0 0

Things unseen and fforgotten...................................   1 0 0

.... £282 6 0
                                                    (actual total £280 9s 4d)
Appraised by us
Richard Sempole
John Weaver
John Turner

Much discussion regarding the position of the various rooms has taken place, and while the 'salting room and buttery' may be identified from the witness marks left by the cheese press there is some doubt about the location of the hall, the kitchen and the cheese chamber. Logically the hall should be the room in the north wing which received an inserted floor in 1620, and in the inventory the upper chamber contains bedroom furniture and has a fireplace. The kitchen, therefore, must have been one of the rooms in the crosswing, with the cheese chamber above. The peripatetic nature of the kitchen has caused much deliberation and is, even now, open to question. Mr. Hughes reports that he converted the bakehouse to a laundry room. If the kitchen was the eastern room in the crosswing and if there was a door in the north wall then access to the bakehouse would be easy. Later, of course, the hall became the kitchen and was so in Mr. Hughes's boyhood.

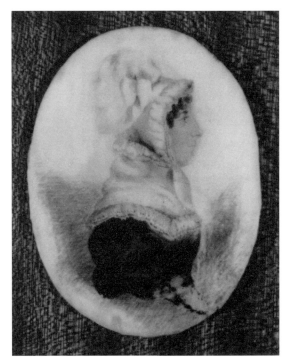

The miniatures of Mary and William Hughes

Miniatures of William and Mary Hughes (née Jones)

William Hughes, son of Richard and Mary Hughes, was baptised on 5th November 1774. He was a tenant of Barhill Farm at Tushingham from 1798 until 1840, while his younger brother, Richard, carried on farming at Ash Wood. He set up a trust for his three children, Richard, Sarah and Jane in 1841. The document gives details of the property he held at that time.

The 'Barhill Account Book' is held at Ash Wood and gives details of farming matters, family history, and some of the contemporary social and economic trends. The Barhill jug and his silver cup are also held at Ash Wood.

On 23rd April 1808 he married Mary Jones, daughter of Richard and Sarah Jones, who farmed at the Grove Farm, Ash. Richard's will and his silver watch and Sarah's sampler are held at Ash Wood. Mary had three brothers, John, Thomas and Richard junior.

The painted miniatures of William and Mary are held at Ash Wood. They are on ivory and were probably made for the occasion of their 10th wedding anniversary in 1818 when William would have been 44. He died in 1842 at the age of 68 and is buried at Ash.

161

Richard Jones's Watch and Sarah Jones's Sampler

These artifacts are held at Ash Wood. Richard and Sarah Jones were the parents of Mary who married William Hughes (see above).

The sampler (see alongside) is dated September 24th 1801. The letter J is missing from the alphabet, although it had been in common use for the consonantal form of I since the middle of the 17th century. Including the frame it measures $23^{1}/_{2}$ ins. x 17 ins. It is backed by part of the *Staffordshire Advertiser* for Saturday 23rd June 1877.

The silver double-cased verge watch (see previous page) is engraved 'B. Clowes Liverpool', is numbered 3995 and hall-marked for Birmingham, 1775/6. The face is unique, the owner's name replacing conventional numerals, and 'Ash' engraved on the upper half.

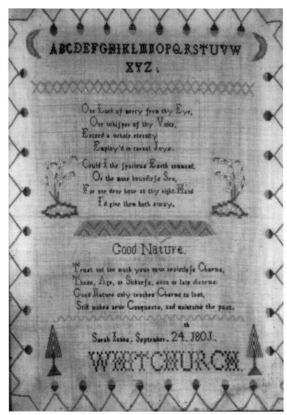

Grove Farm, Ash Parva

Grove Farm presents a very different appearance at present than it did in 1990. At that time it had been severely truncated, and what was left was derelict. However, beneath the applied roughcast and ivy growth was a timber-frame of considerable interest. The owner, Mr. Roger Rowland, intended to demolish the Victorian additions, restore the framework, reinstate the hall range to its correct length, re-build the missing western wing in timber-framing and add a modern brick extension.

It was clear from the OS maps of 1880 and 1901 that the basic structure was H-shaped, but with extensive additions. The owner commissioned an archaeological excavation which confirmed the suspected former existence of a west wing and determined the extent of the hall range. According to the line of the foundations the west wing was of the same width as the surviving east wing, projected forward in a similar way and had two rooms at ground level.[1] Of course, there was no evidence of the style of the framing of the missing wing, and so it was decided to model it on the surviving one and thus balance the frontage on the north elevation.

The Whitchurch class was invited to record the building before the work of restoration began, but, as time was short, it was decided to omit most of the additions. The following is therefore based on the evidence that was available in 1990.

The East Wing
a) External features

It was in the two-storied east wing that the quality of the framing was most noticeable. The plan was of a two-bayed range with two rooms at ground level, each *c.*12ft. square, although it is likely that the space was not partitioned originally and that the accommodation consisted of a large

The front of Grove Farm after restoration

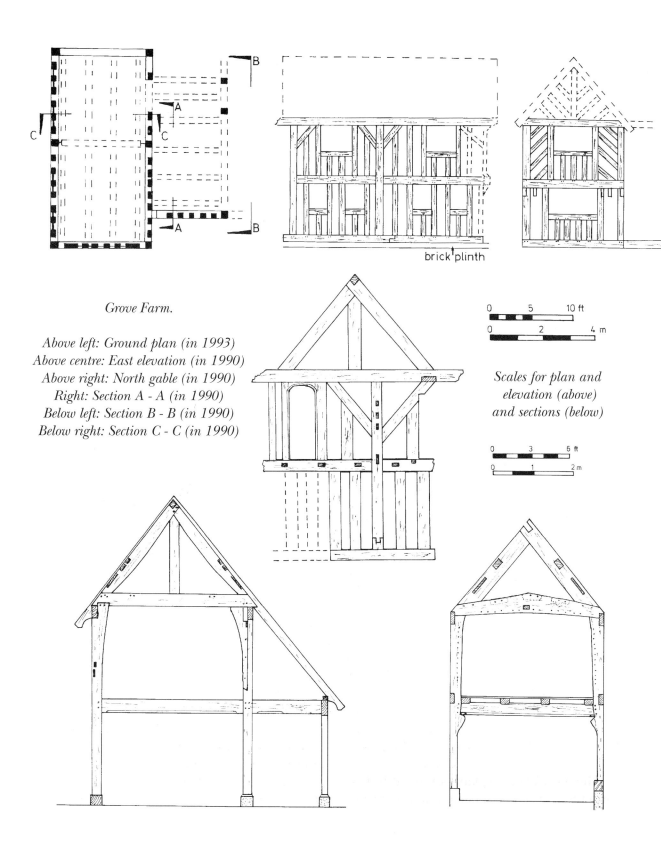

brick plinth

Grove Farm.

Above left: Ground plan (in 1993)
Above centre: East elevation (in 1990)
Above right: North gable (in 1990)
Right: Section A - A (in 1990)
Below left: Section B - B (in 1990)
Below right: Section C - C (in 1990)

Scales for plan and elevation (above) and sections (below)

single chamber on each floor. On the front (north) elevation the wing was jettied both at first floor and tie-beam level. The framing was a mixture of close-studding and chevron-work, the latter carried around to form a feature on the extent of the projection on the east and west walls. In the gable there was a king-post with chevron design worked to a herring-bone pattern. At ground level the moulded sill of a projecting window was *in situ* although the then window was a modern replacement. Three coved timbers springing from a rail on either side suggested that the window reached to the height of the moulded and brattished bressumer beam which supported the upper storey. A similar oriel window, but without the coving, served the upper chamber.

The long side wall of the wing (east elevation) had framing which reflected the internal plan form: fully two-storied and two-bayed with windows regularly spaced, four at ground floor level and two in the upper storey. These windows were of much plainer form, amounting to no more than gaps in the framework. Diagonal wall-braces between the main posts and the wall-plate demarcated the bay divisions in the upper storey.

The studs themselves were fashioned from 10in. square timbers, the interstices were only 12ins. and the overall scantling of the framework suggested an excess of strength throughout the work.

b) Internal Features

One of the most interesting internal features of the crosswing was the truss which formed the division between the two bays (C - C). The floor beam carried a narrow chamfer with pyramid stops at either end and on all four arrises. It was properly tenoned and pegged into mortices in the posts which had thickened heads and were themselves chamfered on both sides. This suggested that the lower half of the truss was contemporary with the external framework, although the posts themselves were L-shaped, raising the possibility that they may once have occurred at an intersection of two ranges.

The upper half of the truss was even more problematical. The cambered tie-beam had empty mortices and peg-holes on its upper face which appeared to relate to crown-post roof construction, the side mortices fashioned to receive down-swinging braces from the head of the crown-post in the standard Shropshire way. An inexplicable feature was the off-centred position of the mortice and peg-holes relating to the assumed crown-post. These were carefully studied and drawn exactly as they appeared. The lower edge of the tie-beam has a series of closely-spaced peg-holes which were matched by a corresponding series on the upper halves of the wall-post, suggesting that the tie-beam was supported by large arch-braces. There was slight evidence that a decorative boss of some kind occupied the centre of the tie-beam. All these features were smoke-blackened and rather worn, suggesting that this part of the truss was once part of a medieval open hall which had an open hearth at ground level. But above the tie-beam there were no further indications of crown-post roof construction, no collars or collar-purlin, and, of course, no crown-post or attendant braces. In fact the roof timbers looked clean and comparatively new. The principal rafters, threaded side purlins, small curved windbraces and common rafters appeared to relate to the bulk of the late 16th or early 17th century framework described earlier.

The most likely explanation for this dichotomy is that in assembling the crosswing the carpenter reused a tie-beam and posts from an old open hall which may or may not have

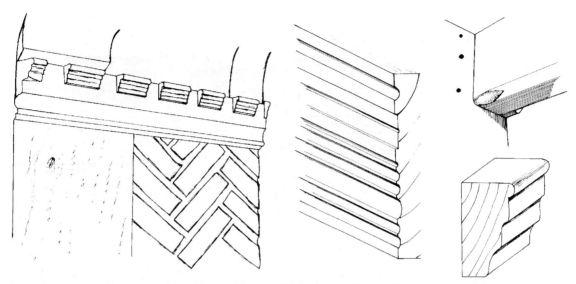

Various details (n.t.s.). Left: Brattishing and brickwork. Centre: Section through bressumer. Top right: Detail of beam with pyramid stop (see section C - C). Lower right: Section through brattice

come from the site. The alternative, that the tie-beam truss was *in situ* and the later framework grafted on to it is not convincing because the smoke-blackening indicated that an open hall, not a floored crosswing was its provenance, and the configurations of the site plan strongly suggest that the hall range would have been set parallel to the road, as it is at present. But a difficult question is why it was thought necessary to reuse timber when, clearly, no expense was spared on the rest of the framework of the wing.

On the ground plan a small area at the southern end of the long west wall is shown devoid of framing. When the survey was made this area was particularly obscure. A doorway giving access to the hall was suspected, but this was only confirmed during the later restoration work. Similarly, on the southern gable wall, timbers are not shown; they had been removed. In the upper chamber a shaped doorhead in the north-west corner provided evidence for access at that level and this is shown on A - A.

The Hall Range

As mentioned above, the hall range had been truncated at its western end and consisted of a 9ft. bay and a 4ft. half-bay, each 12ft. wide and set back from the crosswing by 4ft. 6ins. A ceiling beam appeared to mark the original bay division in the hall (B - B). On the front (north) elevation a nondescript brick wall had replaced the timber-framing to first floor height, but the upper storey retained close-studding without a mid-rail and there was evidence for a window at the present western end which would have lighted the upper chamber.

If Grove Farm had a medieval open hall, it is reasonably certain that nothing remained of it; the roof height and the eaves level matched those of the crosswing, the framework of the hall range was separate from that of the crosswing in places, and it was clear that much remodelling had taken place at different times. At the rear a catslide roof filled in the space between the rear walls of both units, bringing the plan shape virtually to the form of a rectangle. Close studding without a mid-rail suggests a date range from the mid-15th to the mid-16th century and may represent Grove Farm's first major remodelling.

Interpretation and Dating

At the end of the group's survey work the conclusion was reached that the

The front elevation before restoration

hall range was remodelled *c.*1500, with the proviso that this could have occurred 50 years either way. There was little to be deduced from the unit; the eastern parlour crosswing was the more important not only because it contained part of a medieval truss, irrespective of its origin, but because of the style and quality of the framing. A late 16th or early 17th century date seemed appropriate, but whether it replaced an earlier solar or service end is impossible to say. It is feasible that, as remodelled at that time, the house was H-shaped and had a marked similarity to Lower Carden Hall near Malpas.[2] The framework of the crosswing shows a distinct Cheshire influence in the coving, brattishing, chevron-work and oriel-type windows.

Unfortunately the group's findings were at variance with those of the Royal Commission on Historical Monuments of England.[3] Their report raised the question of whether truss B was of base-cruck construction before the remodelling of the late 16th/early 17th century, and quoted as evidence for the comparative shortness of the tie-beam and the presence of two sets of long paired mortices in its soffit which would have received the tenons of the base-crucks and the curved braces between the cruck blade and the tie. The tie-beam in question measures 12ft. 9ins., and is, in fact, 7ins. longer than that in the east wing which is clearly a standard tie-beam and not the first horizontal

The rear elevation after restoration and an extension on the left

beam of a base-cruck truss. If the measurements of the seven known base-cruck hall-houses in Shropshire are compared, the longest first horizontal is 17ft. and the shortest is 11ft., giving an average of 12ft. 10ins. This would appear to support the Commission's reasoning, but if the shortest is discounted the average is 15ft. 2ins. It could be argued that the beam is in the normal tie-beam position and relates entirely to the remodelling of the hall. The king-strut is a timber which was probably added after the remodelling. It is not morticed, tenoned or pegged to either the principal rafters or the tie-beam. As the drawing shows, the group found no evidence of soffit mortices on truss B although mortices and peg-holes relating to large arch-braces are present on truss C. It is possible that in the Commission's report the two trusses were confused.

The group begs to differ on several points, some more important than others. The chief contention is the postulated base-cruck, another relates to the bracing of the missing crown-post on truss C. The Commission's report specifies that it had up-swinging braces, while the group's view of the mortices on the upper edge of the tie-beam is that they were cut and angled for down-swinging braces of the type normally found in Shropshire crown-post roofs. As the crown-post was missing, it was difficult to understand where evidence for up-swinging braces was found.

Further confusion occurred because the trusses were not drawn in the Commission's report, and where they occurred on the plan the labelling did not relate to references in the text. The group also thought it unlikely that the western wing was three-bayed and could not agree with the way in which the hall was shown at a peculiar angle to the east wing.

It was with some relief that it found agreement in assessing the east wing as originally entirely unheated, the lateral fireplace in the northern bay, which has not been reinstated, clearly a later addition.

As far as dating is concerned the two bodies were in reasonable agreement. It seems likely that there was a hall-house on the site in the mid-to-late 15th century, although the Commission estimated a mid-14th century date. Whether this house was the fully developed H-plan that it later became is impossible to decide. If it developed along the lines noted in several other Shropshire farmhouses it is more likely to have been T-shaped. Drastic remodelling in the late 16th/early 17th century provided a two-storied hall in place of the open hall, and a prestigious two-storied parlour wing at the eastern end which was balanced by a larger service wing at the western end. This was the climax of the structural evolution, historically speaking. From then on it was a case of debasement, although no doubt the later 18th and 19th century owners would not have regarded their numerous truncations, additions, alterations, divisions and piecemeal projects in those terms.

The Restoration
As the 'before' and 'after' photographs show, Grove Farm has been restored with spectacular success. Throughout, Mr. Rowland insisted on historical accuracy, was meticulous in details of mouldings, basing everything on original evidence or on contemporary examples, and using new or second-hand materials only when it was absolutely necessary. His insistence that the new brickwork should be aesthetically correct meant that, in addition to using large quantities of local material, he had to resort to purchasing second-hand

narrow bricks from a demolished prison at Bruges. These form a delightful feature in the chimneystack and in part of the walling of the entirely reconstructed south elevation of the east wing.

The group was able to follow the work of rehabilitation and to examine the framework closely as it was dismantled, treated and re-erected. It was interesting that opinions formed in 1990 regarding the structural evolution remained valid, no startling new evidence was uncovered, the only new discoveries being the missing doorway in the south bay of the east wing and the presence of cellars, one beneath the northern bay of the east wing and the other below the corresponding bay of the missing west wing.

Not only has Mr. Rowland recreated the true form of an historic building, he has enhanced the parish and the environs of Whitchurch generally to a degree unsurpassed in modern times.

Tenurial History and the 'Wedding-Feast Annuity'[4]

Ash Parva, despite its name, is a township larger in area than its neighbour, Ash Magna.[5] Although Grove Farm became part of the Bridgwater estate for a time, presumably after 1598 when Sir Thomas Egerton bought the manor of Whitchurch from the Talbot family, it appears to have been a freehold property for much of its life.[6] It is first mentioned in 1520 when Richard Sandford, a local farmer, gave a fat bullock to each of the Ash townships on the occasion of his marriage. There followed what can only be described as a drama with strong biblical overtones. The men of Ash Magna slaughtered their bullock and had a great feast, but the farmers of Ash Parva sought to increase their 'talent' and sold their bullock for £32. With the money they leased a parcel of land of one acre, two roods and 32 perches known as the Pingle which they renamed the Town Croft. The land formed part of the acreage of Grove Farm, the occupier of which paid rent annually to 'The Wedding-Feast Annuity'. Thus the farming community of Ash Parva was able to enjoy an annual feast and this continued until the Second World War rationing restrictions caused it to fall into abeyance. On Michaelmas Day, 29th September 1738, Samuel Jackson 'entered as tenant at Candlemas last on the town croft' and paid £1 8s. Four years later he bought Grove Farm from the Duke of Bridgwater, but agreed to continue to pay the annual contribution to the Annuity. The head of the Hughes family of Ash Wood was always sole Trustee of the Annuity and Ash Wood is included among the surveys in this volume.[7] The Town Croft is listed in a conveyance of 1895 but is not shown on a later plan of Grove Farm of 1918.[8] The 1841 Tithe Map Apportionment shows an area labelled the 'Town Field' and it is likely that the Town Croft was part of that.[9]

The Jackson family may have been in possession of Grove Farm as early as 1630, and it is not clear when Thomas Taylor, the next owner, took over—the Annuity book gives 1766 but the Rate Assessments 1783.[10] However, it is clear that the Taylors were absentee landlords as was Ashton Beckett, described as 'gentleman' from Cranage in Cheshire, who bought Grove Farm in 1823. On this point there is documentary agreement.[11] The Rev. William Dodsworth Bate Birtles, a representative of Ashton Beckett, is given as owner up to 1856, but clearly the Beckett family still had an interest in the property as in September 1918 the Misses M.B. and F.A. Beckett and their sister, Mrs. A.M. Thimbleby of Harrogate sold to their tenants Ralph and Arthur Dodd who became the first working owners since the Jacksons' time.[12] By this time the property had been divided into two dwellings and is so described on the tithe apportionment of 1841. Since 1918 it has changed hands several times. In October 1927 Mrs. Edith Boughey inherited from her mother, but sold it in November of the same year at a public auction to her husband. He paid £5,100, £2,500 of which he obtained on mortgage. Their daughter Beatrice sold it in 1940 to a Miss Palmer whose brothers inherited in 1942. They sold to Mr. Roger Spencer Rowland, a prominent Whitchurch business man and town councillor who, on his death in October 1970, left Grove Farm to his nephew, Mr. Roger Bromfield Rowland.[13] After complete restoration by Mr. Rowland the house was sold to Mrs. J. Hinchcliffe, the present owner.

The rate assessments show the Jackson family as owning seven properties in the area, but occupying only one. If, as seems likely, that property was Grove Farm and it was regarded as the family home, it would explain the comparatively lavish expenditure on the crosswing and the other up-dating phases.

The Richard Jones Connection[14]

Richard Jones was a tenant farmer at Grove Farm and his name features in the Wedding-Feast Annuity book. There are closer links with Ash Wood, however, and artifacts in the possession of Richard Hughes of Ash Wood bring a close personal touch to the link. One is a silver double-cased verge watch which belonged to Richard Jones, another is a sampler worked by his wife Sarah and dated 2nd September 1801. Their daughter Mary married William Hughes who farmed at Barhill, Tushingham but whose ancestral home was Ash Wood, and their miniatures on ivory are held at Ash Wood. These items are illustrated in the Ash Wood chapter. The watch is engraved 'B. Clowes Liverpool', is numbered 3995 and hallmarked for Birmingham 1775/6. It has a unique face, the owner's name replacing conventional numerals and 'Ash' engraved on the face. It passed to Mary and is mentioned in her husband's account book, opened when he started to farm at Barhill in February 1799.[15] Sarah died in October 1823. A copy of her husband's will is held at Ash Wood, and, because it includes some revealing human touches, notes from it are given below. Richard Hughes also has several other pieces of silver inherited from Mary.

Richard Jones's Will

The will is dated 29th April 1806 and Richard Jones describes himself as a farmer of Little Ash. He makes it clear that he has already given money, furniture, household dairy and husbandry implements, horses and cows in equal shares to his eldest son John and daughter Mary, and therefore does not intend to leave them further bequests, but recommends them 'to live with and act to each other with true brotherly and sisterly love and affection.' To his sons Thomas and Richard he leaves £200 each and entreats 'all my said children to continue dutiful and obedient to their mother.' His 'dear Wife Sarah Jones' is appointed sole executrix and receives 'all my Leasehold estate and all my other personal estate.' The will is signed and witnessed by John Knight, solicitor of Knight and Brookes of Whitchurch and John Turtle, a clerk in the firm.

Manor Cottage, Prees

Manor Cottage in Prees is on the eastern side of the road which loops round the church and the old churchyard. In this area the church, vicarage, school and hall form the nucleus of the old village, some distance from the later development alongside what was, before the by-pass was recently constructed, the main trunk road from Whitchurch to Shrewsbury. Appropriately, Manor Cottage has early origins. It was divided into two dwellings some time between 1905 and 1911,[1] but in 1987 was restored to a single house. Recent documentary research and scientific analysis of the timbers has produced strong evidence that the site is that of the manor house and that the present house is a rebuilding in the middle of the 16th century. It contains a two-bay open hall and demonstrates a contemporaneous use of two historic structural forms, the cruck and the box-frame. The architectural evidence supports a late date in the chronology of cruck construction.

The Plan

At present the plan is that of an in-line three-bayed dwelling which incorporates a two-bayed open hall and one further bay to the west. It is difficult to be certain whether there was a bay beyond the hall as the gable at the eastern end had been completely rebuilt prior to the recent restoration programme. If there were only three bays the structure would come into the category of an 'end hall house', but the possibility of a further unit cannot be ruled out. There is no evidence that the house had either a screens passage or a spere-truss and so the entrance was probably directly into the lower bay of the hall. This is the larger of the two hall bays and probably accommodated the entrance area at the western end. There is a blocked doorway in the appropriate position in the north wall of

Manor Cottage, Prees

Manor Cottage.

Left: South Elevation.
Centre left: North elevation.
Lower left: Ground floor plan.
Upper right: Section A - A.
Lower right: Section B - B
(both sections to same scale as
that for the west elevation on
page 174)

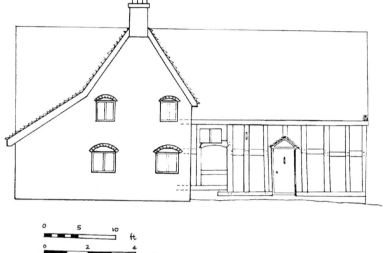

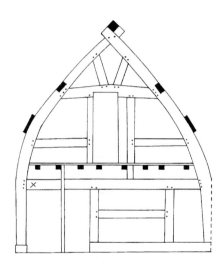

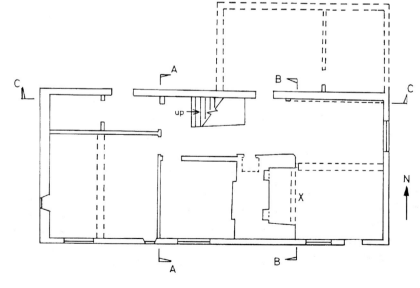

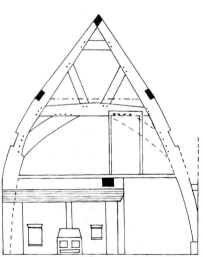

the lower bay, but unfortunately a modern window on the southern side obscures the evidence for an opposing doorway to complete the cross-passage. The truss at A - A is a closed truss and, unfortunately, it is difficult to determine how many doorways it contained originally. At present there is only one, and that may be a later insertion. Certainly the central section of the frame was always filled in, but there could have been a door on either side of it giving access into two service rooms, normally a buttery and a pantry. However, the westernmost bay is comparatively large (16ft. x 19ft.) and contains no evidence of an original partition. If there was only one doorway in the truss, it raises the question of whether animals were housed in the end bay and that would put the house into the additional category of 'longhouse'. Lower end byres are often associated with single doors in the partition. The lower section of truss A - A has redundant fixing points on both sides of the frame, showing that at some time it supported a built-in feature. This is unlikely to have been a high seat on the eastern side as it is at the wrong end of the plan, but it could have been a feeding trough facing into the byre, in which case the cross-passage, postulated above, would have done double duty as a feeding-walk, a not uncommon arrangement.

1) Section B - B

This is an open cruck truss and is the central truss of the two-bayed hall. On the southern side the cruck is partially obscured by the inserted chimneystack but is visible to its full height on the northern side. The cambered collar beam is supported by arch-braces which are so carpentered that the sweep of the central arch is uninterrupted. The apex joint is type 'A', the blades hardly touching but held together by a yoke.[2] The blades are chamfered on both sides up to the level of the collar-beam and possibly rested on stylobates. At present, on the northern side, the foot of the blade and the projection on which it stands are plastered over, but it it clear that the foot was not tenoned into the sill beam, as is the case on truss A - A. The soffit of the yoke and the top section of the cruck on the southern side carry a groove, the purpose of which probably relates to the fixing of a 'fumbrell' or wattle and daub firehood which preceded the present chimneystack. As there is no smoke-blackening on the roof timbers it appears that the house never had an open hearth but was furnished with an efficient means of smoke extraction from the start.

2) Section A - A

As stated above, section A - A is a closed truss which divided the lower bay of the hall from the outer room which may have been a byre. Its apex is Type 'D' in which the blades cross, one tenoned and threaded through the other, forming a cradle to support the ridge purlin. This is described as 'late and unimportant' compared with other apex types.[3] While such a description may be considered over-dismissive, it does emphasise the difference between the prestigious open truss at B - B and the purely functional one at A - A. Not only did A - A demarcate the end of the open hall, it supported a floor over the outer room. Perhaps because of its work load, extra care was taken to ensure that it was fully integrated into the frame, the feet tenoned into the sill instead of resting on stylobates.

On the western side of truss A - A at the northern end, that is, facing into the supposed byre, is a scratched mark on the timber which is shown as a detail at 'X' on the drawings.

It is not a carpenter's assembly mark, but its strange form suggests that it is a ritualistic charm mark, perhaps of runic derivation, intended to ward off cattle disease or some other disaster.

3) The West Elevation
In contrast to the internal cruck trusses, the frame at the western end of the house is of box-frame construction. As the

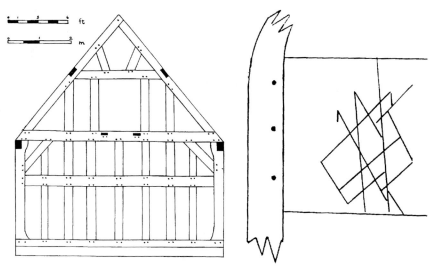

Left: West elevation. Right: Detail at X on section A - A (n.t.s.)

drawing shows, it is of a simple straightforward design, typical of many in the West Midlands. Two features are worthy of special mention: the jowelled feet of the outer posts and the projecting brackets in the centre of the tie-beam. The latter probably supported an oriel window, now blocked, which lit the upper chamber of the outer room.

4) Section C - C
The longitudinal section shows the pattern of the windbraces which are either present in each bay or can be deduced from their dead mortices. They are large straight unchamfered members, tenoned and pegged into the principals and into the purlins. It could be significant that they are absent on both sides from the upper bay of the open hall. If the plan has been interpreted correctly, this area would be the dais end of the hall and may have had its raised dais secured by a method that obviated the need for windbraces at this end. The section also shows some of the detail of the original floor over the outer room, with its large spine-beam and floorboards. The floor level shown above the boards is modern.

Additional Details
Most of the cruck trusses in Shropshire are sawn timbers which give an identical pair of blades for each truss, but at Manor Cottage each cruck blade is fashioned from a whole tree. Because of the irregularity it was necessary to employ posts as part of the wall-framing and on each blade crude cruck spurs effect the connection. The spurs emerge below the wall-plate and are clearly visible on the exterior.

On the long outer walls all the verticals are continuous timbers; the horizontals, which divide the surface into two equal parts, are all short timbers. This is an unusual practice; continuous verticals are normally associated only with the area of an open hall, which, of course, had no upper floor;[4] but here, because the joists in the outer room run in a west-east direction, there was no need to use interrupted verticals on the side walls, and, significantly, they are confined to the gable frame.

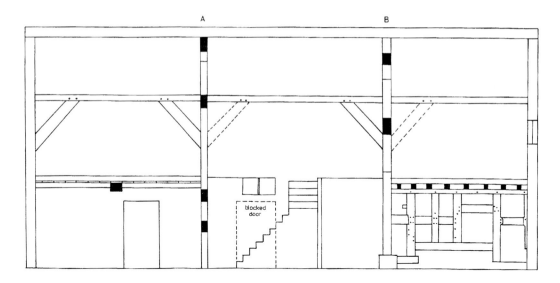

Section C - C (to same scale as west elevation and other sections)

The use of box-frame construction for the end gable wall, while employing cruck trusses internally is interesting. It is not common in Shropshire, although individual cruck and box-framed units occur frequently in houses of one build. Only two other Shropshire houses are known to employ the two techniques in the same unit. One, nos. 6-10 Dodington, Whitchurch is the subject of another chapter, the other lies in south Shropshire.[5]

The box-framed end raises the question of the missing truss at the eastern end and whether it was a box-framed end truss or a partition between the dais end of the hall and a solar bay. If it was the latter, then it may account for the ease with which it was destroyed if and when the house was truncated. It would also account for the fact that level ground is present beyond the modern end wall, sufficient to accommodate a solar end, and for the fact that the well is located beyond the rise in the ground level, now rather a long way from the house.

Assuming that the hall had a distinctive dais end and that the dais was destroyed when the house lost its solar, it is possible that the elaborately moulded beam above the fireplace in the upper bay of the hall once functioned as a beam above the dais. A similar situation occurs at the Guildhall in Newport, Shropshire, and at Wolverton Manor in South Shropshire.[6] That alterations were made at this end is suggested by the presence of a 'scotch' or prop-mark on the exterior of the southern side. It is not on an end timber which would denote propping during original assembly but seems to relate to later shoring up of the frame.[7]

Forming the hearth of the fireplace in the upper bay of the hall, now the dining room, are large brown glazed tiles which do not seem to be particularly old, but whose provenance is puzzling. During restoration it was necessary to excavate below ground level in the north-east corner of the room. Here, below about 6ft. of sand was a layer of tiles of which the hearth tiles are a sample. They were laid on a bed of black ashes and soil, about 1ft. 6ins. in depth. Below this was another layer of tiles, but, unlike the first layer, this did not span the width of the room and was left undisturbed.[8]

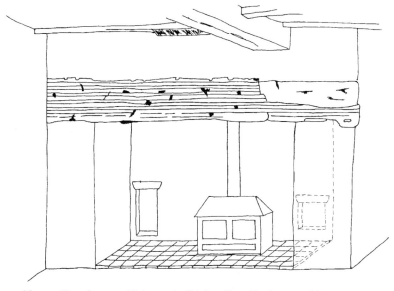

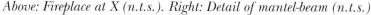

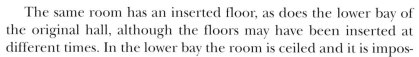

Above: Fireplace at X (n.t.s.). Right: Detail of mantel-beam (n.t.s.)

The same room has an inserted floor, as does the lower bay of the original hall, although the floors may have been inserted at different times. In the lower bay the room is ceiled and it is impossible to examine the joisting system, but in the dining room there is a large spine beam, 1ft. 1in. square, chamfered and stopped, but at the fireplace end only. The joists run in a north-south direction and on the northern side they are supported by a ledge which is secured to the wall. It is impossible to see whether there is a similar ledge on the southern side as the wall is thickened, presumably with a modern inner skin, and plastered over. The joists measure 4ins. x 3ins. and are set at intervals of 1ft. 3ins. Each is chamfered and stopped, and where they join the spine-beam on the northern side the scantling is reduced beyond the stop. On the southern side the stops are obscured by the modern wall but are visible at the junction of the spine beam. Here there is no reduction. In both halves the joists are without tenons and are simply lodged into the spine-beam.

A more satisfactory method was used for the original flooring in the outer room. Here the joists measure 5ins. x 6ins. and are set at intervals of 1ft. 9ins. There are no chamfers and each joist has a bare-faced soffit tenon which may or may not have been secured with a peg; the floorboards obscure the evidence.[9] A similar joisting system was used at the High Street Garage in Whitchurch.

Another detail which has similarities with the High Street Garage is the joint on the wall-plate. Though obscured at present a photograph taken when the house was stripped out shows a bridled scarf-joint with two edge pegs.[10]

Historical Note

The location of the episcopal see whose bishops owned Prees had a complicated history, moving several times before and after Domesday. At the time of Domesday Prees was held by the Bishop of Chester, but soon afterwards, in 1102, the see was moved from Chester and the bishop's title became Coventry and Lichfield.[11] Therefore until 1646, when bishoprics were temporarily abolished and their estates transferred to trustees, the lord of the manor of Prees was an absentee ecclesiastic, although no doubt he or his steward could and would demand accommodation at the manor when visiting this distant part of the diocese.

In 1448 the bishop had received permission to demolish all his residences except those in Coventry, Lichfield and London and three in Staffordshire. He could use the materials to repair those that survived. His residence at Prees, may therefore, have been pulled down.[12] In 1550 the bishop leased the manor of Prees to a Londoner, Richard Cupper, and the manor remained in lease thereafter for as long as the bishops owned it, that is, until 1794. The 1550 lease, however, has not survived, so it is not known whether the site of the manor house was excepted from it and let separately. Certainly it was the invariable practice to lease the manor and the site of the manor house separately by 1676-7, and may have been from 1550. When the parliamentary trustees sold the bishop's manor in 1647-8 the site of the manor house was sold to Thomas Harpar for £147 13s 5d, the rest of the manor having been sold four months earlier to Henock Smith for £1,122. If the manor and site of the manor house had been let separately from 1550, the new tenant of the site of the latter, who was probably a relatively small occupier of land in Prees, would be the prime candidate for the builder of Manor Cottage.[13]

In c.1835 the house was occupied by Samuel Hopwood, at which time it was said to have been received earlier by the Hill family, who held the manor on lease from the Bishop of Lichfield and Coventry, in exchange for lands in Coventry.[14] Since Hopwood's father-in-law, Samuel Booth, (d.1833) was occupying the 'scite of the manor house' in 1794, the time of the exchange, it seems reasonably certain that the house under review is on the site of the manor house.[15]

Summary and Conclusions

Dendrochronological sampling and analysis, carried out in 1994, produced a felling date in the winter of 1551/2, and proved that the floor in the outer room is a contemporary feature.[16] This confirms the supposition that Manor Cottage was built 100 years after the bishop obtained permission to demolish many of his palaces. It is frustrating to know nothing of the man who took advantage of episcopal leasing arrangements at that time, and particularly whether he was influenced by the fact that he was building on the site of the manor. Certainly he built to the standards of many a small manor house, and the fact that he incorporated a byre at the lower end is not unusual.[17] Like any lord, he and his family would take their meals on the dais at the upper end of the hall, warmed by a fire that had its smoke properly chanelled and which did not obscure the view of the superior carpentry of the central truss. He would not be content to sleep above his cattle, but would be comfortably accommodated in the solar end of the house.

As the house represents a rebuilding in the middle of the 16th century, it is interesting to note some of the trends at this time. The provision of a smokehood was an improvement on the old concept of an open hearth, and the style of the box-framing in the end wall is entirely in keeping with such a date. Other details, such as the joints, windbraces, continuous posts and cruck treatment appear to be entirely traditional. It may be thought that the use of whole trees indicates a late date, the better trees already used. But this is not necessarily the case. To the north of the Severn cruck distribution thins out considerably, and it is likely that in this area better trees were never freely available.

It is unusual to find a house of cruck construction where so much of the original wall framing survives. Walls of cruck buildings are, by definition, independent of the trusses and could be easily replaced. Perhaps the combination of cruck and box-framed construction, seen at Manor Cottage, means that the walling was better integrated, was of good quality and therefore did not need to be renewed.

Providence Grove, Prees

Providence Grove is a timber-framed house set gable end on to the western side of Shrewsbury Street, about 170 yards south from the crossroads from where routes lead eastwards to the nucleus of the old village of Prees and westwards to Prees station. The house presently relates to a smallholding of just over 3½ acres, the land lying to the west of the house. Box-framed throughout, the house is of two distinct parts. Old illustrations show that about the time of the First World War it had a thatched roof and that until *c.*1978 most of the framing was concealed with either pebble-dash or cement render, but since that date there has been a continuous programme of restoration, and tiles have replaced the thatch.

External details

Viewed from the south, the earlier two-bayed unit, at the western end, displays open framing with two large curving angle-braces set between the end posts and the wall-plate. A doorway in the eastern corner serves as the main entrance to the house, but is not necessarily marking the original entrance position. Above the wall-plate there is evidence that the height has been raised by 1ft. 8ins. There is a large chimney-stack at the western end. This is brick-built and set internally against the gable frame, appearing externally as a feature astride the roof line.

The later unit to the east consists of a single bay with square-framing and a coved jetty supporting the tie-beam of the eastern gable. The end post accommodates the supporting jetty bracket and a short straight brace to the wall-plate. Like the earlier unit, this later bay has had its roof raised.

For the most part the north elevation repeats the

Providence Grove, south and east elevations, as they are today

179

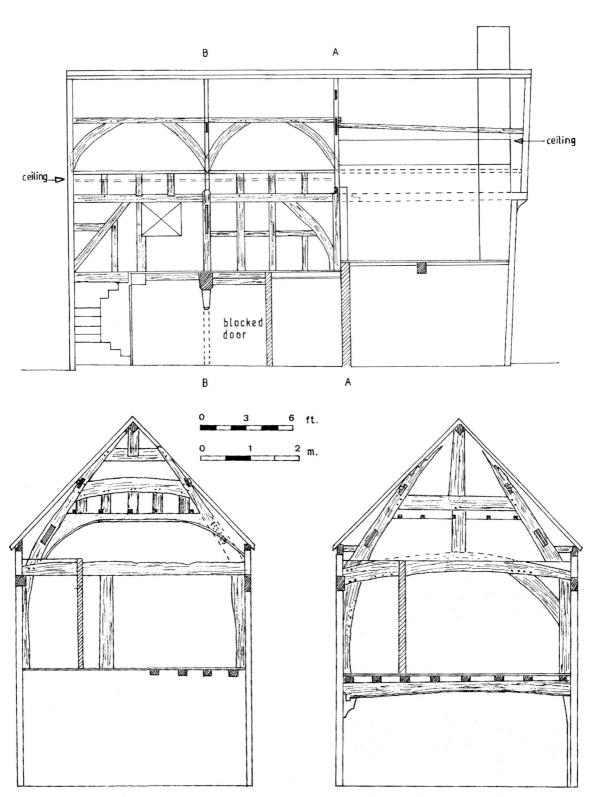

Providence Grove. Sections A - A (lower left); B - B (lower right) and C - C (top)

pattern of the south, and for that reason was not measured and drawn. The main difference is that the chimneystack which serves the corner fireplace in the added bay emerges as a feature piercing the roof in the north-east corner. A modern kitchen is housed in the lean-to against the older unit.

On the west gable wall the timbers have always been exposed, and the amount of weathering is considerable. The posts have jowelled heads, with angle-braces immediately below the jowls and connecting with the tie-beam above. Above the tie-beam there is a straight collar-beam with two queen-struts. Rectangular framing occupies the space below the tie-beam. The later roof-raising is a noticeable feature.

The interstices are filled with hand-made bricks which are probably a replacement for original wattle and daub. Though well puddled, the bricks vary in size, averaging 10ins. x 2¹/₂ins. x 4ins. Similar bricks have been noted in the area, a characteristic fault—a raised band in the floor of the mould, appearing as an irregular feature—providing the distinguishing mark.

No firm evidence that the building ever continued westwards was found. Several enigmatic holes and empty mortices occur on the posts, but none that would positively relate to a further bay. The truss is flush-jointed and it seems reasonable to suppose that any extension westwards would have been single-storied. Structural details below first floor level have been lost or are obscured. The original wall-plates are present, but appear not to have continued beyond the wall-face—they are secured in an unusual way by slight projections at the ends of the tie-beam.

The east elevation faces the street and consists of the gable end of the added bay. It has the date 1611 attached to the gable but this was added recently and may be described as

West (left) and south elevations

'inspired guesswork' on the part of those involved. Old inhabitants of Prees are said to remember such a date being on the building before it was first rendered.

The pattern of the framing is distinctive and reminiscent of the 'Cheshire school' of carpentry which is sometimes found filtering through to north Shropshire. In the gable herring-bone work occurs above the collar-beam, while between the collar and the tie-beam three quatre-foil panels make an impressive display. Below the tie-beam there is coving, and below the coving the main part of the second storey is divided into three panels of herring-bone work, the 'bonework' pointing downwards in contrast to that in the gable which points upwards. Two sections of the interstices between the 'bones' have been left exposed, though protected by glass. These show the wattle and daub infil. Although a modern window has been inserted, there is evidence for an original

181

South elevation drawn to the same scale as the plan on the page opposite

window, centrally placed and rising to tie-beam level from a sill about half-way up the panel as shown on the drawings. As mentioned above, the ground floor area remains rendered over, the cement scored to resemble stonework.

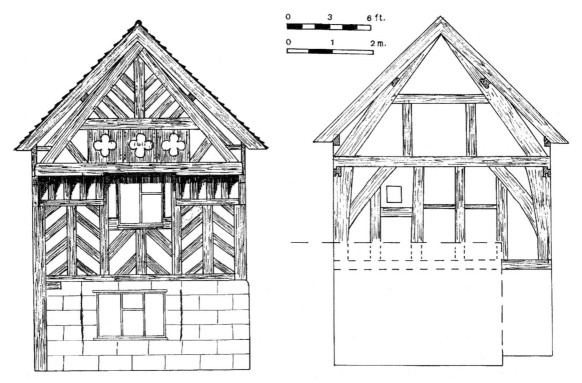

0   3   6 ft.

0   1   2 m.

East elevation (left) and west elevation (right)

182

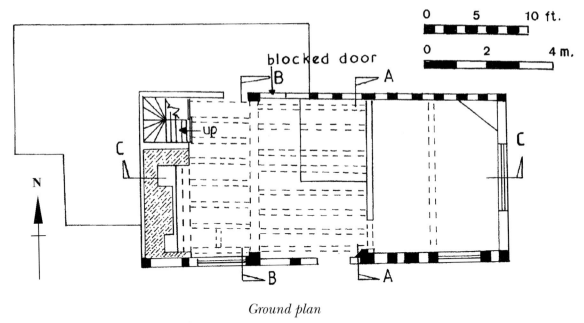

Ground plan

The roof-line is angled out and secondary rafters with connecting spurs have been inserted. This was done, presumably, to bring the whole building into line when it was re-roofed.

The Roof and Sections

Most of the roof-space is accessible with difficulty, and from the minimal amount of smoke-blackening it is clear that the two-bay hall of the earlier unit probably had a 'fumbrell' or smoke-hood against the end truss.

The central truss B has a slightly cambered tie-beam which is supported by two arch-braces, one of which is *in situ*. The other has been removed but the mortices and peg-holes remain. Above the tie-beam is a straight collar-beam, and there is a central strut between the two. The form of the truss indicates that it functioned as the central truss in a two-bay hall.

The eastern truss A was clearly a closed truss and it seems reasonable to suggest that it functioned as the western end of the hall. Below the level of the inserted ceiling which is marked by the five joist-ends shown at the feet of the studs, the arched feature is simply an outline of how the plasterwork appears. There is no reason to suppose that arch-braces occur here.

The windbraces, shown on the longitudinal section C - C, are large curved plain members, tenoned into the soffits of the purlins and into the principal rafters. In the westernmost bay on the south side the windbraces are triple-pegged, but elsewhere double-pegging is employed. On the end truss it is impossible to see whether there is evidence for the windbracing to continue westwards as the area is plastered over. This is unfortunate as it would have provided firm evidence for the house to have continued in that direction, if such was the case.

One tier of purlins occur in each slope of the roof. They are threaded through the principal rafters.

The Plan, Internal Features and Dendrochronological Evidence

In the absence of contradictory evidence it must be assumed that the original plan consisted simply of a two-bay hall. It seems reasonably certain that any units beyond the hall, if they existed, were single-storied. While structural features indicate that the hall was open, and received an inserted floor at a later date, probably in two stages, dendrochronological sampling and analysis gave a felling date of 1468 for the joists which suggests that it was a floored hall from the start. Unfortunately, samples taken from main fabric of the house would not date, but a date of *c.*1468 would stylistically accord with the framing, with, for example, its jowelled heads to the posts and curved windbraces.[1] The transverse beam is roughly chamfered and stopped and rests on two posts which appear to be insertions. Although both halves of the floor are at the same height, the joists don't align either side of the beam. They are set flat and measure, on average, 8½ins. x 6½ins. x 4ins.., varying in quality. The bay containing the smoke-hood may have been left open for a time which would account for the difference in the alignment of the joists. It was probably when this was floored over that the smoke-hood was replaced by a permanent brick-built chimneystack, and access to the upper floor was made possible via a ladder in front of the fireplace. The trimmer for this stair-trap remains as a witness mark. Later the stair-trap was abandoned and a staircase was inserted by the side of the stack. To facilitate the insertion of the staircase part of the internal face of the end truss was cut away. The trimming back of the mid-rail has resulted in the exposure of the mortice for one of the vertical studs.

The brickwork of the stack is exposed in the bedroom at the western end. It is in excellent condition, the bricks are narrow and very well made, each measuring 9ins. x 2ins. x 4½ins.

At ground level a blocked doorway is present on the northern wall. When opened the door fouled the transverse beam, and this was trimmed back to facilitate access. This indicates that the transverse beam was inserted while the northern doorway was still in use, which raises the question of the authenticity of the present entrance on the southern side. The panel to the west of the entrance shows signs of disturbance and the horizontal rail is an inserted timber. It is possible that this panel once accommodated a doorway directly opposite to the one on the northern side, creating a cross-passage within the hall, reminiscent of medieval planning practices. If this sequence is correct it would explain the present position of the entrance, clear of the transverse beam, and account for the blocking of the northern door.

The Documentary Evidence[2]

The oldest document in the deeds belonging to Providence Grove is dated 7th May 1726 and is a common type of conveyance of copyhold premises. It is written in 'Secretary hand' and is in Latin. The use of Latin in legal documents was forbidden *c.*1730, so this is a late example. Basically it concerns the sale of the property from Maria Mason, Charles Mason and John Wright to Paul Gregory, although the exchange of money is not mentioned. Because the property was copyhold, however, the parties were obliged to go through a fictional procedure whereby the vendors surrendered the property to the lord of the manor 'to the use of' the purchaser, to whom the lord was then said to grant the property. There was an annual 'chief rent' of 5s 8d, payable by the purchaser to the lord. This was an ancient customary rent, and not an economic rent. For most practical purposes the purchaser then owned the property. The following is a précis of the document in translation:

Surrender to Uses and Admission

> Manor of Prees. View of frankpledge and court baron of Richard Hill Esq., held 7th May 1726 before Thomas Ball, steward.
>
> Maria Mason, widow of Charles Mason, and Charles Mason their son surrendered (on 29th January last), and John Wright now surrenders, a customary messuage or tenement in Prees in a street called Wallend, now occupied by John Simpson, and customary lands in Prees called Hempbutts, Loweryard, Moore and Higher Croft, now occupied by the said Thomas Simpson. The premises were formerly those of Francis or Laurence Simpson. The surrender is to the use of Paul Greggory, miller, his heirs and assigns for ever. The steward, on behalf of the lord, delivers the premises to the said Paul Greggory, to hold of the lord at will. Paul Greggory pays an entry fine of 100s, does fealty, and is admitted as tenant.

A run of deeds from 1750 to the present time show that until 1876 the Gregory family occupied Providence Grove, although the house was not known by that name until the 20th century. Shrewsbury Street is called Wall End in the earlier deeds.

The Gregory family were millers and farmers. Paul Gregory, presumably the son of the Paul of the 1726 deed, and his wife Elizabeth were admitted tenants on 23rd April 1750 and paid £4 14s 6d entry fine and the 5s 8d annual customary rent. Paul was succeeded by his son, another Paul, whose wife's name was Sarah. She was illiterate—her will, made on 14th January 1815 is signed with a cross. They were succeeded by their son, yet another Paul, whose wife's name was Hannah. Paul III died in 1827, leaving his son, John Paul, who was a minor, £75 4s 4d in trust. Although the rent remained at 5s 8d, the entry fine had increased to £34 and a further £10 was levied for Heriot.

In 1876 the property was sold to John Thomas Hodgkin of Marbury, a farmer, for £600. At this time the tenure was still copyhold and did not become freehold until 1894 following bankruptcy proceedings against Rowland Clegg, Viscount Hill. Hodgkin's land is described as 'that copyhold or customary messuage or tenement with the garden, slaughterhouse, outbuildings, hereditaments and appurtances ... and also those several pieces of land adjoining to the dwelling house and commonly known as Higher Croft, Lower Croft and the Meadows containing 4 acres, 2 roods, and 23 perches.' The inclusion of a slaughterhouse in the schedule confirms the statements of the present owner and local residents that the front room of the ground floor was once a butcher's shop which was entered from a door, now blocked, on the northern side. The census return of 1841 records John Paul Gregory, a butcher, as resident. John Paul's widowed mother, Hannah, and George Drury, a cooper, were also resident.

In 1923 the property was sold to Richard William Cartwright and the run of five generations of male Gregories, all named Paul, came to an end. It remained in the Cartwright family until 1959 when it was bought by Alfred John Roberts who died in 1980. His widow, two sons and daughter continue in residence. The present acreage is *c*.3.8 acres, a little less than was specified in the 1876 deed of sale.

A Note on the Manor of Prees

At the time of Domesday the manor of Prees was held by the Bishop of Chester, but soon afterwards, in 1102, the episcopal See was moved from Chester and the bishop's title became Coventry and Lichfield.[3] In 1646 bishoprics were temporarily abolished and their estates transferred to trustees, but until some time in the 18th century the bishop of Coventry and Lichfield was the titular holder of the manor of Prees. There is some doubt regarding the date of the transfer of the manor by sale to the Hill family of Hawkstone. One source gives 1794,[4] but it must have been earlier than this because in the Surrender of 7th May 1726, quoted above, Richard Hill is named as lord of the manor. The Hon. & Rev. Richard Hill (1655-1727), known as 'The Great Hill', became deputy to the Earl of Ranelagh and Paymaster to the Forces of William III during the war in Flanders. He amassed a fortune and invested much of it in land and property, thus providing a great inheritance for his family.[5] Hawkstone Hall, the main family seat, built by him in *c*.1720, lies about two-and-a-half miles to the south-east of Prees.

Prees manor remained in the lordship of the Hills until August 1894 when the third Viscount, Rowland Clegg-Hill was declared bankrupt.[6]

Oldfields Farm, Moreton Say

Oldfields Farm was recorded before the Whitchurch class was formed, but it is included because of its structural importance and the added dimension that it brings to the study of north Shropshire houses. The class visited it as part of their field studies and had the experience of seeing a dendrochronologist at work. While continuing as a working farm, the house is currently in use as a high-class restaurant, trading under the name of 'Bennett's'.

Oldfields Farm stands in an isolated position about 1$^1/_2$ miles to the north-west of Moreton Say parish church, about four miles to the north-west of Market Drayton and about six miles from Whitchurch.[1] The farm is approached via a track on either side of which are fields containing evidence of medieval ridge-and-furrow ploughing. The name 'Oldfields' is significant. It suggests a continuity relating to the management of arable land in early times. When the system changed from the two field Infield - Outfield system in which the infield was continuously cultivated along with a portion of the outfield, a system common at the time of Domesday, to the more efficient three field system, in which one of three fields, on a rotational basis, was left fallow and grazed by livestock, about 1250, often the old 'Infield' was called the 'Oldfield'.[2] The site of the farm is too removed from Moreton Say itself to be considered as a candidate for that village's infield; it is more likely to have been the centre of a small isolated settlement in its own right, not large enough to be classed as a village. It is possible that there were several houses in the settlement, and that it later shrank to one farm, the subject of this chapter.

The Exterior

Like many other Shropshire farmhouses, from the exterior Oldfields gives the impression of piecemeal development, with units added when necessary; some fully two-

Oldfields Farm, from the north-west

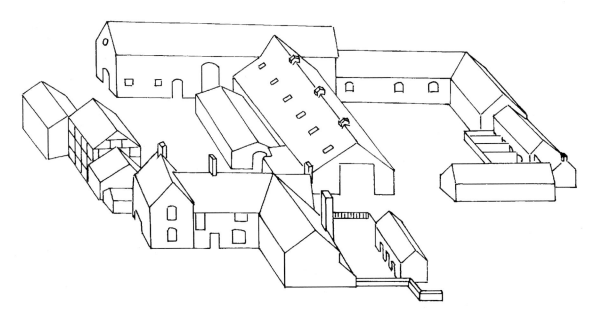

Above: Sketch of Oldfields Farm layout.
Below: Ground floor plan of the house

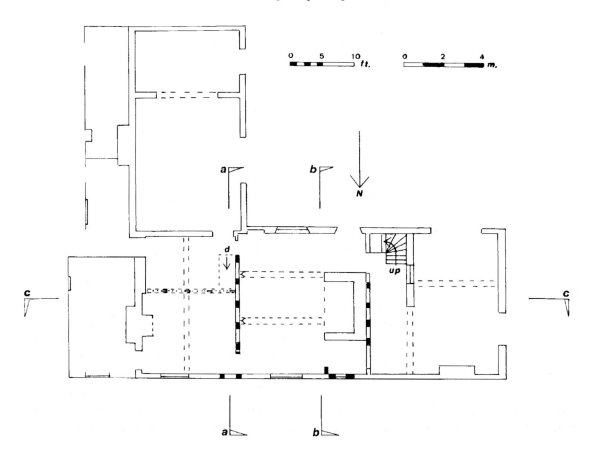

storied, others simply lean-tos. Four large chimneystacks, two outbuilt, one axial, and one integral with an end gable, pierce the skyline and two dormer windows interrupt the roofline on the northern side. At present the house conforms to a basic L-shape, no timber-framing is visible, and the whole complex is whitewashed. However, there is one clue which suggests that Oldfields could contain remnants of a medieval house, and this is the position of the dormer windows. They are set fairly close together at eaves level on a roof slope which is deeper on that side. This suggests that the dormers are lighting a chamber contrived by inserting a floor into an old open hall and thus acquiring two rooms where previously there had been only one; and the hypothesis is borne out by the internal evidence.

The Interior
a) The Hall Range
There are two framed trusses in the unit on the northern side. Section B - B was easily identified as the central truss of a two-bay open hall of base-cruck construction. The section drawing shows the base-cruck rising to support the cambered tie-beam in typical fashion. The cut-out on the back of the blade housed the lower purlin which was set square like the arcade-plate of an aisled hall. The arch-brace which is fashioned to form an integral part of the blade is morticed and tenoned into it and into the tie-beam. These details survive on the northern side only, but the broken lines show the missing components. A decorative chamfer on the base-cruck continues along the arch-brace, and, as the arch-braces were designed to meet in the middle of the tie-beam, the effect, before the floor was inserted, would have been that of a vault in the centre of the open hall. With the exception of the principal rafter joint the truss is flush-jointed on the eastern side, a point which lends weight to some of the discussion below.

Section A - A presented more difficulty. At first, the aisled form suggested that this was the spere-truss, the fixed decorative screen which separated the hall from the screens passage and the service end, and through which access into the hall was gained. However, closer inspection revealed that the 'nave' section was fully filled in, the upper part by timbers whose positions are pinpointed by peg-holes and the lower part by properly morticed and tenoned framing below a transverse member set at about 6ft. above the sill beam. On the drawing the frame is shown as seen from the western side, that is, the side away from the hall. On the hall side there are holes in the lower section which suggest fixing points for a bench seat against the framework. If the evidence has been interpreted correctly, it means that section A - A represents the dais end truss of the hall, the truss which accommodated the high seat at the upper end of the hall where members of the family would take their meals at a table on the raised dais and from where all business connected with running the estate would be conducted. Such trusses in Shropshire have a lower survival rate than spere-trusses. At present 15 spere-trusses have been identified, compared with only three other dais trusses.

Again, because the frame is drawn from the western side, the mortices for the arcade-braces are not shown, but they are present on the hall side. There is no chamfering or ornamentation of any kind on the truss, but the carpenter took care to present the sawn side of the timber to the hall. On the outer face in the upper section, where it is compar-

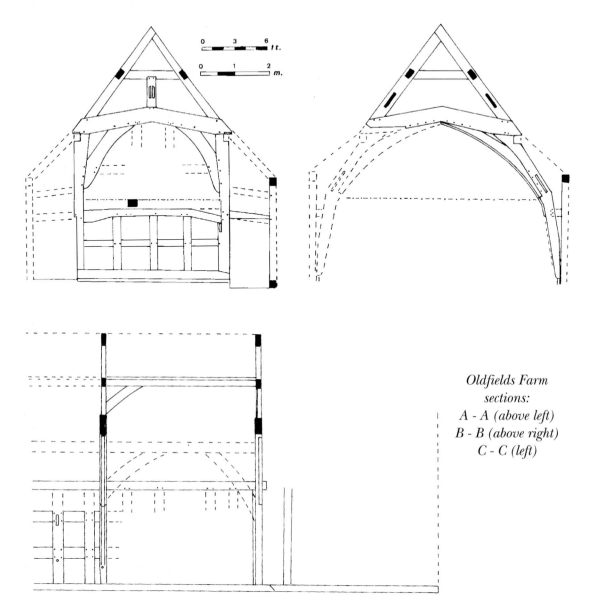

*Oldfields Farm
sections:
A - A (above left)
B - B (above right)
C - C (left)*

atively untouched, the frame shows no sign of weathering which suggests that the house
continued beyond this point. In all probability this would have been a floored bay incorporating a private solar at first floor level.

About 6ft. west of the central base-cruck truss is a timber-framed screen which is independent of the wall-framing and does not now rise above the level of the upper floor, although pegs in the upper surface of the head-beam suggest that perhaps it once did. It appears to have functioned as a partition at the lower end of the hall. Although this would be the logical position for the spere-truss—if the argument for the aisled truss to be at the dais end is accepted—the form of the framing suggests that this was a partition which replaced the spere-truss when the lower end was rebuilt. In its present form the lower end comprises a small non-projecting crosswing with a gable-end chimneystack. Between the partition and the brick wall of the crosswing is a 6ft. space which accommodates the staircase at the southern end. It is tempting to see this width as the 'ghost' of the original screens passage, but there is nothing further to support the idea. The walls have been entirely rebuilt, thus removing any evidence of doors at either end.

The space between the central base-cruck truss and the framed partition is occupied by the inserted axial chimneystack which heats the upper and lower rooms on the eastern side only. The fireplace in the ground-floor room has a mantel-beam whose form and position suggest that it has been turned from end to end and through 90 degrees. It may have functioned previously as the bressumer of a smoke-hood or 'fumbrell' inserted as stage two in the heating sequence, that is after the open hearth was abandoned but before the present chimneystack was built. Such sequences have been found in a number of Shropshire houses.[3]

The whole room is now in use as a dining room, and, in addition to the inglenook fireplace it contains other interesting features, the most significant of which is the lower section of the base-cruck against the north wall. Panelling is present on the western wall and the two spine-beams which relate to the inserted ceiling have quarter-round moulding along their length. There are decorative stops on the moulding at the western end, but the moulding runs into the stack at the eastern end. This supports the theory of a three-stage development in the heating sequence and suggests that the inserted ceiling was in use before the stack, in its present form, was added.

To the east of the aisled truss, in the area which would have functioned as the room below the solar, the space is divided by a timber-framed partition into two rooms, one larger than the other. The larger room, which faces north, was, at one time, the kitchen, although originally this would most probably have been housed in a detached building. When it became a kitchen it was served by an outbuilt chimneystack. There is a doorway in the partition which communicates with the smaller room, but mortices in the sill-beam indicate that originally the two rooms were separate. At present each wall of the smaller room contains a doorway; that on the south gives access to the present kitchen, on the north to the larger of the two rooms, on the west to the upper bay of the hall and on the east into the lean-to addition which once functioned as the dairy. In addition there is a trap-door in the floor which gives access to the cellar. Not surprisingly the small room is currently used only as a circulation area. It was from this part of the house that the only successful dendrochronological date was obtained.

b) The East Wing

The long range on the eastern side which forms the short stem of the L was built as a large dairy with cheese chambers above. The ground floor area is divided into one large room, the main dairy, and a smaller storeroom. The block is served by a large outbuilt chimneystack which had fireplaces at both the lower and upper levels. This suggests that perhaps the unit had a domestic function before it became a dairy. If this is so it has now returned to a previous role as it is currently in use as the kitchen.

c) The Roof Structure

It would be normal, in Shropshire, to expect a base-cruck hall house of the quality of Oldfields to have crown-post roof construction, but there is no trace of this form and it appears to have been designed for side-purlin construction. Unfortunately, both the roof structure and the walls have been drastically altered, and so it is only possible to describe what is present and to attempt to draw conclusions from that. On the hall range both angles at eaves level have changed, and it will be remembered that the deeper slope on the northern side was noted in the introductory paragraph as one of the indications of the historic nature of the house.

From the roof space and looking towards the base-cruck truss, at first glance it appears that all the rafters on the southern side have been renewed and all those on the northern side are original. However, although the difference between the clean rafters on the south and the smoke-blackened ones on the north is striking, it is also misleading. The purlin, though smoke-blackened like the rafters, has mortices and pegholes on the three visible faces, indicating that it is a reused timber. Furthermore it is not housed into the principal rafter in any way, while the mortice for the original purlin remains empty, as does that for the arcade brace. The purlin continues past the base-cruck truss for about 4ins. before it meets the brickwork of the main chimneystack. The rafters are joined, not aligned, at the purlin which suggests that they are probably the original rafters later cut and reused. Section B - B reconstructs the original positions of the purlin and the arcade-brace.

The top of the cambered tie-beam on the base-cruck truss is largely obscured, but where examination is possible there seems to be no mortices and pegholes for a crown post and its attendant lateral braces. This tends to confirm the unusual concept of a Shropshire base-cruck hall without a crown-post roof.

On the aisled truss (section A - A) mortices for the arcade braces are present on the western side but not on the eastern side, from which the section is drawn. Clearly the aisled element terminated at the dais truss. On neither side of the truss is there provision for windbracing. It was impossible to see whether windbracing was provided on the western side of the base-cruck truss, but the surviving member on the eastern side indicates that this facility extended into part of the upper bay of the hall, although it was not designed to reach the dais truss. These details are shown on section C - C.

Centrally placed between the tie-beam and the collar-beam is a vertical timber, 2ins. thick, which is morticed, tenoned and pegged into the tie-beam and half-lapped and

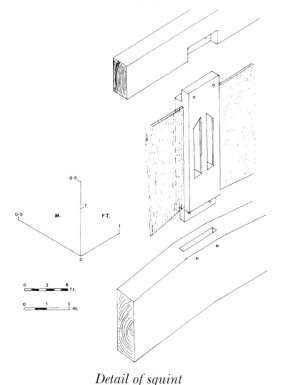

Detail of squint

192

pegged into the collar-beam. It has a pair of 'squints' or vents which are well-carpentered with chamfered sides. There is a heavy encrustation of smoke on the hall side of the truss, including the wattle and daub infil on either side of the vents and in the space above the collar-beam. The 'outer' side, however, shows only traces of smoke seepage. This suggests that the vents are an original feature, probably designed to draw the smoke from the open hearth away from the dais end—a 'wind-eye' in the original meaning of the word before it became corrupted into 'window'.

On the eastern side of the aisled truss and 3ft. 6ins. from it is part of another transverse frame which bears no real relationship to the ground floor plan. The parts that are visible include a short length of a tie-beam, a principal rafter on the northern side, and a vertical strut which is pegged into the rafter and appears to connect with the tie-beam. There is a purlin on the northern side and this is chamfered and stopped on both arrises. From the principal rafter the purlin continues 1ft. 4ins. towards the aisled truss, but there is a gap of just over 1ft. before the projecting purlin from the hall side is encountered. There is no smoke-blackening on the frame, and although it is difficult to find a reason for the inclusion of a structural truss in this position it is connected to the frame at the gable end of the solar which terminates the roof structure. On the eastern side of the frame only are two slightly curved windbraces, one on either side of the purlin. These are fashioned to provide an up and down bracing action and they are matched by similar ones on the end frame. The purlin also continues to the end frame, and the chamfered and stopped arrises suggest that these features are original to the solar end of the house.

The frame at the end of the roof is of more conventional form and is reasonably intact. It consists of a tie-beam, collar beam, three vertical struts between the horizontals, a central vertical strut from the collar-beam to the apex and principal rafters which, as normal in a primarily box-framed medieval house, had no provision for a ridge-purlin. On the southern side the pitch of the roof has been reduced and, of course, the effects of this are present along the whole length.

d) The Wall Framing

No framework is visible on the exterior of the house, but section C - C shows how a pattern of small rectangular framing, three panels high, may be reconstructed. This is done from the evidence of pegholes in the wall-plate on the north side and the small section of wall framing which remains to the west of the base-cruck. However, sections A - A and B - B show that the wall-plate is at a height not compatible with a continuous roof-line, that the wall frame is connected to the base-cruck with a short spur set well below the level of the wall-plate and that the outer edge of the base-cruck has been cut back and sharply angled. Although the scantling of the wall-framing is substantial, with the studs and rails 11ins. wide, the pegs and pegholes are smaller than those employed on the transverse trusses. These factors combine to suggest that the wall-framing is not contemporary with the transverse frames and probably represents a replacement at some time.

Analysis, Summary and Dating

Oldfields Farm presents many problems of analysis. If the aisled truss is accepted as the dais truss rather than the spere-truss, it is reasonable to suggest that originally the house consisted of a two-bay open hall of base-cruck construction with a solar end beyond the dais and a service end at the lower end of the hall. In other words it followed the normal three-part plan of most substantially-built medieval hall-houses. But there are several unanswered questions: was there a screens passage and, if so, was it part of the lower bay of the hall or was it treated as a half-bay in its own right? Why was the hall not built with crown-post roof construction? At present it is the only known base-cruck hall in Shropshire not to have a roof of this form. Is the paucity of windbracing indicative of the difficulty of 'marrying' the base-cruck and the aisled forms? Has there been a reversal in the roles of the two ends? It seems likely that the enigmatic truss, described above as at 3ft. 6ins. from the dais truss is *in situ* and represents part of a rebuilding of the solar at that end. But this probably took place less than 100 years after the house was built and was overtaken by a later remodelling which has left evidence in the roof end-frame. It continued to function as a solar end until the service end was rebuilt in crosswing form and became a parlour, at which time the solar end became demoted to a service end. The flooring over of the open hall and the insertion of the chimneystack as stage three in the heating sequence probably precipitated these major changes in the way in which the house was regulated. The renewal and the re-alignment of the wall-framing was probably all part of the same refurbishing programme.

Although the above development is speculative, it is based on the architectural features which are present. Dating is, of course, extremely difficult. Base-cruck halls with aisled trusses, whether spere-trusses or dais trusses or both are unlikely to have built after *c.*1485 or before 1300.[4] The lack of crown-post roof construction does not necessarily imply that that Oldfields comes late in the evolution, but, coupled with the comparatively crude carpentry and lack of mouldings and cusping, it may be pointing to a building date in the first half of the 15th century. Some alterations were made to the unit at the eastern end about 100 years later, but the great wave of modernisation began with the remodelling of that end in 1573. This is the only firm date that the dendrochronological testing produced. Samples were taken from the aisled truss and the open truss but the timbers were fast-grown, producing a tree-ring growth with too few rings to be suitable for analysis. No documentary evidence that would throw any light on Oldfield's origins has been found.

North Shropshire has few surviving medieval timber-framed hall-houses compared with the wealth of such buildings in south Shropshire. This makes Oldfields Farm significant both from the rarity factor and for its own intrinsic structural interest.

Alkington Hall, Whitchurch Rural

Alkington Hall is about $1^1/_2$ miles south-west of Whitchurch. A date of 1592 appears on a wooden plaque that once surmounted the back door, but which is now preserved as an internal feature. Recent (1994) dendrochronological work has established that this is correct, the timbers being felled in 1591, but this only applies to the bulk of the house; the quadratic plan is completed by a unit in the south-west corner which comprises the remains of an older building, the timbers of which have a felling date of 1572.[1] The house has been described as 'a fragment of an Elizabethan mansion', but this cannot be sustained—it is likely to be as complete as it ever was.[2] At present a working farm, the house is of double-pile form, having brick exterior walls with Grinshill-stone window dressings, finials, copings, quoins and plinth. It has a three-bayed frontage, two-storied, but with full use of the roof-space. A fully three-storied square brick-built unit with a crow-stepped gable forms an extension to the southern wall. At first glance this has the appearance of a large stair-tower, but clearly it never served this purpose, being designed to provide three rooms in a vertical living idiom, and served by its own staircase and entrance.

Plan and Construction

If the tower is disregarded, the house presents an almost square plan, the entrance centrally placed and a passage currently linking the front and back doors. However, the units which make up the double-pile plan are not of the same size, the front is larger than the back, the internal partitions are timber-framed, the rooms are not symmetrically arranged, there is neither an entrance hall nor a grand staircase as might be

Alkington Hall, north elevation

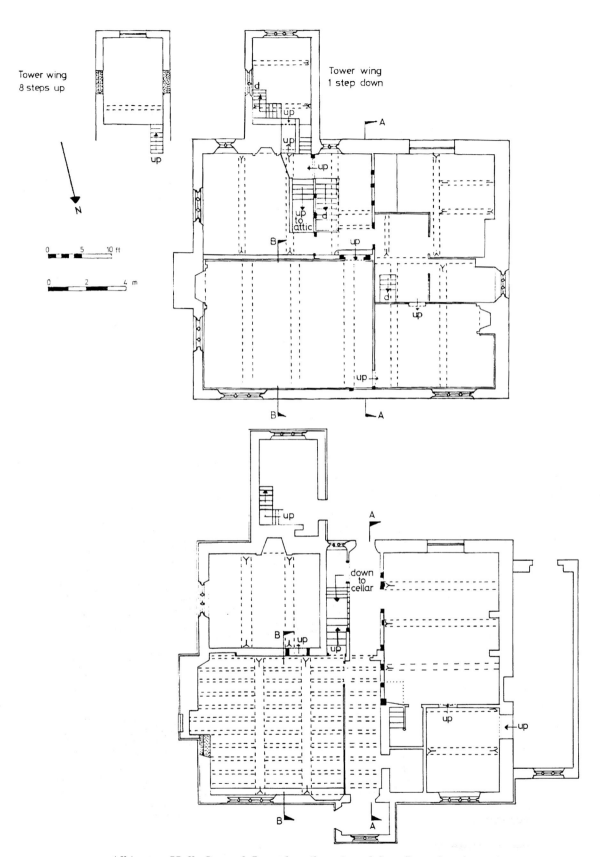

Alkington Hall. Ground floor plan (lower) and first floor plan (upper)

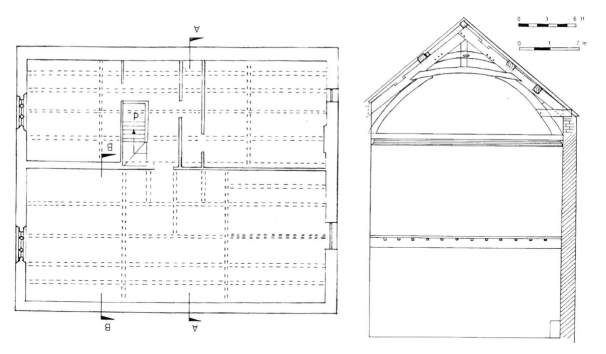

Attic plan (upper left) to the same scale as floor plans opposite, Section B - B (upper right) and east elevation (below)

inserted window

197

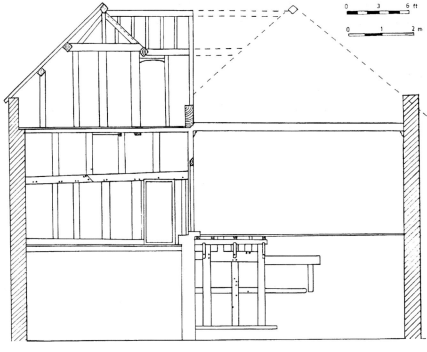

Section A - A

expected in a house of this size, only the roof trusses in the front unit are regularly spaced, and there is evidence of internal jettying. These details confirm that Alkington Hall is a house of at least two periods. With the benefit of dendrochronology, the constructional history can be seen to have a logical development, although some of the details remain puzzling. Many alterations have taken place and have been very well absorbed, and now that the earlier date for the south-western unit has been established, its relationship with the rest of the structure is clear. At present in use as the kitchen with a bedroom and attic above, it represents the remains of a timber-framed house which was incorporated into the remodelling of 1592. Later, the framing was encased in brickwork, presumably to bring it into line with the rest of the house. It displays a mixture of brick bonding, and no diaper-work is present. There are no stone dressings, copings or finials and the stone plinth is not carried around. Much timber-framing occurs at ground-floor level internally in this unit and it has a different roof-structure and fenestration to the remainder of the house.

The older (1592) brickwork is good quality English bond and has vitrified headers forming diaper and zig-zag patterning on the northern front and on both units of the eastern side elevation. The front porch, which is entered from the side, also has diaper-work, but the bricks are machine-made and it is clearly a later addition, probably of the 19th century. There is a tradition that, before the porch was built, an external staircase gave access to the great chamber at first floor level. Certainly the brickwork above the porch shows signs of disturbance, but it is unfortunate that the inner doorway contained in the panelling in the great chamber is sealed, making it impossible to examine the walling. It is possible that the external staircase was contained in a two-storied porch. This would account for the absence of patterning in the brickwork above the present porch, the lack of witness marks for such a staircase and, perhaps for the non-provision of a grand internal staircase.

The Fenestration

On the front elevation the four windows each have Grinshill-stone dressings. Each is mullioned and transomed with an ovolo-moulded profile. Although the openings are of uniform size, those in the lower storey are emphasised by having eight lights, while the upper story has six. All the original windows in the house have stone dressings, but not all are ovolo-moulded, the less important ones have a straight chamfer and are constructed with a mason's mitre. Several windows have been replaced and there are some examples of blocked openings. It is noticeable that no old windows occur in the south-western block. Those lighting the kitchen and the chamber above have segmental heads. The main windows in the tower are similar to the less important ones described above, and are of two or three lights according to their own relative importance, but high under the eaves on the south-eastern side is a small blocked two-light window which has a wooden frame and a central plain chamfered wooden mullion. This is the only example of the use of external wooden dressings, although its opposite number on the south-western side, now entirely blocked, was probably of a similar design. The wooden sill remains visible.

The Chimneystacks

When approaching Alkington Hall, a prominent landmark is the array of tall chimneystacks on the skyline. Of these, the largest is the outbuilt double stack located on the eastern side, but it serves only the northern unit and its location, slightly overlapping the southern unit, gives an unbalanced appearance to the elevation as a whole. However, it appears to be an original feature, the diaper and zig-zag-work is continued in the brickwork and the stack is surmounted with two diagonally-set shafts. Similar twin shafts are set at the junction of the south-eastern unit and the tower. The only square-set chimneys are those wholly contained within the gable of the present kitchen and the one which serves the western ante-room to the great chamber. These are each likely to be later additions.

It may be thought that plain diagonally-set shafts are not appropriate to a date of 1592, but although some of the brickwork shows signs of renewal there is no evidence that they replaced star-shaped shafts. This raises the question of whether the shafts have been rebuilt. Usually chimneys of the late 16th century are massed closely and the shafts are joined with elaborate oversailing brick capping. Here the shafts stand apart and are not joined at the top. Even more intriguing is the omission of Alkington Hall from the Hearth Tax register of 1672.[3]

Roof Construction

The northern front unit of the double-pile form has a three bayed roof plan, with the two internal trusses almost equidistant. Each had principal rafters and a high cambered collar-beam originally, but later reinforcements were added in the form of a lower collar supporting a king-post, arch-braces supporting the lower collar and spurs connecting the arch-braces and the wall-plate. A ridge-purlin, new side purlins and various bracing members have also been introduced, and the whole roof has been re-raftered. Clearly the roof-space was intended to be used, and it is lofty and well lit from original three-light windows at either end. But the provision of high-collared open trusses with inadequate bracing presumably gave rise to problems, and this would account for the later reinforcements, including an iron tie-rod which runs through the whole house from front to back. Many of the primary members are re-used timbers. At one time at least part of the space may have been ceiled over. On the attic plan the double hatching in the centre of the north-western bay of the northern unit indicates the presence of a beam which has angled mortices, apparently intended to house the joists for a cambered ceiling.

The roof of the rear unit reflects the original L-plan. The south-eastern block has a central truss consisting of principal rafters and a single high collar, but this has had a continuous arch-brace added as reinforcement. The south-western unit has an interrupted tie-beam and a collar-beam, and the principal rafters are inset on the tie-beam. Many of the components are re-used timbers, and the tie-rod runs through this section. There is a small modern window in the gable.

Because so much of the roof structure employs re-used timbers it is difficult to be certain about the chronology, but it is clear that the front unit and the south-eastern block relate to each other and have not been raised, whereas the south-western block has been remodelled and is of a different vintage.

The Cellar

The cellar is beneath the north-eastern front room. It is brick-vaulted and has a brick floor, but on the eastern side large sandstone blocks form part of the walling. It is ventilated from a stone window with a plain chamfer that is on the eastern side of the porch. The cellar steps are lit by a window, also plain-chamfered, on the eastern side of the rear door. Known graphically as a 'wet cellar' its condition was ideal for the storage of dairy goods when farming activities were so centred.

The Great Chamber and its plastered ceiling

The Great Chamber is located on the first floor at the eastern end of the north front unit. It is this room which is thought to have had independent access via an external staircase. The chamber is lit by two windows, one at the front and the other on the eastern side. Each has six lights, but while the front window has ovolo-moulded mullions and transom, the side window has a plain chamfer. Heating is from a fireplace at the southern end of the east wall. This has a flat stone lintel, the chamfer of which continues down the jambs and stops about 1ft. from hearth level. There is a wooden triple-panelled overmantel which has three pilasters with ionic-style capitals and stylised paired leaf carving on the front. The panels are, at present, plain, but on the northernmost (left-hand) one, it is possible to discern the shape of a cross, but it is impossible to say whether this has religious connotations. It may be compared with a similar overmantel at Lea Hall in the parish of Preston Gubbals which is complete and is dated 1584. Incidentally, both Lea Hall and Alkington Hall contain internal jetties, a rare feature in Shropshire.

The oak floorboards are adze-dressed and measure on average 1ft. 1in. in width. Floor-to-ceiling panelling occurs on all four walls; there is a plain panelled frieze and the main

The Great Chamber (left) with a detail of the ceiling (right)

panels are each moulded on three sides and employ carpenters' mitres. Where the panelling covers the position of the supposed external entrance there is a blocked door which is surmounted by a wheat-eared frieze. To the west of this is a smaller door, also blocked, which may have opened into a shallow closet. Elsewhere the panelling is uninterrupted and it appears to have been made for the room, though after the house had settled. This is clear from the way in which it is tailored to accommodate the distortion.

The division between the chamber and the ante-room to its west is the width of the panelling only, and the panelling in both rooms is of the same kind. This raises the question of whether the whole of the first floor of the northern unit was once used as either a hall or a great chamber. If the additional plasterwork on the spine beams of the larger room is taken into account, the beams are equidistant, and because the division left a smaller ceiling panel on the western side it suggests that the plastered ceiling in the great chamber was applied after the space was divided, as was the panelling. The front windows are symmetrically placed, and the reputed external entrance door would then have been centrally placed. Heating from the fireplace located on the eastern side would, admittedly, have been inadequate, but this may have led to the decision to divide the room, introduce a smaller fireplace into the western room and insert the present staircase. If the whole heating arrangements for the house were re-planned at this time it might account for the form of the stacks.

The plastered ceiling of the great chamber is, arguably, the most important feature of Alkington Hall. Spine-beams divide the area into four panels, the westernmost being smaller than the others. There is much fleur-de-lis ornament and the concave lozenge-work is interrupted with square panels containing various motifs: flowers including the marigold, rose and eglantine, oak leaves, acorns, grapes, vine-leaves, a heraldic beast, and a pomegranate peeled to expose the seeds. All these reflect the taste for allegory deeply engrained in the thinking of the time. Outstanding in the overall design because they are not positioned symmetrically are two panels with human heads. The legend of the house maintains that the male is Henry VII and the female his wife, Elizabeth of York, who are

0 1 2 3 ft
0 1 m

W

The plasterwork ceiling of the Great Chamber (left) and details of the two human heads (above)

reputed to have stayed here. Neither is crowned, but the legend has an answer for this: they are depicted before the battle of Bosworth. Such a tradition is, of course, open to question, and if true they must pre-date the rest of the plasterwork by over 100 years. But there has to be some reason for the inclusion of such masks and the most likely explanation is that they represent members of the Cotton family who had strong associations with Alkington in the 16th and 17th centuries.

The Ante-chambers

To the south of the great chamber is an ante-room which has two plaster roundels in the ceiling, one depicting two birds in oak-foliage with acorns, and the other a griffin (see below). The other ante-room, to the west of the great chamber, is panelled in the same manner as the great chamber and has a communicating door. In this room the window,

Assorted details (n.t.s):
Frieze and panelling on door
of south-east ground floor
room (top left).
Bedding locker in north-east
ground floor room (top right).
Panelling in
Great Chamber (centre).
South doorway to Great
Chamber (lower left).
Internal jetty (lower right)

being front-facing, is ovolo-moulded, and the chamber is heated by a small fireplace in the south-west corner. At present it contains a Victorian grate. Its possible one-time integration with the great chamber is discussed above.

The Dining-room

The room in the south-eastern corner is currently used for dining. It is distinguished by three plaster panels in the ceiling. These are lozenge-shaped and depict a rose, a rose and fleur-de-lis, and a 'green man'. Each has a border of foliage and grapes. (See illustrations (n.t.s.) on left)

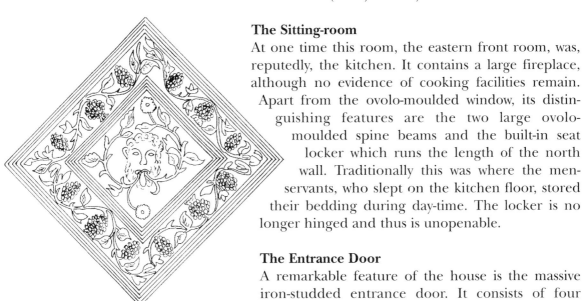

The Sitting-room

At one time this room, the eastern front room, was, reputedly, the kitchen. It contains a large fireplace, although no evidence of cooking facilities remain. Apart from the ovolo-moulded window, its distinguishing features are the two large ovolo-moulded spine beams and the built-in seat locker which runs the length of the north wall. Traditionally this was where the men-servants, who slept on the kitchen floor, stored their bedding during day-time. The locker is no longer hinged and thus is unopenable.

The Entrance Door

A remarkable feature of the house is the massive iron-studded entrance door. It consists of four vertical planks of oak on the outer face and is backed with seven horizontal planks. There are iron strap-hinges, those on the front having decorative curled ends with a tongue. On the inside the door is fitted with a wooden latch and secured by means of a large purpose-made wooden wedge driven into a bolt-hole on the right-hand jamb.

The Timber-framing

The internal partitions of Alkington Hall are timber-framed, but, where they have been exposed, the framing varies considerably and clearly relates to the different phases. Close-studding occurs on the northern side of the partition between the present kitchen and the dairy/cheese room and again on the partition wall between the dairy and the central passage. In each case it is found above rectangular framing and carries enigmatic 'planted-on' internal jetties which appears to serve no purpose. But the wall on the eastern side of the stair-well, that is, on the left ascending the stairs, carries a genuine internal jetty associated with rectangular framing above and below. The overhang is very small, a matter of five or six inches, it serves no function and must have been included for effect.

There is more framing, though rather irregular, in the partition between the kitchen and the passage, and on the landing is a feature which appears to form part of the partition between the Great Chamber and the landing. It has the appearance of a high blocked doorway, but is adjacent to the current entrance into the chamber which shows no signs of disturbance. The arch-brace on the left is original, but that on the right appears to have no pegged joints and is probably an insertion. There is a wooden lintel at normal headroom level and no evidence of any missing horizontals. Both 'doorways', if they may be described as such, are approached via two steps, and they employ the same sill-beam, the blocked opening having bricks supporting the sill.

Dendrochronological sampling produced the felling date of 1591 for the post of the arched opening, suggesting that it was once a grand entrance into the great chamber, but so cleverly was the later doorway contrived that it has every appearance of being original. It was also established that the post and one of the purlins in the northern slope of the roof were obtained from the same tree.

Comparisons

Apart from certain similarities in detailing to Lea Hall, mentioned above, the only other house in north Shropshire which bears much resemblance to Alkington Hall is Soulton Hall near Wem (see p.248). This is three-storied and with a three-bay façade, brick built with stone dressings, is of double-pile form, has mullioned and transomed windows, and the date 1668 occurs on an external date-stone. It is associated with the Hill family. Like Alkington Hall, it has no formal entrance hall or grand staircase.[4] In Shrewsbury the mansion known as Whitehall, though stone-built and with three straight gables to each elevation, is of almost square double-pile form, two-and-a-half stories high. Here the flat-headed windows have an embryonic ovolo-moulding and again there is no formal entrance hall. Whitehall dates from 1578-83 and was built for Richard Prince.[5] It represents the second earliest double-pile house in the country.[6] Acton Scott Hall, supposedly of late 16th century date and of double-pile form, likewise has no formal entrance hall and, on a smaller scale, the Moat Farm at Alcaston, entirely brick-built, had, before its roof-line was altered recently, two parallel ranges and no formal entrance hall.

Crow-stepped gables are not a common feature in Shropshire. Those on the rear tower at Alkington are very similar to those which occurred at Bellaport Old Hall near Market Drayton, and there is a family connection between the two houses.

When comparing the plastered ceiling with other known Shropshire examples, it is tempting to bracket it with examples in such houses as Belswardine, Morville Hall, Upton Cressett Gatehouse, Wilderhope, Plaish and the Abbot's House at Buildwas. In these it seems clear from the repetition of the motifs that a school of plasterers were using their own standard moulds for each commission. But at Alkington Hall, the fleur-de-lis is the only common denominator. For the remainder the work has an individualistic feel, with the masks neither regularly positioned nor facing the same way, some of the motifs reversed and others displaying eccentric designs. This suggests that the craftsman took his basic design from a pattern-book, conceded the fleur-de-lis and used some of the popular emblems, but then gave free rein to his own ideas. He had to work on spaces restricted by the intrusion of the spine-beams, and the treatment of the soffits is reminiscent of similar work at Ludford House and at The Feathers Hotel in Ludlow.[7] Other comparable ceilings occur at Arleston Manor and at Hoo Hall in Preston-on-the-Weald-Moors. Certainly the vine and the pomegranate were favourite themes, although only one panel at Alkington depicts the pomegranate. Further afield, a ceiling at Plas Mawr in Conway includes the fleur-de-lis and an heraldic beast similar to that at Alkington.

Assessment

The structural development of Alkington Hall is made reasonably clear from the tree-ring dating, and there can be no doubt that the south-western unit is part of the 1572 timber-framed building. This was enlarged in 1592 by the addition of an L-shaped brick built unit, resulting in the square double-pile form that presently exists. Several features invite comment. For example, it is unusual to find the use of irregular zig-zags in Elizabethan brickwork, although the salutary lesson of the diaper-work at St. John's College at Cambridge should be borne in mind.[8] Quoin-work and diagonally-set chimney shafts of such plain form are also anachronistic, seemingly ahead of their time. In keeping with the 1592 date, however, is the ovolo-moulding, which had reached Shropshire by that time, and internal jetties, though not common, are also known in the county before then. But had it not been necessary to incorporate the remains of an older house surely the builder would have made provision for a more imposing entrance and staircase. The present through passage is more reminiscent of a medieval house-plan, but the front door prob-ably led directly into the one-time kitchen which would then, presumably, have been classed as the hall. The ovolo-moulded spine-beams are positioned equidistantly across the area and the joists also run continuously. This raises again the question of whether the Great Chamber, as seems likely, was provided with private access from outside and was considered the most important room. It is reasonably certain that the plastered ceiling in the Great Chamber is of 17th century date. Certainly it and the panelling were applied to a frame already distorted, and it may have been then that the internal entrance position on the southern wall of the chamber was changed. At the same time the size of the chamber was reduced. The design of the ceiling may owe much to the many pattern books and emblem books that were available at the time.[9] The chimneystacks may have been remodelled as part of the same exercise, but the omission of Alkington Hall from the Hearth Tax at this time remains a mystery. The only other major remodelling was the brick casing which was applied to the framing of the 1572 unit, and this may be as late as the early 19th century.

Tenurial History[10]

Alkington, one of 13 townships which made up the historic parish of Whitchurch, has the place-name definition 'the Tun of Ealhmund's people'.[11] These were presumably Saxons who had settled in the area in the 8th century. Domesday records that before the Norman Conquest it was held by Aelmar, a free man, and that in 1086 it was part of the holding of William Pandolf whose overlord was Roger de Montgomery, kinsman of William the Conqueror, Earl of Shrewsbury and the recipient of the lion's share of William's favours.[12] Alkington was then part of the manor of Wem although it lay within the parish of Whitchurch, which it still does.[13]

In the 13th century Pandolf's descendant and sole heiress, Maud/Matilda married William de Boteler who became Baron of Wem. Their great granddaughter, Ankaret, was given Alkington, Dodington and Edgeley as part of her dowry when she married John le Strange of Blakemere, Lord of Whitchurch in about 1327.[14] Alkington thus became part of Whitchurch manor throughout the successive lordships of the le Strange, Talbot, Bridgwater and Brownlow families until the estate was finally broken up in the 1920s.

By the end of the 14th century Alkington had become the property of the Cotton family who took their name from the hamlet of Coton in Edstaston, near Wem, recorded in Domesday as part of the manor of Wem after 1086.[15] John de Cotin is mentioned in the Hundred Roll of Bradford in 1254 as lord of a moiety in the ville of Cotin, and in 1356 Alan Cotton of Coton was appointed Forester by William de Botiler, by then lord of Wemme. In 1398 John de Cotin's great-great-great-grandson Roger married Ellen, daughter and heiress of John Gremyton of Alkington. Her family had held the property for four generations, her great-grandfather being Roger Gremyton of Alkington. This branch of the Cotton family was afterwards referred to as 'of Coton and Alkington'.[16] Roger and Ellen's son John married Katherine, daughter and heiress of Thomas Constantine of Dodington, and it was their eldest son Thomas who carried out the wishes of John Talbot, Rector of Whitchurch, in founding the Whitchurch Free Grammar School in 1550.[17] Thomas Cotton married an heiress, Alice, the only child of Ralph Johnson of Whitchurch. He died in 1559, and from the inventory of his goods, described below, it is clear that as well as farming at Alkington he ran a prosperous tannery at Whitchurch.[18] The named rooms in the inventory include a hall, a nether parlour, a hyre (upper?) parlour and two chambers above the nether parlour, and while it would be gratifying to be able to fit these rooms into the plan of Alkington as it existed before 1592 the evidence on the ground is insufficient.

Alkington passed to Thomas's son William who was childless and so when William died his nephew, another William, inherited. This William was one of the six sons of Ralph(e), another of Thomas Cotton's sons.[19] Ralph was a mercer in Whitchurch, having been apprenticed to Roger Luter of Salop, and he was also a churchwarden. In 1528 he married Jane Smith of Newcastle-under-Lyme and they produced a very talented family of whom Allen was probably the most gifted. A draper (wool merchant) like his brothers, Allen became Sheriff of London in 1616-17, Lord Mayor of London in 1625-6 and was knighted in 1626. It was probably Allen who rebuilt Alkington Hall, but the ceiling in the great chamber is likely to have been added by Rowland Cotton, son of William, grandson of Ralph, and nephew of Allen, who would have been about 46 in 1626. Perhaps it is his mask

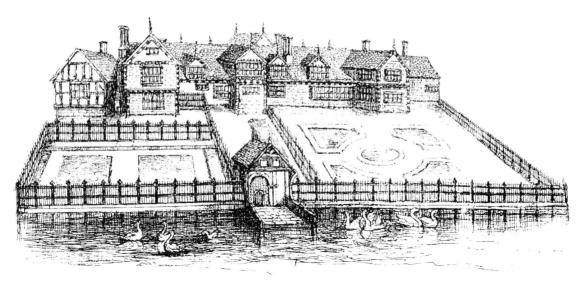

Bellaport, Norton-in-Hales, home of the Cotton family.
The drawing is a copy by Frances Stackhouse-Acton of a watercolour owned by Mr. R.J. Hall
of Bellaport Old Hall

and that of his wife that adorns the ceiling. Rowland was in possession of Alkington in 1619 and had himself been knighted in 1608. Although largely resident in London, he appears to have had strong county connections, held many titles, was a close personal friend of the Prince of Wales, the future Charles I, and added to his estates by buying Bellaport near Market Drayton.[20] However, a sidelight on the state of his finances occurs in the inventory of Roger Poole of Dodington, a moneylender who died in 1615. Sir Rowland Cotton is listed as owing 17s.[21]

The large house at Bellaport, illustrated by the old drawing above, has been destroyed but it is interesting that the house that reputedly served as the Home Farm and is now known as Bellaport Old Hall had, until comparatively recently, crow-stepped gables very similar to those on the tower at Alkington.[22] The raised platform in front of Bellaport Old Hall is reputedly the site of the large house, and the moat is discernible. The theme of 'Dutch-type' gables is repeated on the nearby Bellaport Hall Farm where they have the curvilinear form, and this house also has a nearby site on which stood a large house known as Bellaport Towers on account of the several turrets and towers which were a feature of its composition. Sir Rowland and Lady Cotton have an elaborate monument in Norton-in-Hales' church, the parish in which Bellaport stands.[23] On it is depicted the new coat-of-arms: a chevron between three cotton hanks, a play on the family name.[24] It is very likely that the monument was designed by Inigo Jones. Both Jones and Cotton served the Prince of Wales and were involved with the court masques that were a notable feature of the time. They also had a mutual literary acquaintance in Thomas Coryate, a courtier. A sketch by Inigo Jones on which the monument is based is held by the Royal Institute of British Architects.[25]

Sir Rowland died childless and was succeeded first by his brother William and then by William's son, another William, who inherited Bellaport and entertained Prince Rupert there in May 1642.[26] He also was buried in Norton-in-Hales as was his grandson, another Rowland, who died in 1753. This Rowland was the last Cotton to be styled 'of Alkington', but in 1746 his heir, William, had made a settlement by which property in north Shropshire, including Alkington and Coton, was left in trust for his daughters. The trustees were Sir Thomas Aubrey, Bart., and Charles Littleton, Bishop of Carlisle.[27]

Although the Cottons retained their interest in Alkington, the main Shropshire seat seems to have shifted to Bellaport, and Alkington was leased to tenants. For at least the last 150 years Alkington has been occupied by the same family, first as tenants, and since 1937 as owners. The 1841 census shows William Wilson, aged 42, farming there. He was a widower and lived with his son Thomas, 25, and three daughters, Mary, 21, and twins Martha and Kate, 17. Three male farmworkers and two young female domestic servants aged 18 and 10 were also resident. Sometime around 1924 Thomas Wilson Fearnall, son of Kate Wilson and Thomas Fearnall took over the tenancy before purchasing the property from the Woods estates of Shrewsbury in 1937. Alkington Hall is still the home of the Fearnall family, Mr. & Mrs. John Fearnall having taken over from John's aunt, Miss Ann Fearnall who has now retired.[28]

Appendix I The Cottons and Whitchurch Grammar School[29]

When Canon John Talbot, the Rector of Whitchurch, decided to found a school in his native town of Whitchurch he asked Thomas Cotton to carry out his wishes, leaving £200 for this purpose when he died in 1549. In the preamble to the statutes of the school Thomas Cotton wrote 'John Talbot, before his death, committed the accomplishment of his resolute determination (to found a school) to me, the said Thomas Cotton.' With a further £40 subscribed by parishioners Cotton purchased a 150-acre estate with a farm called Cow Hall at what is now known as Caughall in Cheshire, the income from which was to form the school's first endowment. This was in September 1550. The school was built in Bargates, on a site just to the north of the parish church, but it was not the first Grammar School in Whitchurch. John Gilbert was licensed to keep a Grammar School there in 1326, and William Grophule was similarly licensed in 1358. Talbot's school was rebuilt in 1848 on the same site, moved to a new building at Mossfields, Heath Road in 1937, became a co-educational Grammar School in 1963 and since 1978 has been known as the Sir John Talbot's School, a comprehensive. The tomb of the founder is in the parish church, north of the chancel, but any memorial to Thomas Cotton, who was also buried in the church when he died in 1559, disappeared when the medieval church collapsed in 1711.

Of the 12 feoffees (trustees) selected by Thomas Cotton to run the newly-founded school, his son Ralph was the first-named and chief feoffee, while two of the others were William Chidlow and William Cowper, his sons-in-law.

The estate at Caughall was sold in 1884 and became the site of Chester Zoological Gardens.

Appendix II Thomas Cotton's Will and Inventory[30]

In his will, proved at Lichfield on 25th January 1560, Thomas Cotton left 3s 4d for repairs to St. Alkmund's church and 'to every poor man, woman and child that shall resort to my funeral one penny ... to pray for the health and salvation of my soul.' After monetary bequests to his children and grandchildren he left his son William 'my house and burgage wherein I dwell' together with 'a fourth part of Great Blakemeare field after the death of my wife Alice.' (Blakemeare was the manor house to the east of Whitchurch, the seat of the le Strange and Talbot families.) To his son Ralph(e) he bequeathed 'my best salt of silver overgilted, my standing cup of silver overgilted and half a dozen of the best silver spoons with apostles at the ends, to him for life and then to his son and heir, together with a parcel of ground and a parcel of Alkington wood.' His third son, Roger, received part of Tilstock wood and one tenement in Much Parke Street, Coventry, of which he was already tenant. The residue of his goods, plate, jewels, ready money and chattells were left to his wife Alice for life, 'but if she marry again she shall have only the third part of my goods', the remainder was to be divided equally amongst his children.

The Inventory of Thomas Cotton's goods was taken on 17th October 1559. Two of the four Appraisers were his sons-in-law Thomas Hulse of Astley, Gent, and William Cowper. In it, after lists of sheets, towels, bedding etc. there is mention of 'hanggyng in one hyre parler, 10s; iiii chestes in one hyre parler and a prasse, [press] £1.0s.0d., vi gratte platers in the hall, £1.0.0d; hangynges in the hall 6s.8d; hangynges in the nether parler 6s.8d; hanggynge in the ii chambers above the nether parler 6s.8d; in the nether parler a Coboard 10s.' There was a 'parsell gylte plate' worth £30 6s 8d, but his main wealth is shown as 'xv dyker of leather and xvi doz of skynnes' together worth £76. (A dicker or dyker was 10 hides.) This does seem to indicate that Thomas Cotton had a prosperous tanning business in Whitchurch from which his wealth derived, rather than from the farm at Alkington where he lived. The livestock and crops, presumably at Alkington, included 'xii kynne, vi oxsen, iii wenying calvis, xiii yong beasst, a gyldng, a mare and collt; Rye, barley and ottes.' Most of the items are easily identified: 'chaffyng dyshes', 'brochys', 'a chest bown with iren', 'iiii masslen bassyn', 'quysshyns' etc. But included in the list is 'ii hanggyng for ii beddes of Saye.' Saye was a cloth of fine texture resembling serge; in the 16th century sometimes of silk, subsequently entirely of wool.[31] The total value of his movable goods was £257 7s 2d.

Appendix III The Will of Ralph Cotton
Ralph was the eldest son of Thomas Cotton. Ralph died in 1563 and the terms of his will indicate some disharmony between himself and John, his eldest son. John inherited nothing apart from 'my best silver salt and half-a-dozen of Apostle spoons, a ruff garnished with silver and my best gown.' Furthermore he stipulated that John would 'according to my promise made take to wife Ellen Whitley or else one other daughter of the said John Whitley, deceased.' Clearly John had a mind of his own for he rejected all the Whitley girls and married Jane Dod of Claverley.[32]

Appendix IV The Cotton Crest
The tomb of Sir Rowland Cotton and Lady Cotton in the church at Norton-in-Hales shows the Cotton crest, a chevron between three cotton hanks. Pure cotton fabric made from the pods of the cotton plant was not in general use in England before the mid-18th century, but the term 'cotton' was applied to a coarse woollen material whose nap was raised with teasles, or 'cottoned' to give the softer, fluffy appearance of true cotton.[33] There was also

Fustian, a term applied to a fabric with a linen warp and a cotton weft with a brushed pile like corduroy, and also to a fabric made from a mixture of flax and wool. Thomas Cotton's inventory of 1559 includes 'iiii pyllos of fostion' which, with 'iii of tycke' were worth 12s.

Cotton family crests

The Cotton badges are depicted in the volume of Shropshire Genealogies.[34] They are from left to right:

1) Cotton of Coton and Alkington - argent, chevron sable engrailed, 3 mullets gules. (argent = silver, sable = black, gules = red)

2) Drawing of seal, William Cotton of Alkington, seal vis 1663. The crest is described as: 'An eagle wings expanded beaked and legged and holding in the dexter claw a belt buckled of two.'

3) Cotton of Coton, Alkington and Bellaport: argent, chevron sable between 3 cotton hanks.

Appendix V The Alkington Family

Local tradition, documentary evidence and, to a lesser degree, architectural features appear to equate Alkington Hall with the Cotton family and for these reasons emphasis has been laid on the family in this report. However, the family known as Alkington of Alkington features in several documents and within the same date range as the Cottons.[35] At present nothing is known about their dwelling-place or whether they were connected with the Cottons.

Park Farm, Alkington

Park Farm is situated within the township of Alkington at the end of a lane which leads south-westwards from its grander neighbour, Alkington Hall.[1] It lies about half a mile from the Shropshire Union Canal which itself runs very close to the Cheshire border. Externally the house is unremarkable, and is overshadowed architecturally by Alkington Hall, but its origins are earlier and, as its farm buildings are reasonably complete, it represents a microcosm of the type of farming practice prevalent in north Shropshire until after the Second World War.

The house is two-storied and has a three-bayed frontage with end chimneys, but the asymmetrical appearance of the brick façade and the way in which the upper windows are set tightly under the dentilated eaves cornice suggest that the brickwork, although well crafted in Flemish bond, is a casing applied to an earlier timber-framed house. Internal inspection confirms this hypothesis. One timber-framed truss (A - A) has been stripped of its plaster and it was this which, when dendrochronologically sampled and analysed, yielded a felling date of Spring 1556.[2] The bricks themselves are dull red and measure 9ins. x 3¹/₂ins. x 4ins. They are hand-moulded and set in lime mortar. The voussoirs are not rubbed, but are purposefully cut to a wedge-shape.

Section A - A

The frame has a straightforward design, of tie-and-collar-beam construction with angle-braces. It was a closed truss, with much original wattle-work and mud and straw infilling remains in the roof space.

The eastern face is dressed to a smooth finish, but the tree bark was left on the western side. This gave rise to the thought that it was an end truss, but the bark is not weathered, neither is there

Park Farm, south-east elevation

213

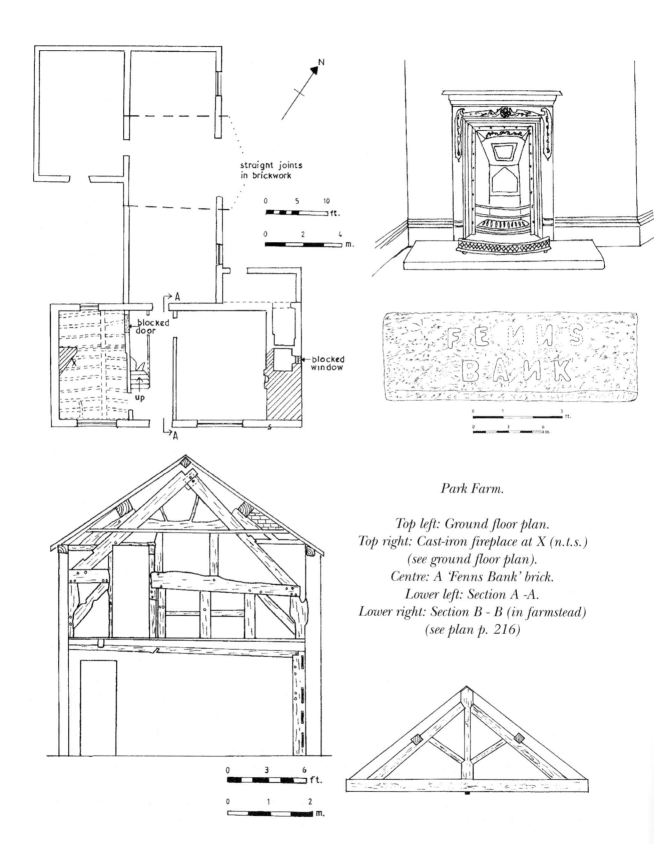

straight joints
in brickwork

0 5 10 ft.

0 2 4 m.

→ A

blocked
door

X

up

→ A

blocked
window

FENNS
BANK

0 1 3 ft.

0 3 6 m.

Park Farm.

Top left: Ground floor plan.
Top right: Cast-iron fireplace at X (n.t.s.)
(see ground floor plan).
Centre: A 'Fenns Bank' brick.
Lower left: Section A -A.
Lower right: Section B - B (in farmstead)
(see plan p. 216)

0 3 6 ft.

0 1 2 m.

214

evidence of weathering lower down. Furthermore, the purlins, although reset, appear to be original timbers and are continuous. There is no evidence of smoke blackening on any of the roof timbers.

The principal rafter apex joint is secured with a slip-tenon, rather than with the normal mortice-and-tenon joint. This appears to be an example of cost-cutting, but, despite movement elsewhere in the frame, the apex joint remains so tight that it is almost impossible to insert a fine knife-blade into it. It is only because the infilling in the top stage has partly fallen out, revealing the slight protrusion of the slip-tenon that the device employed by a mid-16th century carpenter has come to light. There is also housing for a ridge-purlin.

The corner-post on the eastern side is L-shaped. Various interpretations may be suggested for this, probably the most likely one is the simplest, that the carpenter was obliged to work with an imperfect log. Below the level of the first floor the post has every appearance of being a reused timber. The opposing post is of the normal rectangular form. This raises the question of the general quality of the basic material. The impression is gained that carpenters were working with oak which would have been rejected as unsuitable in earlier times. Although it is an accepted fact that the oaks available in north Shropshire were inferior to those south of the Severn, the timbers at Park Farm have distortions suggesting a degree of desperation on the part of all concerned with the timber-framed phase of building.

The Plan

It is evident from the plan that the present lay-out owes much of its form to the remodelling that took place in the 19th century, and much of what is considered to be later extension work is shown in outline only. There is a space behind the chimneystack in the eastern room which is difficult to interpret, but it is clear that it had an intended purpose because there is access to it from the north side.

It is possible that the remodelled house was T-shaped. What now appears as a linking block could have terminated on the first line of the straight joints.

The Farm Buildings

The lay-out of the farm buildings at Park Farm is purposefully planned on model-farm lines. The date of 1883 on the main range with the initials MSW (Marianne Sophia Wood) confirms the impression that at this time there was a confidence in the future of dairy farming in north Shropshire which merited the erection of quality buildings. The bricks on the dated unit are from the local Fenn's brickworks, vertically extruded and set in English Garden bond, that is, three rows of stretchers and one row of headers. This unit and the long south-western range appear to be a little later in date than the adjoining range which continues and completes the south-eastern elevation. Here the bricks appear to be early Fenn's, horizontally extruded and set in Flemish Stretcher bond, that is, three rows of stretchers and one row of headers and stretchers. Hard blue vitrified Staffordshire bricks are used for all the dressings, including the pitch-holes, for part of the lower courses and for the pigeon loft on the north-eastern gable. They also occur randomly elsewhere in the brickwork. Small blocks of sandstone are also included in the fabric and are used to accommodate some of the door hinges. On the north-western elevation rounded bricks are used on the corner of the projection which has the lower roof-line.

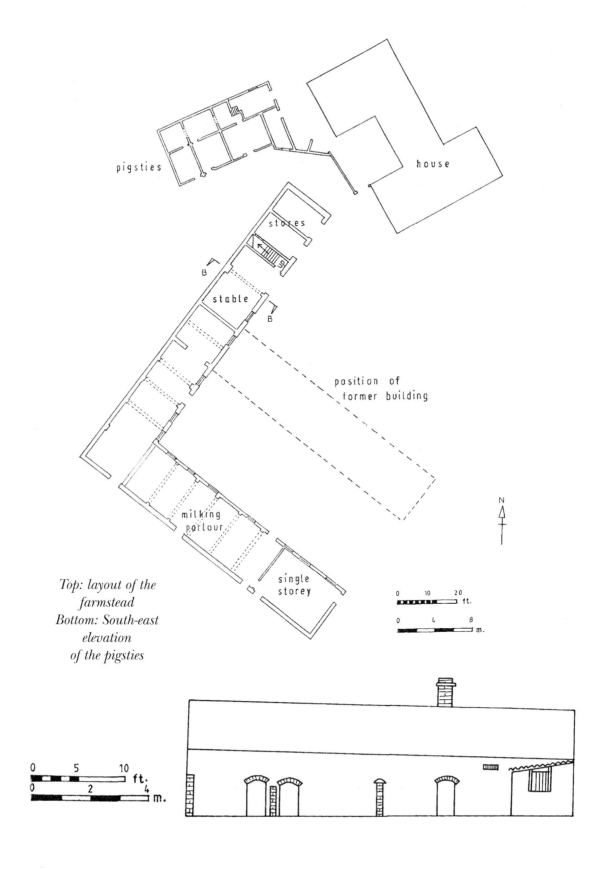

pigsties

house

stores

B

stable

B

position of
former building

milking
parlour

single
storey

N

Top: layout of the
farmstead
Bottom: South-east
elevation
of the pigsties

0   10   20
ft.

0   4   8
m.

0   5   10
ft.
0   2   4
m.

216

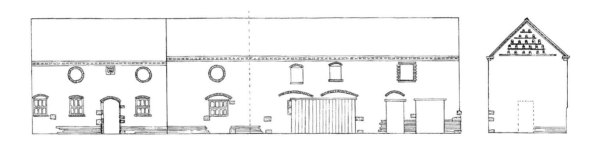

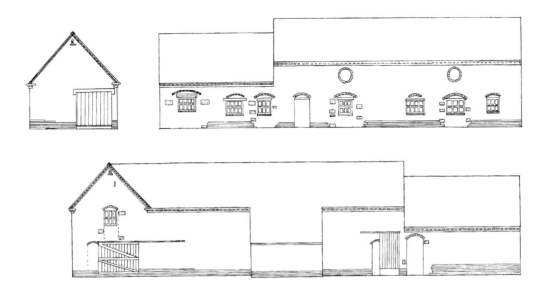

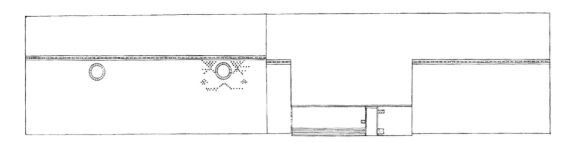

The Farm Buildings.

Top row: South-east elevation (left) and north-east gable (right).
Second row: South-east gable (left) and north-east elevation (right).
Third row: South-west elevation.
Fourth row: North-west elevation

On the south-eastern gable there is an owl-hole (ulenlok) at the apex and another on the south-western side. The latter also has an opening below the owl-hole for a hoist.

A vanished range about which nothing is known, is shown in outline on the plans. In certain lights the outline of its gable end shows against the brickwork of the earlier range. It would have enclosed two sides of an inner yard in the same way that the south-western range enclosed two sides of an outer yard. It has not been removed in living memory.

In the boundary wall of the pigsty block one brick is stamped with the name 'Fenns Bank' and is shown on the drawings. This local brickworks which ceased production *c.*1936, must have produced millions of bricks during its working life, but the isolated example at Park Farm is the only one known to bear the firm's name, and it was thought worthwhile to record it. The chimneystack in the block was necessary for the preparation of the potatoes, bran and other foods for the pig-mash and poultry-feed.

The Later History[3]

It has not been possible to trace the occupants of Park Farm before the 19th century. Originally the land, as part of the township of Alkington, belonged to the lord of the manor who was, by the 17th century, the Earl of Bridgwater. Several farms in Alkington had been sold by the early 19th century, some to members of the Wood family, for a Thomas Wood is noted as owning 36 acres in 1825.[4] At the time of the Tithe Commutation Act in 1837 Mrs. Anne Wood of Shrewsbury owned Park Farm, and her tenant was Thomas Cook.[5] However, his 28 acres constituted less than half the acreage of the present holding, the rest was owned by John Richard and Thomas Roe and tenanted by Thomas Jones.[6] Mrs. Wood owned three other farms in Alkington at this time.[7]

In the 1850s Park Farm was tenanted by the Davenport family and they remained in occupation until 1912.[8] It continued to be owned by the Wood family, and in 1883 passed to Mrs. Marianne Wood, widow of the Rev. Robert Faulkner Wood, rector of Moreton Corbet.[9] The Rev. and Mrs. Wood had carried out a programme of improvements to their Alkington properties and had either built or re-built the neighbouring Alkington House, for it bears a plaque inscribed 'R.F.W. 1880'. A similar plaque appears on the farm buildings at Park Farm, inscribed 'MSW 1883', evidence that they were erected by his widow. Probably around this time Park Farm was remodelled and encased with brickwork.

Mrs. Wood died in 1893, by which time the family's estate in the area consisted of six farms: Park Farm, Alkington Hall, Alkington Grange, The Chain House and Cloverdale, all in Alkington, and Ivy House Farm in the adjoining township of Tilstock. The estate had been divided between the two daughters of the Rev. and Mrs. Wood, and it was the son of one of the daughters who in 1937 sold all six farms to the sitting tenants.[10]

At this time Walter Windsor was the tenant of Park Farm and it is his grandson, Eric Windsor who, with his wife Elizabeth, at present farm the 90 acres as a dairy farm. They have a herd of over 100 cattle and no arable land. During the last ten years they have uncovered much of the early structure.

The Ditches Hall, Wem

The Ditches Hall, sometimes known simply as The Ditches is a particularly fine two-storied and box-framed 17th century farmhouse located about a mile to the west of Wem parish church. The farm acreage is at present *c*.200.

The External Details

Outstanding in many respects, probably the most eye-catching feature is the close-studded framing on the front and on both side walls. Each storey has a mid-rail, and the lower storey has a straight tension-brace at each corner. The house was originally jettied on all four sides, but the jetty detail has been lost on the south side as the south gable wall has been rebuilt, but four internal dragon beams confirm the fully-jettied form. There is a central brick chimneystack in line with the integral porch which, in itself, contributes greatly to the aesthetically pleasing basic design.

The windows are original. Each has the dropped sill, indicative of purposefully designed openings which were not just a gap in the framework. Those in the lower storey are larger than those lighting the bedrooms, but each is fitted with ovolo-moulded mullions and transoms.

The Porch

Fully two-storied, the porch is jettied and has its own pitched roof which breaks the otherwise uninterrupted roof line of the house. At ground level the porch is fitted with seats and two side windows, unglazed, but with four ovolo-moulded mullions. The door latch has the date 1612 inscribed upon it. Above the tie-beam there is the only piece of free-style decoration in the form of a fleur-de-lis.

The Ditches Hall, east elevation

The North Elevation

The same attention to detail occurs on the north gable wall as is seen on the frontage. One slight variation occurs in the gable where some diagonal struts are used. This is not true herring-bone design and detracts from the regularity of the verticals used elsewhere.

The Plan

The internal plan is entirely predictable from the external appearance. The porch gives access to a lobby-entry plan with two equal-sized rooms, one on either side of the large central chimneystack. The house has been extended by numerous additions at the rear, one of which contains the present staircase, but there is evidence to show that originally the staircase was located not at the rear of the stack, which would be the usual position, but in the south-west corner of the northern room, currently the dining room, but thought to have originally been the kitchen on account of the style of the fireplace.

Each ground-floor room has the ceiling divided into rectangular panels by spine-beams, and a part-chequerboard design is effected by the joists on the long axes being set at right angles to those in the centre. All the joists are chamfered and stopped, and the spine-beams are ovolo-moulded.

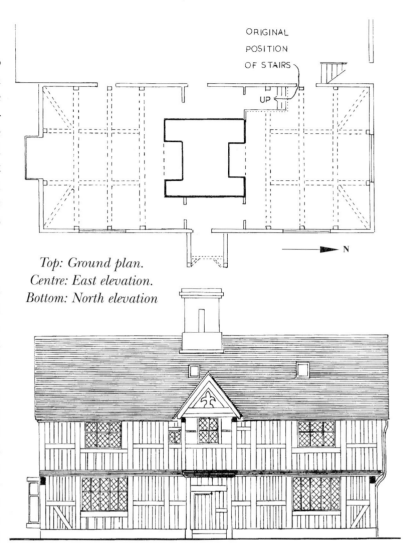

Top: Ground plan.
Centre: East elevation.
Bottom: North elevation

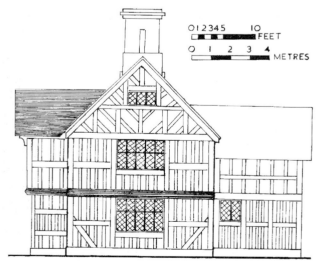

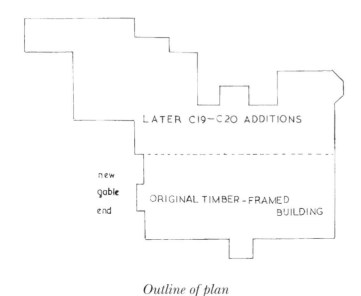

Outline of plan

The Fireplaces

In each of the ground-floor rooms the fireplace is of Grinshill-stone construction. That in the southern room, the parlour, has ovolo moulding on the jambs. There is a high mantel-shelf and a lower shelf incorporated in the overmantel, each with classical moulding, and between the lower shelf and the lintel is a plain deep stone surface which contained a large shield bearing coloured heraldic designs. It was divided into numerous sections, each with blazons which presumably relate to families connected with the house. Full interpretation of the blazons would require the services of a genealogist skilled in heraldry, but those families that can be identified without too much difficulty seem to be mostly from the north: Brereton, Saumon and Saighton from Chester; Ashton, Anderton, Thurston and Greenhaugh from County Lancaster; Cunliffe from Liverpool, and Bassett from Wales. These are deduced simply by relating known armigerous families to their crests. Often, more than one family would use recognised symbols. Perhaps the most significant family is the Breretons. The fleur-de-lis is the cadency mark for a sixth son, and, as noted above, this occurs as a decorative feature above the porch and on the shield.[1]

The fireplace in the northern room is plainer and is fitted for cooking purposes, but the jambs are chamfered and have decorative stops incorporating lozenges and trellis work in the Grinshill-stone.

The Roof

The roof structure is consistent with the 17th century framework and includes two tiers of purlins and straight windbraces. A plaque attached to the chimneystack in the attic has the inscription 'Samuel Haycocks ... reperaed in 1822.'

The Gas Plant

Many additions have been made to the rear of the house, and in *c.*1909 provision was made for a domestic gas plant to supply

Fireplace with blazons, now gone

light and power.[2] The engine was housed in a brick outbuilding attached to the house, and the gas was made from petrol. To the side of the engine house there is a well into which the weights dropped from a pulley-and-hoist system. The engine house, the pulley and the well remain.

Assessment

Few houses in Shropshire are as ordered and uncomplicated as the Ditches Hall, and few are as aesthetically pleasing. Admittedly, the doorlatch is a strange place to find an inscribed date, but 1612 seems consistent with all the architectural features and with the plan. Jettied on all four sides, close-studded and with a two-storied projecting porch, the house is a text-book example of a newly-built lobby-entry-plan-type of that date. While the site is probably ancient, nothing remains of any earlier structure within the present building.

Notes on the Documented History

The following notes are taken from those made by Mr. Raymond Elkes.[3]

In the 16th century the house was held by the Twyfords who had the title 'gentlemen'. The last Twyford died in 1603, and 'The New Ditches' was built eight to nine years later, its first owner-occupiers being the Kilverts. George Kilvert was in possession by 1622 and was succeeded by his son Richard, gent, who died in 1644. Richard's own son, George was born at The Ditches and baptised at Wem on 20th January 1621, but after Richard's death in 1644 the estate was sold to John Barnes of the Lowe Hall, less than one mile to the north-east. It appears that the property was then leased out for a while, initially to the Shenton family; Randolf Shenton, son of Randolf and Elizabeth Shenton of The Ditches was baptised on 13th October 1665. Sometime in the next nine years the tenancy must have then passed to Richard Jebb, for on 15th January 1674 Ursula, daughter of Mr. Richard Jebb and Elizabeth 'at the Ditches Hall' was baptised.

In the meantime, in 1658, ownership of the property had been passed to John Edwards of Wem as a marriage portion for his daughter Dorothy. In about 1663 John Edwards sold it to Mr. Barnet of Ryton. They resumed actual possession, for on 12th June 1676 a son of William Barnet 'of Ditches Hall' was buried. The original Mr. Barnet's son, Roger, married twice, firstly Ann Day of Wem and then Martha Donn of the Lowe Hall. The Ditches Estate was settled on the issue of the first marriage, a sole daughter Elizabeth, who in turn married Richard Tyler of Horton. They had two daughters who inherited the freehold portion of the estate. One daughter married William Barnet—her uncle on her father's side, and the other 'one Longford of Ellesmere' by whom she had a son who inherited the copyhold portion of The Ditches. The Barnets remained as owner-occupiers at least until 1713 when Anne, younger daughter of Roger Barnett, presumably by his second wife, was born there on 2nd October.

Subsequently the Barnets leased The Ditches out, initially to the Farringtons, and some-time between the death of Thomas Farrington on 19th September 1761 and 8th June 1771 the lease passed to the Haycocks, for on that day Ann, daughter of Thomas Haycock of The Ditches was baptised in the Noble Street chapel. In October 1778 Mr. Samuel Haycock of The Ditches died. Samuel left his estate to his brother John Haycock, yeoman, of Iscoyed in the parish of Malpas, Cheshire, who moved into The Ditches with his wife Mary.

Meanwhile ownership stayed with the Barnets. Roger Barnet's grandson owned the estate in 1753, which was still the position *c.*1757 when Garbett's *History of Wem* was written, Garbett himself being related to the Barnes and Edwards families. A William Barnet witnessed a tenant's will in 1788.

Mary Haycock died in January 1804, and John on 6th June 1812, leaving 'the tenant rights of the farm and lands now occupied by me as tenant and lessee to my son Samuel Haycock for his own use.' Samuel married Sarah Slack, but they had no family. He died on 28th December 1839 aged 53 and his widow was still farming The Ditches at the time of the 1841 census. Meanwhile Samuel's sister Sarah had married Edward Elkes, eldest son of Thomas Elkes of the Lowe Hall on 15th April 1823, and they farmed the adjacent Pool's Farm. In the 1840s Edward Elkes began to farm The Ditches, and by 1857, now a widower—his wife had died in November 1846 aged 57—his brother-in-law was his farm bailiff at the Pool's.

Edward was a prominent farmer, a churchwarden at Wem and a leader of the agricultural community. He was head of a large extended Elkes family in the area. His eldest daughter Susanna married her cousin Samuel Elkes, the youngest son of Thomas Elkes of the Lowe Hall. But Edward's life also had its tragic side. His second daughter, Margaret, married The Ditches' cowman Joseph Barnett, much to Edward's disgust. Margaret and Joseph had a large family, two surviving daughters of which became their Aunt Susanna's heiresses, who died in 1866 aged 41. The eldest son, John died in 1848 aged 29 and the third daughter Sarah Mary died in March 1860 aged 30. The youngest son, Thomas Edward died, aged 27, in June 1860 as a result of an injury incurred when he went to help a man who had a wheel of his cart stolen in a street in Wem.

When Edward died at The Ditches on 9th June 1868 he was followed as tenant by his daughter Susanna and her husband Samuel who had acted as her farm bailiff. It was a double wedding at Wem on 10th May 1876. The other couple were Richard Gough of Whettal, Ellesmere and another Susanna Elkes, Samuel's sister.

Samuel Elkes died in January 1895 from pneumonia caught when he became wet through when shooting. It was planned that his nephew John Elkes, (Raymond Elkes' father), son of his eldest brother Henry Elkes of Newport should succeed him at The Ditches, but John was only 15 when his uncle died, and so his aunt Susanna had to give up the tenancy. She bought the Old Mill House in Wem and died there in 1906, leaving that property to her Barnett nieces.

Less is known of the intervening owners. They included John Lee, though he had died when the Lowe Hall estate, including Pool's Farm, was sold in 1874. The Cunliffes owned it after the Elkes family gave up the tenancy. More recently Mr. & Mrs. Clement E. Pickmere were owner-occupiers in 1951.[4] Mr. & Mrs. John Williams are the current owner-occupiers.

According to Arthur Mee[5] there is a 'hiding hole in the attic'. Another story has it that Charles I is reputed to have spent a night in the house, but the building had more notable links with the Puritan and non-conformist movements in north Shropshire. Iris Woodward in her *Story of Wem* (1951) says that Mr. Richardson, the Puritan Rector of Myddle, moved there when he was ousted at the Restoration but had to move again because the Five Mile Act forbade him to live within that distance of any part of his former parish. Certainly the

Bassetts, Farringtons and Haycocks had links with the Presbyterians at Whitchurch and the Congregationalists at Noble Street, Wem; and, while Edward Elkes was a churchwarden, his brother Thomas had married Sarah Dudleston, a member of a Baptist family, who joined the Noble Street Chapel in 1832.

Andrew Parsons, the Puritan rector of Wem built himself a black and white house on Shrewsbury Road, later called the Old Mill House and it was this house which Susanna Elkes bought for her retirement after her husband's death at The Ditches.

Ridgwardine Manor, Norton-in-Hales

Ridgwardine Manor, once a farmhouse, is one of three such houses in the hamlet. It lies about a mile and a half from the parish church and about $2^1/_2$ miles from Market Drayton. The place-name suggests a ridge of some kind with a homestead upon it and that exactly describes the situation at Ridgwardine Manor.[1] A ridge of sandstone underlies the site, creating a slight rise in the ground level, sufficient to be noticeable in the otherwise flat plain of north Shropshire. Only one field drains towards the house, the remaining fields drain away and the house is located about 4ft. below the ridge.

The adjunct 'Manor' is modern. The medieval manor is that of Betton, and the present Ridgwardine Manor was, until *c.*1800, a farmhouse on the Betton estate simply called 'Ridgwardine'. The first reference to it being called 'Manor' occurs in the Tithe Assessment of 1841. Then it became 'Ridgwardine Manor Farm' and at present it is known as 'Ridgwardine Manor' to distinguish it from 'Ridgwardine Farm', another farm in the hamlet.

The house is approached from a drive leading from a minor road which winds from

Top: Ridgwardine Manor, front or south elevation.
Below: East and north elevations

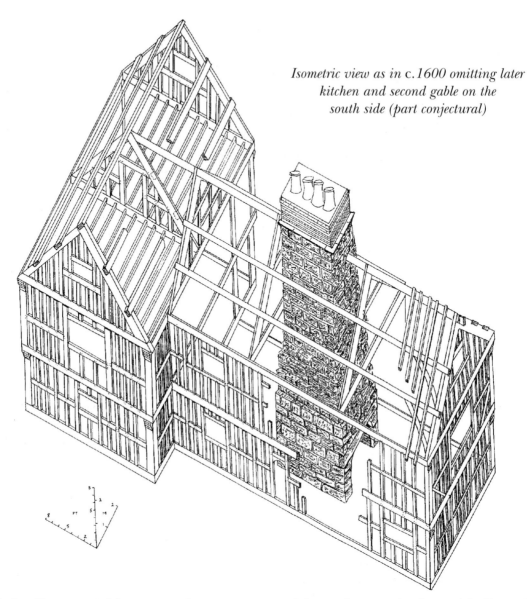

*Isometric view as in c.1600 omitting later
kitchen and second gable on the
south side (part conjectural)*

Market Drayton and loops round to serve many of the settlements in the parish. From the
front the dominant features are two large gables, the central chimneystack and extensive
brickwork, but basically the house is T-shaped, only one of the large gables truly relates to
the plan and the brickwork is mostly cladding or replacement for timber-framing.

The Exterior
The Rear (North) Elevation
It is here that the timber-framing is best preserved and the true form of the house is
reflected. The upper stories in both the hall range and the crosswing retain close studding
with a mid-rail; only at ground floor level has the framing been replaced with brickwork.
Also from this aspect it is clear that the bay at the western end is a later addition, for the

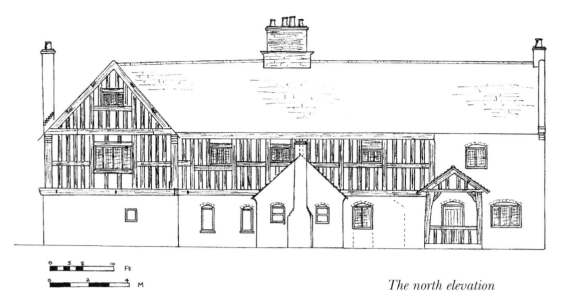

The north elevation

peg-holes on the ultimate vertical timber of the hall range make no provision for the framing to extend beyond this point. The end unit is entirely brick-built and there is additional evidence internally for it to be an addition.

The brick built single-storied extension at right-angles is also a later addition and the porch was added very recently.

Many of the timbers are replacements, but care has been taken to preserve the close-studded design. The gable of the crosswing retains its small jetty which is supported by an ovolo-moulded tie-beam above carved brackets. Again, unfortunately, the plate is a replacement timber, but the jowelled foot of the corner-post and the fact that the new plate runs continuously below the vertical studding in the manner of a bressumer suggests that the first floor was also jettied.

The East Elevation

It is clear that this, the side wall of the crosswing, was also close-studded as peg-holes for the studs are regularly placed along the wall-plate. Nothing remains of framing on this side, it is entirely bricked, although the brickwork abuts rather than covers the surviving corner post at the north-eastern corner. There is a slightly outbuilt chimneystack almost mid-way along the wall and this serves what has been called the 'Georgian' room. It has a small lean-to extension at the base, the purpose of which is to give depth to the fireplace in the parlour.

The Front (South) Elevation

A major refurbishment took place *c.*1810 or later when the kitchen bay was added at the western end, and the bulk of the house was clad in brickwork. At this time the front elevation was given the greatest attention in order to emphasise its importance. No framework is visible, all is brick, and an attempt to at least give an impression of symmetry was made by creating an entirely false gable to match the gable of the genuine crosswing. This neces-

227

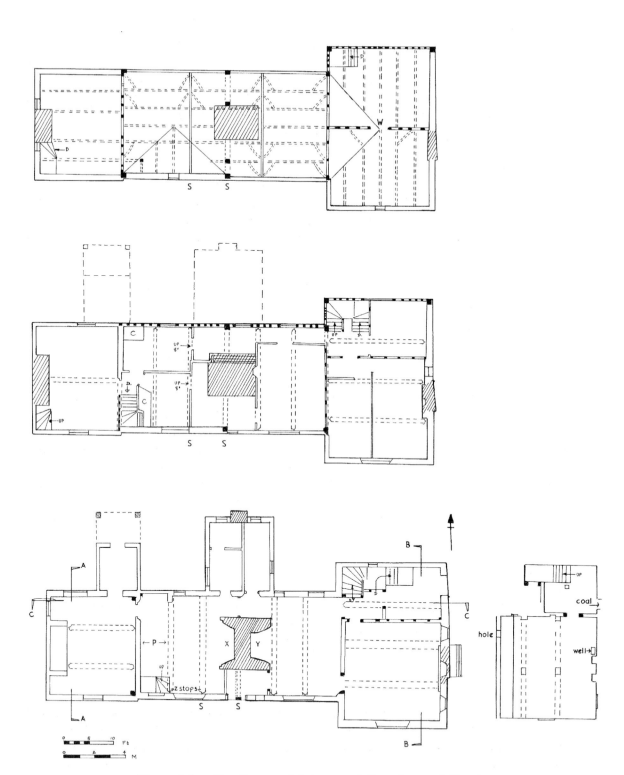

Plans of the cellar (bottom right), ground floor (bottom left),
first floor (centre) and attic (top)

sitated cutting through the roof purlin and windbraces in order to insert a matching window in the roof space. The main entrance door is awkwardly placed and its position may be the result of second thoughts. There is a blocked door to the west of the ground floor window in the false gable, and this may have a significance which is discussed later.

The added (kitchen) bay is finished with a raised gable, coping stones and kneelers, but care was taken to keep the roof ridge at a uniform level throughout.

The Brickwork

The bricks are of a fairly consistent size, 9ins. x 2½ins. x 4ins., reddish in colour, kiln-fired, dense but soft-textured and with a high pebble-content. They probably came from the brickworks at Betton. The site is now no more than humps and bumps in a field but water-filled pits and a raised track which supported a tramway bear witness to clay extraction and brick firing there at one time. The site is not shown as such on the Tithe Map of 1841 and although it features on the OS maps of 1880 and 1902, the brickworks do not appear in any of the directories of the time and it is possible that, although fairly extensive, it was a short-lived enterprise set up solely to provide bricks for use on the Betton estate. A few 'wasters' recovered from the site are similar to those at the house and to other houses in the area.

In the projecting crosswing the bonding is mostly of the English Garden type, that is, three rows of stretchers and one row of headers, although in the gable the use of headers is kept to a minimum. A three-brick plat-band indicates the level of the first floor on the crosswing. There is no plat-band on the main section of the frontage but it occurs again on the added kitchen bay where it is only two bricks in depth. On this bay the bonding, though not consistent, appears to be mainly of three stretchers and a header in each course. This is Flemish Garden bond, sometimes known as Sussex bond.[2] The same bonding occurs in the main section of the frontage, where, to the right of the main door, there is even more inconsistency, with more stretchers involved.

Many of the bricks display what seems to be a fault in the mould, a feature which has been noted often in north Shropshire.

The Interior
The Plan

Before the kitchen bay was added at the western end the basic plan at Ridgwardine Manor consisted of a three bayed hall range with a large central chimneystack, and a two bayed crosswing, jettied certainly at the rear and probably also at the front.

The Roof Space
a) The Hall Range

Above the added kitchen the framing of the gable end of the earlier build is fully exposed (section A - A). This is weathered on the western side, confirming that the kitchen bay is indeed an addition. Also it is clear that the door giving access to the next bay is contrived from an earlier window; three mortices for mullions remain as does part of the window frame. Another piece of evidence is provided by the ridge purlin which comes through from the next bay and terminates in its original housing on the principal rafter. This has

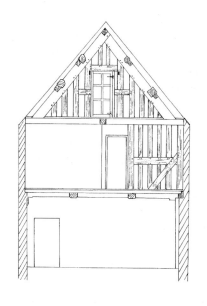

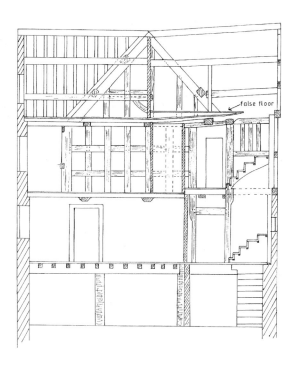

*Sections A - A (above), B - B (right)
and C - C (below)*

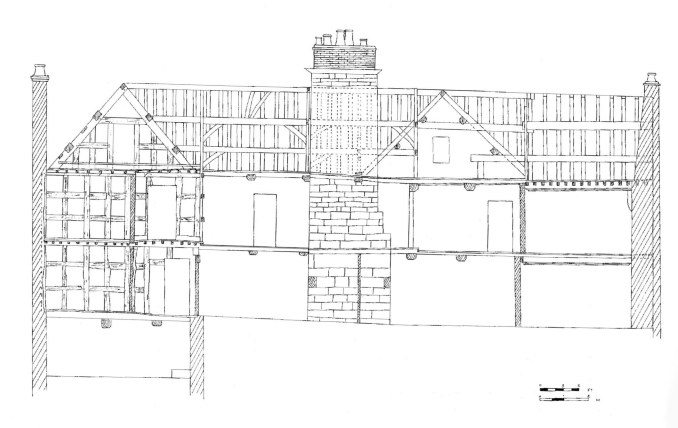

230

a projecting tenon providing seating for barge-boards and some kind of finial and/or pendant. The window indicates that the roof space in the house was always intended for use, a point confirmed by the amount of headroom and the treatment of both tiers of side purlins which are chamfered and stopped. It seems likely that when the gable functioned as an external feature there was a hoist to raise sacks or perhaps cheeses into the attic space. The evidence for this lies in two through mortices in the longest verticals of the framework which are cut with an angle of 45 degrees for the supports. Similar hoists have been noted elsewhere in the area. A small staircase is located in the south-western corner of the attic chamber and this, though no longer in use, connected with the bedroom below and the kitchen on the ground floor.

In the bay to the west of the stack the purlin has been cut through in order to create the false gable on the front and to insert a window matching that on the crosswing. The removal of a windbrace at this juncture enables their original form to be examined. Tenoned into the soffits of the purlins they are mostly straight timbers, although some are slightly curved, and are butted and pegged on the backs of the principal rafters.

The stone chimneystack is a dominant feature of the roof space and shows no sign of settlement at all, but the framed floor around it has a marked downward movement.

A truss in the bay to the east of the stack is set very close to it and has evidence of joists going in a westerly direction, that is, into the stack itself. The truss has stave holes on the soffit of the collar suggesting that it was a closed truss at one time. This in turn suggests a separation of the servants. The men probably accessed their sleeping quarters from the kitchen stairs and the females from the stairs in the crosswing.

b) The Crosswing

In the crosswing the space divides into two clearly defined bays. The northern (rear) gable retains its framing and is identical to that of Section A at the original end of the hall range. At attic level the central truss is remarkable for the extraordinarily large rush-taper marks upon it. Clearly when this part of the attic was in use as sleeping quarters the rush lights were not moved about and their positions were maintained over a long period of time.

Each bay has two tiers of purlins and the windbraces make an interesting study. Some are straight, others are curved, some are set in a convex arc, others in the more conventional concave arc and some are missing. Section B shows how a false floor was inserted into the northern bay presumably to facilitate its use for sleeping purposes and in the same bay the intrusion of the head of

The attic stairs (n.t.s.)

231

the main staircase necessitated the removal of the lower windbrace, the insertion of a supporting strut mid-way, and part-replacement of the lower purlin while further along access into the roof space of the hall range necessitated the removal of the lower windbrace although the mortice remains for it as does its stub on the back of the principal rafter. These features raise the question of whether the staircase was originally intended to reach attic level and were the two units always intended to communicate at attic level? These points are discussed later.

The First Floor
The bay divisions noted in the roof space are echoed at first floor level, and the later partitions are easily distinguished by their lighter scantlings and lack of proper

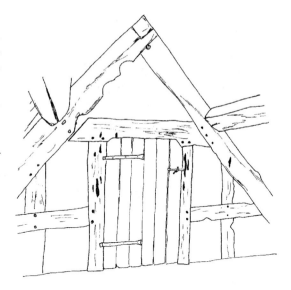

The attic with rush taper marks at W (n.t.s.)
(see attic plan p.228)

pegging. At Section 'A' further proof that this was the end truss of the hall range before the kitchen bay was added is apparent from the weathering upon the timbers, the flush jointing and the slight jetty formed by the positioning of the ovolo-moulded tie-beam.

The massive stone chimneystack dominates the lay-out. At this level it is stepped in four uneven stages and there are signs of disturbance in the centre of the second stage, but the reason for this is unknown.

The Ground Floor
Some of the features at this level have a bearing on the overall assessment of the house and are discussed under that heading.

The Central Stone Chimneystack
Unmistakable from outside and dominating the interior is the very large stone chimneystack. It is reasoned below that its position was changed while the house was being built and that this accounts for some anomalies. The stone is from the ridge of Ruyton and Grinshill sandstone (Wilmslow sandstone) of Triassic age which extends from north-east of Market Drayton to Norton-in-Hales. It is a current bedded coarse sandstone with many clay castes or inclusions and is an excellent freestone—being able to be cut freely in any direction without shattering. The quarry is most likely to have been that located at SJ 688360 and shown on OS maps of 1889 and 1954, two and a quarter miles away. At present woods cover the uneven ground of the old stone diggings, but part of the quarry face along the strike of the rock is still visible and there is a large water-filled pit. Clearly the stone was well used, it may be identified in local farm buildings, boundary walls, in significant village sites along the clay ridge, in the older parts of Market Drayton parish church and in the parish church at Norton-in-Hales.[3]

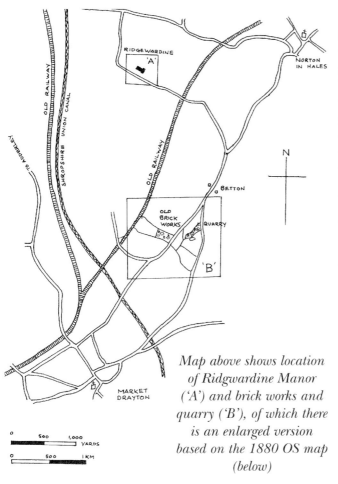

Map above shows location of Ridgwardine Manor ('A') and brick works and quarry ('B'), of which there is an enlarged version based on the 1880 OS map (below)

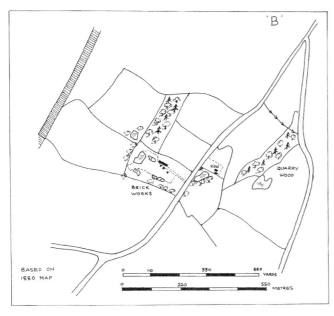

In the house the blocks used at ground floor and first-floor levels were finished with a lime plaster skim, since removed, and this has bleached the stones, but in the attic they retain their original orange/red colouring and the tooling marks with their characteristic herringbone patterns are crisp. The stones have been squared but not ashlared, and the courses are of random depth, those on the ground floor have a maximum depth of 15ins. and the longest stretcher face is 4ft. As expected, the whole structure tapers towards the top and the blocks reduce in size.

It has been estimated that inside the house *c.*12,496 cubic feet of stone are present. This does not take into account that needed for the foundation and that which shows externally above the roof line. On a basis of 26 cubic feet per ton this gives 480 tons of stone, all of which would have to be horse-drawn. The Barhill account book records a wagon and two horses able to transport three tons at a time which means that on that basis more than 148 trips to the quarry were necessary.[4]

The Fireplaces

The stone chimneystack provides back-to-back fireplaces for the two main rooms at ground floor level and probably two at first floor level, but the attics were apparently unheated. As sandstone is well known for its heat retaining properties the stack would act as a massive night-storage heater, that is, if fires were maintained on the ground floor hearths.

There is a difference between the main fireplaces. That on the east in the present dining-room has chamfered jambs finished with broach stops, while the timber lintel has evidence that it was once plastered over. The cast-iron fireback is thought to be an original feature. Clearly this was the more prestigious of the two fireplaces, although in the other the wooden lintel is arched, chamfered and stopped. This fireplace is distinguished by a series of redundant recesses in the overmantel, possibly for a smoke canopy of some kind or for fixtures for smoking meats. It seems to have been where cooking was done, and there is evidence for fixtures of various kinds. The inside area has been lined with brick-work, possibly to repair damage from long use.

The Cellar

The cellar is located below the crosswing. It is mostly of brick, divided into two compart-ments, and has a blocked coal chute. There is a well on the eastern side. The steps are of sandstone and there is some stonework at the foot of the steps on the northern wall. It remains an open question whether the cellar is an original feature or whether it was inserted when the house was remodelled.

The Stable Block

Most of the farm buildings belonging to Ridgwardine Manor have been demolished. One brick-built barn has been converted into a house, but the stable block remains in use and is shown opposite. The brickwork is similar to that on the house and the general quality of the building is very good. The recording team was impressed with the regularity of the right-angles and the mathematical precision of the components.

Assessment and Dating

At ground floor level several features occur which suggest that the house was not built entirely from new in the 17th century. The first is the image of a screens passage at the lower, western, end of the hall range. The dimensions, about 6ft., are in keeping and the soffit of the beam has a regular set of mortices which held verticals for a partition of some kind. At the northern (rear) end the beam is supported by a projection, but this could be a later insertion. There is evidence of a blocked doorway at the end of the 'passage' on the external brickwork and at the opposite (front) end another blocked doorway appears in the brickwork. As mentioned above, the present main doorway is awkwardly placed and the blocked doorway may represent the traditional entry position. At present the small staircase which gives access to the upper floor is housed behind the blocked door.

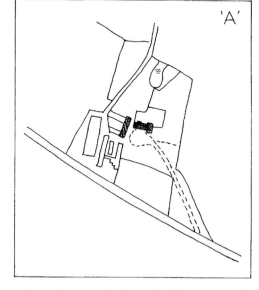

Plan showing the farm buildings (n.t.s.)

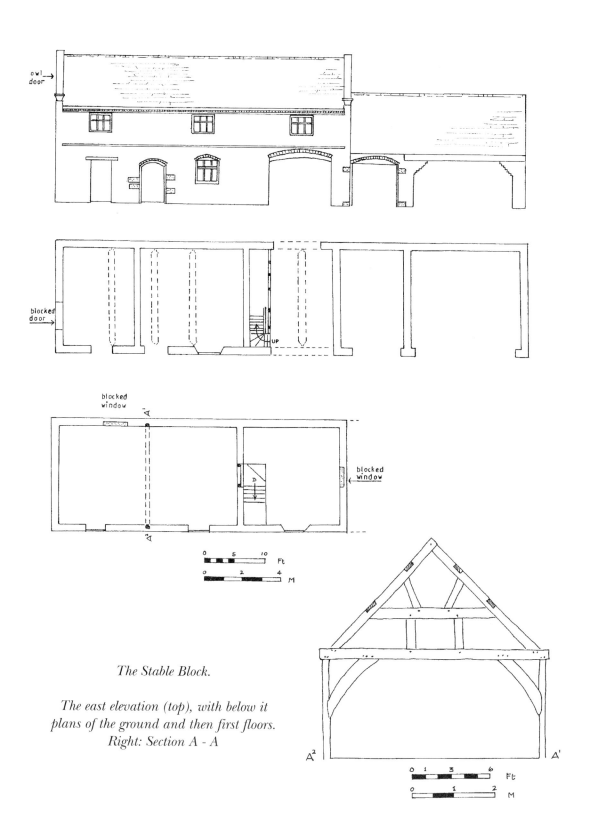

owl door →

blocked door →

blocked window

blocked window →

A¹

A²

UP

D

0   5   10   Ft
0   2   4   M

The Stable Block.

The east elevation (top), with below it plans of the ground and then first floors. Right: Section A - A

A²   A¹

0   1   3   6   Ft
0   1   2   M

235

Another puzzling feature also relates to the entry position. At present the door opens onto a lobby-entry, but it is only possible to turn right, whereas in the classic arrangement it should be possible to access the rooms on either side of the stack. Furthermore, centrally placed above the doorway is a transverse beam with mortices similar to those in the 'screens passage' beam, but here the beam goes into the stack and does not appear on the other side. The beam is supported by the remains of a post which, if continued, would come in the centre of the doorway. From this it is clear that the lobby-entry on the south side is a later contrivance.

This raises the question of whether the stack was inserted into the remains of a medieval house which had an open hall, a screens passage and perhaps a spere truss. While this is possible, there are factors which suggest an alternative development. The bulk of the present house can be shown to be of one build with the stack forming the 'anchor' around which the framing was set. In this phase there was never an open hall and a building sequence with the stack as the pivot may be postulated. In this the stack was probably planned as a smaller feature, occupying a central position in the space marked S - S on the plans. This would account for joists in the attic on the truss immediately to the east of the stack to appear to go into the stonework and for the same situation to occur at ground-floor level. The house would still have had a lobby-entry, but on the northern side. The isometric drawing shows the position of such an entrance, marked by its arched door-head, the remains of which feature in the house.

Then a change of plan occurred, the stack was made larger and its position altered. The effect of this is noticeable at all levels in the house. A significant factor is the presence of ovolo-moulding on all the main ceiling beams and its absence on the one that appears to go into the stack. Ovolo-moulding is also a linking feature on the tie-beams of the cross-wing and the end wall of the hall range. Without doubt the present kitchen bay was added and the most likely time for this to occur was when the front was remodelled, the back partly bricked, the great parlour 'Georgianised', the main entry position changed and access made from the attic in the crosswing to that over the abutting bay of the hall range. It is possible that, at this time, the 'front' became the 'back'. A fossilised lane runs on the western side of the house and still provides access to the road.

In its final form, apart from the fact that it has a crosswing instead of a parlour end, it is remarkably similar to Peter Smith's 'Type C Severn Valley three-unit lobby-entry' houses.[5]

Dendrochronological sampling and analysis had to be discounted at Ridgwardine Manor. The timbers were too fast-grown, many had come from pollarded oaks and were distorted, shaken and split. While this in no way affects their strength or stability it makes tree-ring dating impossible.[6]

Dating, therefore, rests with the architectural analysis and on the basis of style, plan and features the suggested date for the timber-framed house with its central stack is c.1600 with a major remodelling taking place c.1810 or later. William Church Norcop, lord of the manor of Betton, 'enlarged and beautified' his home, Betton Hall, about this time and it is likely that Ridgwardine Manor received similar treatment.[7]

It seems strange that until comparatively recently, as the tenurial history will show, Ridgwardine Manor was not owner-occupied. When it was completely timber-framed the close-studding employed on each elevation, not just on the front, suggests wealth and importance. Similarly, the cost, time and effort involved with the stack, the quality of the fireplaces and the stable-block relate more to a gentleman's residence than to a tenanted farm. Perhaps the Church family, the probable builders, had intentions to live there. Another anomaly is the absence of any other than one-hearth houses in the 1672 Hearth-Tax for Betton.[8]

The Tenurial History[9]

In Saxon times Ridgwardine came within the Hundred of Hodnet and under Drayton which was held by Lady Godiva, Earl Leofric of Mercia's countess.[10] The earliest name to be linked with Ridgwardine is that of Ulfketel, a Saxon, who held the manor of Betton which included Ridgwardine.[11] After the Conquest the new Norman overlord was Thorold de Verley and he gave Drayton Parva to Shrewsbury Abbey after which it was treated as a member of Betton.[12] At the time of Domesday (1086) Betton was held by the Abbot of Shrewsbury who had received it as a gift from Gerard le Torney. Gerard, who held his lands under the great Earl Roger de Montgomery, probably died soon after 1086 and his lands, though held for a time by Hamo Peverel, his son-in-law, were regarded as having reverted to the crown.[13]

In 1200 Nicholas de Rugwrthin, with the consent of the Abbey, granted all his lands at Rugwrthin (Ridgwardine) to Alured, son of Gerard de Norton, for three marks and three shillings. In addition Alured was to pay Nicholas half a mark on St. Martin's day and 12d on St. Giles's day each year.[14] A few years later, *c*.1210, Alured granted all his lands in Ridgwardine to Abbot Hugh of Shrewsbury and at the same time Nicholas's son Thomas quitclaimed all his rights in Ridgwardine in return for one mark from the Abbey.[15]

But in 1241 the abbey surrendered to Hugh, son of Hora de Rugwrthin, all the lands which his father had held in Rugwrthin together with the assart (cleared woodland) which his father had made. Hugh was to do suit to the abbey's court at Betton and was not to sell or alienate the land providing that the abbey bought it at its market value. He was to pay 6s per annum and 8d for the assart, and one large pig if he had enjoyed pannage rights, but only a reasonably sized pig if not.[16]

In 1276 there was an agreement between Shrewsbury Abbey and Combermere Abbey in Cheshire concerning the tithes of land newly brought into cultivation in the manor of Betton in Hales which the latter claimed belonged to its parish church of Drayton. After examining the special rights exhibited by Shrewsbury, the Abbot of Combermere abandoned his suit on condition that he was allowed to collect his accustomed tithes in Betton, Ridgwardine and Tunstall. Shrewsbury Abbey was to pay two marks a year to Drayton church.[17]

After the dissolution of Shrewsbury Abbey in 1540 Ridgwardine, Norton, Tunstall, Forton, Wollerton and Betton were purchased by Sir Rowland Hill, and when he died he left Betton with Little Drayton to Elizabeth Barker. The Barkers sold Betton manor to William Church, a Nantwich mercer, in about 1600 and thus Ridgwardine came into the hands of the family who built the well-known 'Churche's Mansion' in Nantwich which is dated 1577.[18]

The Church family was wealthy and had seats at Nantwich and Tunstall, but William Church is recorded as 'of Betton' in 1623, his father Richard being 'of Nantwich'.[19] Five generations later William's great-great-great-granddaughter, Mary Church married Laurence Norcop of Betton and their son was baptised William Church Norcop in January 1744.[20] The latter became High Sheriff of Shropshire in 1813 and died in 1822.[21]

At the time of the 1841 Tithe Assessment another William Church Norcop, the Sheriff's son, owned Ridgwardine, but lived as his family before him, at Betton Hall. He died a bachelor and his property was inherited by his sister's son, Alexander William Radford. On 8th April 1862 A.W. Radford was granted Royal Licence to assume the surname of Norcop and further assumptions of the Norcop name occurred, presumably in order to facilitate inheritance.[22]

By 1904 the estate was mortgaged and in 1921 Arthur Radford sold Ridgwardine Manor Farm to Percy Dobson whose family had been tenants from *c.*1850. Probably for the first time in its history the property belonged to the people who lived and worked there.

The names of other 19th century tenants include the Cartwright family, there in the 1840s, the Evans' in the 1870s, and the Moores in the 1880s, but by 1891 the Dobson family were again tenants and after Percy died in 1958 it was bought through sub-purchase by Lilian Martha Key of Eccleshall. Her son Wesley farmed Ridgwardine and inherited it on her death in 1980.

The Keys still owned Ridgwardine Manor in 1986 although the farmland had been broken up and sold off piecemeal. In 1986, when it was sold to R.A. Wade and his wife Patricia it was specifically called a 'pig-breeding complex'—a 20th-century echo of Hugh Rugwrthin's 13th-century rent to Shrewsbury Abbey.

The present owners, Drs. R.B. and C.J. Johanson, bought the house in 1993 and live there with their young family.

Although seldom owner-occupied, Ridgwardine was clearly an important holding within the manor. The acreage figures, where known, reflect this as does the structural quality of the house. In 1841 the acreage was 142 and it rose steadily to 200 in 1881 although it dropped back slightly in 1871 to 179. Before it was broken up it had reached over 202.

It seems likely that farming was geared to cheese production when that industry was at its height. The provision of a hoist in the attic has been noted and Market Drayton had its own Cheese Fair. An echo occurs in the 1861 census when Anne Jones, a 17-year old living-in servant at Ridgwardine Manor is described as a 'vessel cleaner'. A 'vessel maid' is a dairy-maid and the term is still used in the once great cheesemaking area of north Shropshire and south Cheshire.[23]

Gazetteer of other properties

The following brief descriptions are of properties which, for various reasons, were not fully recorded but which contain details of architectural interest. In addition to Whitchurch Rural, properties in this section lie in other parishes in north Shropshire whose boundaries adjoin Whitchurch. Some buildings may be included in future recording programmes. It is not a comprehensive survey, and while all the properties have been seen by the author, some have been noted only from the outside; the degree of inspection will be clear from the description.

Whitchurch Rural

Ash Hall[1] (SJ 580403)

Apart from the emphasis on the central bay which includes a central pediment and two giant pilasters with Corinthian capitals, this house is very similar to the town house of the Newport family, Earls of Bradford, in Dogpole, Shrewsbury, and is probably of a similar date, late 17th or early 18th century. Each is built of Flemish-bonded brickwork, two-stories high and five bays wide, with a symmetrical front, a hipped roof, an overhanging eaves cornice, sash windows with flush frames, quoins and a plat-band. At Ash Hall the dressings are of Grinshill-stone, whereas at the Guildhall they are of raised brick. But the rear elevation at Ash Hall is unlike the front. Here, although the quoins continue round the corners, the roof is not hipped but is abruptly terminated to form a half gable which contains windows lighting the roof space. A tall recessed archway occupies the

Ash Hall

centre of the elevation and functions as the conjunction between the main block and a modest two-bayed two-storied unit which has a much lower roofline and was probably used as a service block. It is possible that this represents an earlier house on the site and that the classical 18th century structure was grafted onto it. Interior inspection was not possible. Traditionally, Ash Hall has family connections with Benyon's 18th century flax mill in Ditherington, Shrewsbury, the world's first iron-framed building, and with the Fergusson family from whom is descended the present Duchess of York.

Ash Grove, Ash (SJ 565403)
Three-bayed, three-storied with end chimneys and a central entrance, Ash Grove has a very symmetrical appearance, but this is the result of the addition of a Regency unit to an earlier house, creating the double-pile plan-form that it has at present. Even the Regency frontage was altered in Victorian times to provide two bay windows and an entrance porch at ground level, and a balcony above. In all, five different building periods can be identified in Ash Grove. The roof trusses in the Regency unit are of the indus-trial king-post type, in wood, and

Ash Grove (now the Lady Lambert Nursing Home)

without the later refinement of the adjustable screw at the junction of the king-post and the tie-beam. The date of 1678 appears on a stone tablet between the two units, and this could date the oldest part of the house which is contained within the rear unit. Here the ground floor room has ovolo-moulded spine-beams with cyma stops, very similar to those seen at 38 High Street, Whitchurch. To the north of the house is a fine 18th century stable-block.

Wren's Nest, Ash Parva (SJ 580403)
Basically, this is a small box-framed cottage, one-and-a-half stories high and two bays wide, originally with only one of the bays heated. Formerly called 'Church Cottage', it has recently been enlarged by an extension which contains three dormer windows and a veranda. The window in the gable roof gave access to the upper floor of a

The Wren's Nest

shippon, enabling the cattle to be fed from above without the farmer having to leave the house. This arrangement has been noticed in other Shropshire farms.[2] All the timbering on the exterior is fake and has been carried out using the same technique that was noted in the houses in Dodington.

Ightfield Parish

The Gables (SJ 594386)

A box-framed T-shaped farmhouse on the Cloverley estate. Square-framed throughout, the plan appears to be that of hall-and-service range and a parlour crosswing. The hall range is one-and-a-half storied, but has a large added dormer-gable at the service end which dwarfs the other dormer window over the hall or house-place. Such is the emphasis on 'black-and-white' that the outbuilt brick chimneystack has mock timbering painted on. At the rear there is an additional service wing which has a flight of steps giving access to what was probably the mens' room, known in Cheshire as the 'shant' from which the term 'shanty town' is thought to be derived. Adjoining is a converted ginny-ring.

The Gables

Barn at Ightfield Hall

Basically square-framed but incorporating some re-used cruck trusses, this is a long six-bayed building which may have served more than one farm. It measures approximately 78ft. x 26ft. The two end bays are derelict. It dates to the mid-to-late 16th century and is similar to one standing in the grounds of Hodnet Hall.

Barn at Ightfield Hall, dendro dated 1567

Prees Village

1 Shrewsbury Street

Situated at the crossroads in Prees, on the corner of Shrewsbury Street and Church Street, no. 1 is a box-framed, two-storied and double-celled house which has a two-storied timber-framed projecting porch. There is a central chimney-stack which, in conjunction with the porch entrance, creates a lobby-entry plan. The ground-floor timbers have been obscured, and what appears to be a shop window has been added to the room on the north side of the porch. The square-framing is original, but that on a rear wing is painted on. Some of the windows have 'Yorkshire'-type sashes, that is, they slide horizontally.

2 Shrewsbury Street

This property is immediately opposite no. 1 (above), and occupies the corner of Shrewsbury Street and Mill Street. It is box-framed, one-and-a-half storied, three-bayed and with three dormer windows, but timber-framing is only visible on the gable elevation to Mill Street. The remainder has been brick-skimmed. It appears to have a lobby-entry plan.

Tudor House, Whitchurch Road

The overall H-shape is the result of the addition of a brick built unit to the southern side of a hall-and-cross-wing house which is timber-framed and appears to date from the 17th century. Both the hall and the cross-wing are two-storied and two-bayed,

1 Shrewsbury Street

2 Shrewsbury Street

Tudor House

242

and the original framing is square-panelled. The added unit has Flemish bond brickwork and quoins, and its roof is hipped on all four sides, but mock-timbering is painted on to give cohesion to the H-plan. An old sketch made in 1900 shows that it may be another example of the lobby-entry plan, but the stack is no longer visible from the outside.

Shirley House and Devonshire House

Shirley House and Devonshire House, Whitchurch Road

This block is entirely different from the timber-framed genre encountered in Prees. It consists of one double-fronted and one single-fronted house, each of three stories. An integral rear unit results in a double-pile plan, the M-shaped gable ends clearly indicative of the builder's intention. Though obviously brick built, there is rusticated stonework to the ground floor, and at present the upper stories are roughcast. The bay windows on the larger house are probably additions, and the northern ground floor window has also been altered, but both door cases are original and are identical in form. The houses probably date from *c.*1840, and are quite stylish.

The Cottage, Church Street

The term 'cottage' is a little misleading. Though box-framed and 17th century in origin, it has had several additions and many alterations, resulting in a spacious and elegant house. Though plastered over, there is the suggestion of a hewn jetty on the front, and the oldest part has an end lobby-entry plan. It was known as the 'Dowager Cottage' at one time, the Hill family being lords of the manor of Prees. Certainly it was the home of Miss Harriet Hill *c.*1841.

The Cottage, Church Street

Prees Parish

Hazlewood Farm, Darliston
(SJ 580335)

A T-shaped farmhouse, at present entirely roughcast, though clearly the hall unit is timber-framed and jettied. Exposed at jetty level is a recessed plaque with the date 1655 and the initials T+C. These are contained in a shield which is flanked by two symbolic dragons with protruding arrow-shaped tongues, very similar to those which adorn the frieze in a panelled room at Boreatton Hall in Baschurch parish. That house is dated 1675. In 1987 some of the roughcast fell away from the gable wall, revealing a carved bressumer with dragons or dolphins, a hewn jetty which had carved decoration, and some star panelling in the upper storey. Clearly the hall unit has a very decorative frame, now concealed.

Top: Hazlewood Farm, with (below) the recessed plaque

The internal beams have ovolo moulding, and the whole scheme appears to relate to the 1655 date. The crosswing is of two-and-a-half stories, although the roof lines of both units are at roughly the same height. It appears to be an addition, possibly of the 18th century, replacing an earlier unit.

The Old Post Office, Darliston
(SJ 582334)

Also known as 'Cooper's Cottages' and as 'Bainton Cottages', this is basically a box framed T-shaped house, one-and-a-half-storied throughout. The stem of the T accommodates a long two-bayed house-place which has square framing, three

The Old Post Office, Darliston

panels high. The crosswing appears to be a slightly later addition, perhaps of 1648 which is the date carved on the mantel-beam. The date is followed by the initials S.D. On the crosswing there is a mixture of close-studding and herringbone work, and it has a hewn jetty. Documents relating to the house refer to cheese production on a large scale.

Sandford Hall (SJ 582343)

The present house represents a replacement for a timber-framed house which is thought to have survived until 1772, but on a different site. Though not grand, it is not vernacular, as befits a Shropshire family with a pedigree going back to Norman times and including many titled members.

Sandford Hall (above) with the game larder (below)

Brick built of two stories, it has a five-bayed frontage with two dormer windows, stone quoins and a central projecting three-storied bay which contains the entrance door. This bay is emphasised with its own quoins and a semi-circular pediment to its uppermost window. The bricks are bright red and set in Flemish bond. It has a hipped roof with an overhanging eaves cornice. The windows are flat-headed and have keystones; and dividing the stories is a stone string-course. There are some Regency features, some affecting the ground-floor windows, but the glazing is all of the four-paned Victorian type.

To the right is an added wing which appears to be of Regency date. It has an elaborate dormer window and the date 1689, but this date is more likely to refer to the main block. Another Regency addition is the porch on the left gable wall of the main block. Here an extra line of quoins gives emphasis to the entrance.

As at Ash Hall comparison may be made with the town house of the Newport family, now known as the Guildhall in Dogpole, Shrewsbury. The date is also similar, if the 1689 date at Sandford can be relied upon.

In the extensive grounds is an octagonal game larder which incorporates a dovecote on the top floor. Brick-built, the structure has been re-faced with cement work which is finished to resemble weathered timbers—a practice frequently noted in north Shropshire. The restoration was done in 1930 by 'L.G.S.' according to the inscription. Internally there are two distinct floor levels below the doves' housing which have no evidence of nesting boxes. The birds were confined to the top section which has dormer windows as well as a central cupola or 'glover' for entrance.

Keeper's Cottage, Sandford (SJ 582341)

Formerly part of the Sandford estate, the cottage was originally a single-cell dwelling of box-frame construction, dating from *c.*1620. It was later enlarged to two stories and given an inserted floor. Later still it was extended to create a two-up, two-down cottage and given a pretty single-storied porch. Externally it has the appearance of being entirely brick-built, but a straight-joint in the brickwork is in line with the surviving framed truss which was originally the outer wall of the single-cell. A cellar was added at some time, and this has resulted in curious internal floor levels.

The Moat Farm, Fauls Green

The Moat Farm, Fauls Green (SJ 587327)

An interesting complex, The Moat Farm is basically L-shaped, but a very large dormer window is under-pinned in brickwork to provide the entrance and to create the impression of a crosswing. To the west of the entrance door the wall displays uninterrupted vertical studding, and this area is single-storied with a low eaves level and a raking roof-line. These details suggest a late 16th century small single-bayed open hall. The flanking crosswing to the west appears to be a 17th century box-framed addition, providing a parlour, a dairy and one other room. 18th century additions have been made to the south-east, and over the rear door is a terra-cotta datestone with the inscription 'H.R.S. 1702'.

Wem Parish

Aston Bridge Farm (SJ 529286)
Though much altered and modernised, there are suggestions that this farmhouse was originally a cruck-trussed longhouse. The internal cruck frame has an infil of peat blocks, cut to the size of the average brick. Peat blocks were also noted in the walls. The parlour has a Grinshill stone fireplace with classical moulding and stops.

Aston Bridge Farm, Wem

Aston House Farm
(SJ 531286)
Most of the external framing appears to be a replacement of the original square-framed carpentry. This gives the house the impression of being a sham, which is a pity because it is a good example of early 17th century planning when the fully-developed H-plan was brought up to date by the inclusion of a two-storied hall with a central entrance. Only the disposition of the chimneystacks detracts from a symmetrical appearance. The house is two-storied throughout, the eaves level is continuous, and both

Aston House Farm

wings are jettied towards the front. Internally the parlour wing contains a panelled great chamber at first floor level with a small ante-room behind it. The service wing contains servants' accommodation. The stairs for the service wing are accommodated in a block outside the north-west corner of the hall, but those for the parlour wing rise from the hall. Further emphasis is given to the parlour wing by the provision of a large stone-built chimneystack, while the hall may have been unheated at first. It now has a brick-built stack. Aston House Farm illustrates clearly a stage in the decline of the hall within the concept of the English pattern of living.

Soulton Hall

(SJ 544303)

A gentry house of double-pile plan-form, Soulton Hall is brick-built in English bond and with Grinshill stone dressings. It is three-bayed, fully three-storied, has a symmetrical form and is dated 1668. There is an elaborate entrance porch with fluted Roman Doric columns and a metope frieze. The over-sized pediment was necessary in order to accommodate the Hill family crest and the date. The windows are stone-mullioned-and-transomed. It has a flat roof which gives a cubic appearance to the house, but there is no evidence that it was ever gabled, and the drainage system is very efficient. Internally there are timber-framed partition walls, and it is possible that an earlier house may be encapsulated. There is no formal entrance hall, entrance is into a passage.

Top: Stoulton Hall with (lower) detail of doorhead and pediment

Wem Rural

The Bull and Dog Inn, Coton
(SJ 528344)

The building has been much altered, but it has a pleasant timber-framed single-storied porch which reaches to eaves level. This has its own pitched roof, turned balusters at the front and sides, and is fitted with seats.

The Bull and Dog Inn

Avenue Cottage, Coton
(SJ 528343)

Two distinct units, each two-bayed and two-storied make up this house. The end chimney on the unit which has the lower roof-line has twin brick shafts of circular form. They are probably 19th century in date, but their unusual design is a striking feature of the house.

Avenue Cottage, Coton

Whixall Parish

Gander's Bank (SJ 525341)

The cottage is box-framed, square-panelled, and has been raised from a single-storey dwelling to one-and-a-half stories. Two dormer windows have been inserted above the original wall-plate. The present entrance appears to be a later alteration; the original end-baffle entry has been filled in, leaving the suggestion of a timber-framed fire-hood against the end wall. The barn which adjoins the property at the opposite end may be an original feature.

Gander's Bank, Whixall

15 Waterloo (SJ 502328)

A brick-built canalside cottage of one-and-a-half bays with an end chimney; single-storied, but with full use made of the roof-space. Though small, and with random-bond brickwork, the cottage has a certain style. This is because the gable walls extend beyond the roof and are finished with coping-stones and moulded kneelers. There is also a dentil-course, and brick arches over the windows and door.

15 Waterloo

250

Modern Whitchurch

Whitchurch proclaims itself an 'Historic Market Town'. To those who know it well this is modesty indeed. But three by-passes, the first in 1874, the extension to this in 1924 and the latest and most ambitious in 1992 have ensured that travellers literally pass it by. Only the residents or those with a specific reason to visit Whitchurch are at all familiar with the town. Like many other small English towns in the late 20th century, its character has changed and because of the current pattern of employment it may be described as a 'commuter' town. But it is more than that. It has an ambience which is friendly and relaxing, pressures are few, the facilities available are quite remarkable, car parking is free and people who move to Whitchurch perhaps because of work are soon aware of the community spirit which pertains—and very few choose to retire elsewhere.

Barclay's Bank, in the building that was the town hall in 1718

At the last census (1991) the return was 8,466. Whitchurch is strategically placed mid-way between Chester to the north and Shrewsbury to the south, and between Crewe to the east and Wrexham to the west. The new town of Telford is also easily accessible. Each of those centres is larger and has more to offer in many ways, and therefore it is not surprising that Whitchurch has become a dormitory town. What is surprising is the range of services that it retains. In administrative terms its has a Town Council and still retains a magistrates' court which meets in the Civic Centre on Mondays and even has a single cell for the detention of persons awaiting a court hearing. This cell opens directly into the court-room.

The Civic Centre in the High Street was built in 1970 to replace the old Town Hall, built in 1874, which had suffered a fire in 1941, although the ground floor had continued in use. The 'Civic' as it is colloquially known, serves the community well. In addition to housing the

The 'Civic'

magistrates' court, it has a theatre which can seat up to 500 people, and two multi-purpose rooms, one called the Edward German Room and the other, the Merrie England Room. The latter has a licensed bar and a kitchen. Sir Edward German (1862-1936), originally German Edward Jones, was born and educated in Whitchurch and went on to become a famous composer, although sadly his work is neglected today. He is probably best known for his light operas 'Merrie England' and 'Tom Jones'. Whitchurch is conscious of the honour and certainly makes more of him than Shrewsbury does of its more famous son, Charles Darwin. Another name commemorated in Whitchurch is that of Randolph Caldecott (1846-1886), the author and illustrator of childrens' books who earned the soubriquet 'Lord of the Nursery'. Although not a native of Whitchurch he worked in the town as a bank clerk and insurance agent. The town library, adjoining the 'Civic' is called the Caldecott Library in his memory and both he and Edward German have special sections devoted to them in the new Heritage Centre in St. Mary's Street.

The old Town Hall Vaults,
birthplace of Sir Edward German

Behind the library is a large covered area where various activities can take place and where the weekly market is held on Fridays. This is so popular that it spills over into the passageway that runs between the two main blocks. Whitchurch is at the centre of rich pasture land, renowned for the production of Cheshire cheese and the once great cheese fairs, held every three weeks, attracted factors from a very wide area. There are still a few cheesemakers in Whitchurch although the industry is but a shadow of its former self and the cheese fairs are no more. But many people would still not think of buying cheese other than in Whitchurch market.

In addition to the 'Civic' there is a Leisure Centre at the Sir John Talbot School's campus which includes a small theatre complex and has an all-weather sports pitch. Golfers are catered for admirably at the Hill Valley Club, and other sports including rugby, cricket, soccer (Whitchurch Alport), hockey, bowling, archery, swimming, tennis and badminton all have flourishing clubs. Hunting enthusiasts have a choice between the North Shropshire, the Sir Watkin Williams Wynn and the Cheshire Hunt. There is an 'Operatic and Dramatic Society' and a 'Little Theatre Group' which stage productions at regular intervals. There is no longer a cinema as such, but the 'Civic' has projection facil-

ities and sometimes films are shown there. The local male voice choir and the 'Festival Chorus' also flourish, as does the town band. There is a photographic society, Rotary and Inner Wheel clubs, Round Table and Ladies' Circle, a '41 club' and a Tangent Club. Every August Bank Holiday Monday the town stages a carnival which seems to epitomise the community spirit.

The parish church of St. Alkmund's domi-nates the High Street, crowning the summit of the hill. By any standards it is a beautiful building, inside and out, and has a history stretching back over nearly a thousand years. The church supports a Mothers' Union and a Ladies' Fellowship. Other active churches in the town include the St. John's Methodist, the United Reformed, St. George's Roman Catholic and the Evangelical churches. There were other non-conformist churches at one time, but these have closed, and a chapel-of-ease, St. Catherine's in Dodington, a fine building of 1836 is a building at risk at present.

The High Street looking north towards
St. Alkmund's Church

There are two blocks of almshouses. One set was built in Dodington in 1829 by Elizabeth Langford for the use of four poor widows, and the other in Bargates. These were founded in 1647 for 'six decayed housekeepers', but the dwellings were reconstructed on the same site in 1807. Both are administered by the Higginson Trust, a combination of local charities. To qualify for an almshouse a person has to be resident in the parish.

Whitchurch is not an isolated community. Although the town bus service is minimal, there is a daily service to Shrewsbury and to Chester, and weekly on market days to Market Drayton and to Wrexham. Although many rail services have been axed, the station still operates and provides a two-hourly service to Shrewsbury and to Crewe. Once a day a train runs to Cardiff and another to Manchester.

Health matters are looked after by three medical practices and there is a local commu-nity hospital which was created out of the old Deermoss workhouse. Here there are three modern wards, one for G.P. care, one for geriatric care and one for psychiatric care. There are X-ray facilities and a small Accident and Emergency unit. The hospital actually serves a large surrounding area, with places like Shrewsbury sending patients for convalescence. There is no operating theatre; consultations and operations are usually referred to

Shrewsbury, Gobowen or to Telford. In addition to the hospital and on the same site is the Bradbury centre for the elderly and infirm to receive day care. Here there is a hydrotherapy pool and physiotherapy facilities. Another centre for care of the elderly and disabled is the 'Brownlow' in Claypit Street which was created from a former C of E school.

Education is catered for by the Sir John Talbot Comprehensive which takes 11-18-year

The Heritage Centre in St. Mary's Street

olds, the Whitchurch C of E Junior (7-11), the Whitchurch C of E Infants and Nursery (4-7) and there are several play groups. There is also a private primary school which takes 4-11-year olds. Further Education is provided by a branch of the North Shropshire College which is a tertiary college based at Oswestry but with a department at the Talbot Campus at the Sir John Talbot School. North Shropshire District Council runs evening classes, also at the Sir John Talbot School. Keele University provides a programme of extramural classes and the Whitchurch History and Archaeology Group, founded in 1977, puts on a programme of lectures and field trips and produces a regular newsletter.

Whitchurch lost its museum some years ago, and sadly, with it some of the exhibits, though many were stored in Shrewsbury. But a welcome development in 1998 was the conversion of the old Post Office in St. Mary's Street to a Heritage Centre which includes a Tourist Information Centre. Here there are displays relating to the history of the area, audio-visual presentations, books and leaflets for sale and travelling exhibitions. Supporting the Heritage Centre is a group of 'Friends' who campaigned strongly for its inauguration.

The Jubilee Park, covering 11 acres on the western side of the town provides a welcome open space and it has a bandstand, and an adventure playground for children. The park was opened in 1887, the year of Queen Victoria's Golden Jubilee. To commemorate her Diamond Jubilee 60 lime trees were planted to form the Avenue approach.

A branch of the Shropshire Union Canal once served Whitchurch. There were wharves and warehouses and pleasant walks could be taken along the towpath. But the canal was closed in 1944, much of it filled in during the 1950s and houses built on the site. Recently, however, a short stretch of a quarter of a mile has been reopened, is water-filled once more and is proving a great attraction.

Like many once self-contained communities Whitchurch has lost much of its local industry and no longer has a Smithfield, or livestock, market. The main employers, W.H. Smith and Co., ironfounders and engineers, closed in 1983, their products once having been sold all over the world. But the clockmaking firm of Joyce, though now merged with

Joyce's clock works in Station Road

John Smith of Derby, continues in business. The firm was founded in 1690 and Joyce's clocks are world famous. The oldest working one is thought to be that made for St. Catherine's church in Whitchurch in 1836. The parish church has one of the finest tower clocks in the country, and in the Heritage Centre can be seen the pattern for the firm's largest clock. This was made for the Customs House in Shanghai.

However, Whitchurch has a modern Industrial Estate which supports furniture making, other light industries such as the making of candles and rocking-horses, and several food processing plants. It also retains its long-established weekly newspaper, the *Whitchurch Herald* in Castle Hill which also provides a printing service.

The town is well served for shopping and banking and has a chamber of trade anxious to promote local enterprise. Two supermarkets and a surprising number of chain stores operate successfully, and there is a pleasing range of small specialist shops, including two long-established butchers who have an excellent reputation. About 15 public houses are available, but residential hotels are limited. Conference facilities are available at a centre about five miles away. There are a number of attractive cafés and other eating places, the old-established 'Walker's' in the High Street being a case study in this book. Many of the small shops still observe the traditional half-day closing on Wednesdays, as does the library.

Recently the town underwent a 'Street Improvement' programme which included making the High Street and Green End one-way, resurfacing and narrowing the carriageways, pedestrianising the Bull Ring and installing a Joyce clock there. While undoubtedly the town now looks better than it has done for about 20 years, the changes have resulted in traffic congestion when vehicles are unloading as they block the carriageways completely. But this seems to be the price paid for a resurgence of civic pride and few would disagree that Whitchurch is improved.

The Joyce clock in The Bull Ring

The National Westminster Bank
with its 'pseudo-framing'

Most communities can name their own public benefactors and Whitchurch is no exception. A former Rector of Whitchurch, Sir John Talbot, founded the Grammar School in 1550 as a free school for boys, although this has since become comprehensive. (See the report on Alkington Hall for the Cotton connection). His tomb is in the parish church. E.P. Thompson, a Liverpool banker who built and lived in the house called 'Paul's Moss' in Dodington was extremely generous, giving to the town its free library, reading room, art gallery and museum, and providing equipment in the Jubilee Park. More recently Harry Richards of 'Salopia', a coach-hire firm, later absorbed by a national company, left money to be used at the discretion of his trustees for local projects. He died in 1979 and has a memorial garden in the park. The Bridgwater and Brownlow families as lords of the manor in earlier times were also concerned with the town, and there have been other local benefactors.

The buildings described in this book represent only a selection of the older housing stock. Dodington is always singled out for praise of its eighteenth century structures and there is some good Georgian, Regency, Victorian and Edwardian housing particularly in Chester Road, Station Road and Edgeley Road. During the 1930s it seems that Whitchurch had a brief flirtation with the 'pseudo-framing' passion that had smitten Chester some years previously. The flirtation did not last long, but the National Westminster Bank in the High Street stands as an epigraph to the affair. It is a pity that the planning blight that descended on so many English towns in the 1950s and 60s when the removal of so-called unfit dwellings had priority affected Whitchurch so much, leaving great gaps in the streets, destroying building lines and often replacing traditional buildings with unsympathetic constructions. The 'slum' clearance programme has been savage. Starting in 1935, yards leading off the main streets were cleared, genuine timber-framed terraces were demolished and cruck buildings were flattened. It is true that hindsight is of dubious benefit, but the thought persists that many terraces and cottages could have been brought up to modern standards and that there was no need for such wholesale destruction.

Glossary

Arcade-plate:	Longitudinal timber set along the tops of arcade posts in an aisled building
Arris:	The line along which two timber surfaces meet
Bay:	The area between two main frames of a building, used as a unit of measurement, *e.g.* 'two-bay hall'
Blazon:	In heraldry the science or rules of coats-of-arms
Bolection moulding:	A moulding which projects beyond the surface of the panel, frame or feature
Box-frame:	Timber-framing in which posts and beams form a 'box' which supports the roof directly and in which the walls are integral. *cf.* 'Cruck'
Cadency mark:	In heraldry the emblem or symbol of younger sons
Chamfer:	The surface formed by cutting off a square edge, usually at 45°
Closed Truss:	A cross-frame in which the spaces between the timbers are filled, usually with wattle and daub. Openings may be left for doors and windows
Collar-beam:	A transverse timber connecting rafters or cruck blades at a point below the apex and above the tie-beam
Collar-purlin: only	The longitudinal timber supported by the crown-post. Often the lengthwise stiffening in crown-post roof construction. Sometimes called the 'collar-plate'
Cornice:	The uppermost member of the entablature, projecting above the frieze. The moulding running round a room at the junction of the walls and ceiling
Console:	A form of bracket with a uniform front width and S-shaped profile, the lower curve smaller than the upper
Copyhold:	In law, a right to hold land the title of which is taken from a copy of the manorial court roll. Virtually freehold
Court Baron:	Literally the Court of the Baron who was the tenant-in-chief; in Whitchurch this was the Earl of Bridgwater
Cross Passage:	Entry and exit through opposed doorways and with a wall or partition on the hall side. Sometimes 'Through Passage'
Crown-post:	The upright central timber standing on a tie-beam and supporting a crown-plate or collar-purlin. It does not rise to the apex and is usually braced four ways. Usually not associated with side purlins
Crow-stepped gable:	Where the stone or brick slopes of the gable are arranged in steps
Cruck:	A pair of inclined timbers, usually wrought from a single tree, forming an arch. The roof is supported on the back of the cruck 'blades' and the walls are independent. There are many variants. *cf.* 'box-frame'

Dendrochronology: The science of sampling and analysing timbers to determine the tree-ring growth pattern and thus arrive at the felling date which is virtually the building date

Dentil eaves moulding: Projecting bricks or stones at eaves level resembling teeth

Diaper work: In brickwork where vitrified headers are used to create a lozenge or diamond-shaped patterning

Double-pile form: Two parallel blocks with a common dividing wall. Can be roofed in various ways, but usually separately

Dragon-beam: Beam running diagonally across the ceiling to support jetties on two adjacent sides of an upper floor

Eared surround: The surround of a door or window where extensions at the head resemble squared ears. Sometimes 'lugged'. Popular in 18th century work

End baffle-entry: Where the entry faces the side of the internal end chimneystack

Entablature: In classical architecture the superstructure of an Order, consisting of architrave, frieze and cornice

Fan-light: The semi-circular window over a door. The glazing-bars are arranged in the shape of a fan. Popular in 18th century work

Finial: Upright ornament at the apex of roofs, pediments, gables, etc

Frieze: Any band of ornament or walling immediately below a cornice

Ginny-ring: Horse-engine house or wheelhouse; a round, square or polygonal building connected to a threshing barn, where power to drive the machinery was provided by horse(s) or oxen in circulatory movement

Girding beam: The horizontal beam in a framed wall, at the level of an upper floor

Guilloche: A classical ornamental form consisting of two or more intertwining bands of circles

Hood mould: A projecting moulding over the heads of arches. Sometimes used for dripstones over windows to deflect rainwater

Jetty: Cantilevered overhang of one storey above another. Jettying can take various forms. A 'hewn jetty' is formed by the expansion of the outer face of the wall post rising through two storeys. Gables can be jettied. Internal jetties occur when a first floor internal partition oversails the wall below

Jowelled feet: Where the feet of posts (as opposed to the heads) are thickened

King post: An upright timber standing in the centre of a tie-beam and rising to the apex of the roof

King strut: As above, but not rising to the apex

Kneeler: A short coping stone set horizontally at the foot of the gable slope to stop the coping stones on the slope from slipping down. Sometimes decorative

Mason's Mitre: In stonework where the horizontal member overlies the vertical, the mouldings meeting at the intersection. Different from a 'carpenter's mitre' where the joint is at an angle to both members

Metope:	Part of a classical frieze; the spaces between the triglyphs
Modillion:	Projecting rectangular brackets in the cornices of classical styles
Mullions:	The vertical members between the lights of a window. They may be moulded or of square section set diagonally
Notched-lap joint:	A joint fashioned to resist withdrawal by having a notch cut in one side. They take various forms
Ovolo moulding:	Moulding which has a egg-shaped profile, usually combined with a fillet when used in window mullions. The late 16th/17th century successor to the medieval quarter-round
Passing braces:	Long straight timbers usually running from the wall post and halved across other timbers to reach the opposite rafters
Pentice roof:	The lean-to roof over an adjoining subsidiary building
Pilaster:	A shallow pier-like rectangular column which is attached to a wall. Usually made of stone but Ruabon Pilasters are made from the bright red bricks produced at Ruabon in Denbighshire
Plank-and-Muntin:	A solid wood wall or partition made from upright timbers (muntins) into whose grooved sides planks of thinner scantling are slotted
Plat-band:	A band of projecting brick or stonework usually on the front of a building. Its function is two-fold; to hide the joist-ends and/or to give relief to an otherwise plain frontage
Purlin:	A lateral roof timber supporting the rafters. There are many types
Queen-posts:	Paired posts set on a tie-beam and supporting the purlins. May be straight or raking
Queen-struts:	As above, but supporting the collar-beam
Quoins:	Raised dressed stones or bricks at the corners of buildings. Used for effect
Rat-trap brickwork:	Where the bricks are laid on edge, saving on bricks, mortar and time. So called because the cavities so formed between the leaves resembled traps
Scantling:	The measured size or dimensions of a timber
Scarf-joint:	The joining together of two short timbers to make a longer one. The technique varies greatly
Shippon:	In Shropshire, a cow-house
Spere-Truss:	The fixed decorative truss at the low end of a hall, usually of aisled form. Access to the hall was through the 'nave' section. 'Spere' is old English for 'Screen'. It seems to have been a status symbol
Tie-beam:	The main transverse beam connecting opposite walls at wall-plate level. Applies to box-frames and crucks
Transom:	A horizontal member dividing an opening, usually a window
Triglyph:	A tablet or similar ornament with three grooves set at equal distances along a classical frieze
Vitrified header:	A 'header' is a brick laid end-on as opposed to 'stretcher'. A vitrified header is a brick which has been subjected to excess heat during firing, thus changing its colour and texture. Glass-like

Voussoir:	A wedge-shaped stone or brick forming part of an arch
Wall-plate:	The horizontal timber at the wall-head to which the roof trusses and rafters are fixed
Wealdon House:	Where the open hall and the two storied end bays are roofed in one plane. The hall is usually recessed, the ends jettied and the eaves continuous. Designs and sizes can vary.
Windbrace:	The brace in the plane of the roof usually connecting the principal rafter or cruck with the purlin. Usually paired. Can be straight, curved or cranked. Often decorative. Used to counteract the pressure of wind on the roof and to stiffen it
Witness mark:	Any residual mark giving evidence of a former feature

REFERENCES

Abbreviations used are as follows:

Archaeol. J.	Archaeological Journal
C.B.A.	Council for British Archaeology
C.R.O.	Cheshire Record Office
E.P.N.S.	English Place-name Society
H.M.S.O.	Her Majesty's Stationery Office
L.R.P.	Ludlow Research Papers
L.S.L.	Local Studies Library, Shrewsbury (Now part of the Shropshire Records and Research Centre)
O.S.	Ordnance Survey
O.U.P.	Oxford University Press
P.C.C.	Prerogative Court of Canterbury
P.R.O.	Public Records Office
R.C.A.H.M.	Royal Commission on Ancient and Historical Monuments in Wales
R.C.H.M.	Royal Commission on Historical Monuments (of England)
S.R.O.	Salop (Shropshire) Record Office (Now the Shropshire Records and Research Centre)
S.A.S.	Shropshire Archaeological Society (now Shropshire Archaeological and Historical Society)
S.R.R.C.	Shropshire Records and Research Centre
T.S.A.(H.)S.	Transactions of the Shropshire Archaeological and Historical Society
Vern. Arch.	Vernacular Architecture (Journal of the Vernacular Architecture Group)
V.C.H.	The Victoria History of the County of Shropshire
V.C.S.	The Victoria History of the County of Staffordshire
W.A.A.G.	Whitchurch Area Archaeological Group (Now Whitchurch History and Archaeology Group)

History

1. T.C. Duggan, *The History of Whitchurch, Shropshire,* Herald Press, (1935), 53
2. G. Webster, *The Cornovii,* Duckworth, (1975), 73,4
3. G.D.B. Jones & P.V. Webster, 'Mediolanum Excavations at Whitchurch', 1965-6, *Archaeol. J.*, Vol 125, (1969), 193-254
4. M. Gelling, *The Place-Names of Shropshire, Part I*, E.P.N.S., (1990) 310-11; R.W. Eyton, *The Antiquities of Shropshire,* (1856), Vol X, 14
5. E. Eckwall, *English Place-Names,* 4th Ed. Oxford (1960), 6, 160, 474, 14, 513
6. J. Morris (ed.), *Domesday Book (Shropshire),* Phillimore, (1968), 4,7,4
7. T.C. Duggan, *op.cit.,* 54
8. *Ibid,* 38
9. Bodleian, MS TOP Salop C2; S.R.O. M/F 2172, f. 523
10. R.W. Eyton, *op.cit.,* 15, 25
11. T.C. Duggan, *op.cit.,* 38
12. R.W. Eyton, *op.cit.,* 23

13. T.C. Duggan, *op.cit.*, 87

14. J.M. Barton, *Whitchurch to Castillon*, WAAG (1981), 4-19

15. L.S.L., M/F 43, E. Clarke, A History of Whitchurch Grammar School 1550-1950, unpub. M.A. Thesis, 19. A copy is held in the Caldecott Library, Whitchurch

16. *V.C.H.* (Shropshire) Vol IV (1989), 133

17. Calculated by Dr. P. Morgan, Keele Uni. Research class (1993)

18. R.B. James, *Old Inns of Whitchurch*, WAAG, (1984), 5

19. SRO 212/bundle 472. Photocopy is SRO 399/1

20. This event was paralleled at St. Chad's, Shrewsbury in 1788

21. H. Colvin, *A Biographical Dictionary of British Architects 1600-1840*, Murray, (1978), 88

22. L.S.L. G 32.6/4256, E. Hopkins, The Bridgewater Estates in North Shropshire in the first half of the the 17th century, unpub. M.A. Thesis, 1953. (Copy held in the Caldecott, Lib., Whitchurch)

23. L.S.L., M/F 97, A.J. Pollard, The Family of Talbot, Lords Talbot and Earls of Shrewsbury, unpub. Ph.D. Thesis, Bristol Uni.,(1968), 359; S.R.O. 2683, B. Ross, The Accounts of the Talbot Household at Blakemere 1394-1425, unpub. M.A. Thesis, Australian Nat. Uni., Canberra, (1970), Vol.2, 24, fn.I

24. N. Pevsner, *Buildings of England* (Shropshire), Penguin, (1958), 315

25. *V.C.H.* Shropshire, *op.cit.*, 151, *passim*

26. D.B. Barnard, *Transport in the Whitchurch Area*, part 2, WAAG (1985), 9

27. *Ibid*, 15

28. T.C. Duggan, *op. cit.*, 85,86,89

29. Census returns

30. R. Hughes, *Clock and Watchmakers in Whitchurch*, WAAG (1987), *passim*; WAAG (ed.) *Whitchurch Remembered*, Shropshire Libraries, (1980), 62, 64

31. K. Barnard, *Eminent Men of Whitchurch*, WAAG, (1982), *passim*

Whitchurch Castle & The Star Hotel

1. Gifford and Partners, Report on an Archaeological Excavation, Castle Hill, Whitchurch, 21st June 1993. Copies held by WAAG and the Town Council.

2. *ibid*, 7,8

3. S.R.O. 212/Box 80 (46), Account Roll for the manors of Blakemere and Dodington. We are grateful to Dr. P. Morgan for locating this document and to Dr. D. Cox for help with the translation. See also R.B. James, 'The Castle and Defence', cont., *WAAG Newsletter*, 43 (Jan. 1990), 6,7

4. E.W. Bowcock, *Shropshire Place-Names*, Wilding, (1923), 108

5. R.B. James, *op. cit.*

6. L.S.L. C64 ACC 278, The Rev. Mr Nightingale, *A Topographical and Historical Description of the County of Salop*, (1818), 283

7. Bodleian Lib. MS Top Salop C2; SRO 2172/2 M/F f 523

8. R.C.H.M.E., City of York, Vol II, *The Defences*, H.M.S.O. (1972), 137, pl. 43

9. SRO Box 427 102, Bridgewater Papers, Copyhold Surrenders

10. SRO Box 429 225, *ibid*; quoted by R.B. James, *Old Inns of Whitchurch*, WAAG (1984), 25

11. R.B. James, *ibid.*, 24, 25

12. We are grateful to Mrs J. Green for allowing inspection of the cellar at the Star Hotel

13. R. Hughes, *A Pavement Safari*, WAAG, (1993), 8,9,10

Cruck Construction in Whitchurch

1. M. Moran, 'A Terrace of Crucks at Much Wenlock, Shropshire', *Vern. Archit.* Vol 23 (1992), 10-14

The Use of Peat in Whitchurch Buildings

1. R. Millward and A. Robinson, *Landscapes of Britain: The Welsh Marches*, Macmillan (1971), 78-80

2. Grid Ref: SJ 529286

The Whitchurch Inventories

1. 21 Henry VIII, c 5, (1529)

2. L.S.L. qH 55.5 (2 Vols)

3. B. Trinder & J. Cox, *Yeomen and Colliers in Telford*, Phillimore, (1980)

4. Info, supplied by S. Watts

5. G.M. Trevelyan, *The Journeys of Celia Fiennes*, Cresset Press (1947), 226

6. R.B. James, *Old Inns of Whitchurch*, WAAG (1984), 7, 8, 18, 19

Dodington House

1. J. Morris (ed.) *Domesday Book*, Vol.25, Shropshire, Phillimore, (1986), 256b

2. N. Pevsner, *Buildings of England*, Shropshire, Penguin (1958), 315

3. ex. info. Dr. Mollie Mc Carter, the present owner. She and her late husband Dr. J.B. Mc Carter purchased the overmantel.

4. R.A.F. Reaumur, *The Art of Hatching and bringing up Domestick Fowls of all kinds at any time of the Year*, London, 1750, pl.15, pag.470, no.279 (translated by A.Trembley). I am grateful to Mary Perry for this reference.

5. W.A.A.G. Newletter No. 4 (1978), 10,11; J. Vince, *Fire-Marks*, Shire Album 2, (1973), 25

6. This section is compiled by Joan Barton and Madge Moran.

7. Deeds, *penes* Dr. Mollie McCarter.

8. *Whitchurch Remembered*, Shropshire Libraries, (1980), 33

9. ex. info. Dr. Mollie Mc.Carter.

10. The two main sources for the Henry family are: *The Diaries and Letters of Philip Henry M.A. of Broad Oak, Flintshire*, ed. by Matthew Henry Lee, M.A., vicar of Hanmer, London (1882) and Matthew Henry, *The Life of Philip Henry*, ed. by J.B. Wiliams, London, (1825)

11. C. Stell, *Nonconformist Chapels and Meeting-houses: Shropshire and Staffordshire*, R.C.H.M., (1986), 205; Also see text of 7, Dodington.

12. D. Jenkins, Newsletter 15, W.A.A.G. (1981), 5,6

13. T.C. Duggan, *History of Whitchurch*, 1935, 80; W. M'Reath, *Whitchurch Past & Present*, n.d., 39-40; A letter from Alexander Brown, son or grandson of Dr. Brown who practiced from Dodington House, dated Jan. 4th 1927: 'It is said that Bishop Heber

when he lived in Dodington used to stand in that window....scratched with a diamond on the glass is the name Heber...' (*penes* Mary Perry) There is no evidence at present of such an inscription.

14. L.S.L M/S 43, E. Clarke, *A History of Whitchurch Grammar School*, Sheffield Uni. M.A. thesis, 1953, 123-127

15. R.H. Cholmondeley, *The Heber Letters*, (1950), 77,78. We are grateful to Ms. P.R. Bennion, librarian at the Bishop Heber County High School, Malpas for this ref.

16. D. Hayns, Malpas History, no.8 (1987), 9

17. Heber correspondence in the collection of Mr. Algernon Heber-Percy of Hodnet Hall, 2nd. Feb.- 2nd. Oct. 1824. We are grateful to Marion Roberts for supplying this reference and to Mr. A. Heber-Percy for permission to quote from the correspondence.

18. S.R.O., 3091/3/10

19. Info. via Mary Perry. The Poor Law Relief returns are in a private collection.

20. Deeds, *penes* Dr. J.D. Mc Carter

23 & 25 Dodington (The Old Manor House)

1. J.Morris (ed.) *Domesday Book*, (Shropshire), Phillimore (1986), 4,7,4; T.C.Duggan, *History of Whitchurch*, (1935), 32

2. Census returns

3. Lithograph, *penes* Sylvia Eaton of Whitchurch.

4. R.W. Eyton, *Antiquities of Shropshire*, Vol 9, (1859), 194-5

5. The late G.G.J. Owen's notes, based on the recollections of Mrs Alice Whittingham, and supplied by his daughter, Mrs. Mary Perry, a member of the class.

Ellesmere House (28 Dodington)

1. *Eddowe's Journal*, 15th July 1818

2. *Kelly's Directories*, 1868, 1870-4, 1877

3. L.S.L. qH35, J.M. Barton, *Whitchurch Schools 1550-1950*, W.A.A.G., (1989), 41-47

4. *Kelly's Directories*; G.G.J. Owen, notes supplied by his daughter, Mrs Mary Perry, a member of the class. Mr Owen died in 1982.

The Mansion House, 21 Dodington

1. N.Pevsner, *Buildings of England (Shropshire)*, Penguin, (1958), 315

2. Photographs, W.A.A.G. collection; *Whitchurch Remembered*, Shropshire Libraries, (1979), 51

3. R.C.H.M. Report (1991), n.p.

4. *Whitchurch Remembered, op. cit.*, 62

5. The social history is complied by Joan Barton

6. *Salopian Journal*, 24th January 1798, n.p.

7. S.R.O. 4791

8. *Salopian Journal*, 28th March 1798, n.p.

9. C.C. Brookes, *Fontes Rivorum or The Springs of the Brookes*, Kingston Press, (1931), 37; See Dodington House report for the Henry background.

10. Census Return

11. Notes of the late G.G.J. Owen, *penes* Mary Perry
12. J.M. Barton, *Whitchurch Schools 1550-1950*, W.A.A.G., (1989), 41-2
13. Photograph, W.A.A.G. collection

7 Dodington (The Olde House)
1. Several examples of this practice have been noted in N. Shropshire and in Cheshire. The Old House (modern nomenclature) was treated for Walter Needham in the early 1950s. Ex. info. Mary Perry. See also report for 6 - 10 Dodington.
2. This section is compiled by Joan Barton, mainly from deeds *penes* Mark Vaughan, the present owner, who kindly allowed access.
3. R.F. Skinner, *Nonconformity in Shropshire, 1662 - 1816*, Shrewsbury, (1964), 19, fn. 101
4. See Dodington House report
5. *V.C.H. Vol. 2 (Shropshire)*, 1973, 10
6. L.S.L. H 64 996: G.E. Evans, *Whitchurch Long Ago*, Oswestry, (1893), 18
7. T.C. Duggan, *The History of Whitchurch*, (1935), 60-8
8. *Ibid*, 67-9; C. Stell, *Nonconformist Chapels and Meeting-Houses in Shropshire and Staffordshire*, R.C.H.M., (1986), 205-6

6, 8 and 10 Dodington
1. M.Moran, 'A Terrace of Crucks at Much Wenlock, Shropshire', *Vern. Arch.*, Vol 23, (1992), 10-14
2. N.W. Alcock, *Cruck Construction, An Introduction and Catalogue*, C.B.A. Research Report, 44, (1981), 96
3. It is known that nos. 8 & 10 Dodington were treated in the early 1950s. See also report on no. 7 Dodington (The Olde House)

Barkhill House
1. L. Wright, *Clean and Decent*, Rout. & Kegan Paul, (1960), *passim*
2. This section is compiled by Joan Barton.
3. See chapter on The Mansion House. The Parish Register records the marriage of William Turton and Elizabeth Bulkeley on 14th January 1760. (Parish Rgisters)
4. R.B. James, *Old Inns of Whitchurch*, W.A.A.G., (1984), 26,27
5. Mrs Clay Finch, *Old Whitchurch*, Herald Press, (1920), 7, (quoted in J.M. Barton, French Prisoners of War, *W.A.A.G.* Newsletter, 23 (1983), 4,5
6. H. Temperton, *A History of Craft Freemasonry in Shropshire*, Bewdley Press, (1981), 22; see also J.M. Barton, *supra*
7. Info. from Mrs. Elma Howells, daughter of Percy Williams.
8. Report in the *Whitchurch Herald*, 16th Dec. 1927
9. Info. from Felicity Rogerson.
10. Mr. M. Rogerson, the present owner, has childhood recollections of playing in the orchard.
11. L.S.L. M/S 2358, John Knight's Account books. He probably built and lived in Cherwell House on the corner of Dodington and Rosemary Lane. The Barkhill gardens & those of Cherwell House would adjoin.

12. See report & drawings of Dodington House for a similar mark.
13. A.B. Wyon, *The Great Seals of England*, (1887), 120-1; 105; Pl. XLVI. *Boutell's Heraldry*, Warne, (1950), rev. by J.P. Brooke-Little, 1983, 215, Pl. V. We are grateful to A.C. James of the Soc. of Antiquaries' Library, Dr. D. Cox of the Shropshire V.C.H and Roger Knowles for their help.

17 - 23 Watergate

1. Thanks are extended to A.J. Minshall Ltd. for permission to examine and record 17 and 19, and to the occupiers of 21 and 23 (The Flower Bower and Richards') for permission to include their properties in the survey.
2. *eg.* 41-45, High Street. Until recently the shopping arcade opposite 17-23 Watergate was similarly treated.
3. *eg.* 6-10 Dodington.
4. Pat Gates was responsible for the paintings. She was assisted by Barbara Latham and Richard Hughes. Stencilled decoration was recorded at 60 High Street.
5. *Buildings at Risk in North Shropshire*, N. Shrops. District Council, 1995, n.p.; *Vernacular Architecture*, Vol. 28 (1997), 168, 170
6. M. Toussaint-Samat, *The History of Food*, Blackwall, (1993) 504: 'The English word 'clove' comes from 'clou'; in full the French expression was 'clou de girofle' and in English the spice was originally called 'clove gillyflower'. This full name was then reserved for the clove-scented pink, sometimes further corrupted to 'July flower'... it was widely used in medieval cookery and administered medicinally as a 'panacea ... against plague, impotence and catarrh'; T. Beck, *The Embroiderers' Flowers*, David and Charles (1992), 34, a garden knot design similar to the border on the wall-painting at 17-19 Watergate; a book cushion of *c.*1600 includes a similar flower, 35; 'both carnations and pinks were known as "gillyflowers" in John Parkinson's day (1629),... emblemistic of love and affection.' In Henry Lyte's 'A Nievve Herbal' of 1578 he refers to the flower as 'the clove gillofer', 149
7. W.A. Pantin, 'Medieval Inns', *Studies in Building History*, ed. E.M. Jope, Odhams, (1961) 187
8. P. Smith, *Houses of the Welsh Countryside*, HMSO, 2nd ed. (1988), 662-3
9. *VCH (Shropshire)*, Vol XI (1985), 260; L.S.L. C71 vf, R. Salmon, *Shropshire's Building Heritage* (1984), 17; For an account of Ash Wood see pp.151-62
10. W.A. Pantin, *op cit.*, 182-3, fig 9.6
11. This section is compiled by Joan Barton and Madge Moran. We are grateful to Sylvia Watts for her help with the Inventory and to Messrs A.J. Minshall for permission to examine the deeds of of 17-19. A comprehensive file on the documented history of the Raven is held by WAAG. Extracts only are quoted.
12. Deed dated 24th December 1921, *penes* A.J. Minshall Ltd
13. SRO Box 108, John Eddows, Survey of the Manor of Whitchurch, 1667
14. SRO Box 230, Bridgwater Papers
15. M. Toussaint-Samat, *op cit.*, 572; E. Smith, *The Compleat Housewife*, 1st. ed., 1729, facs. 1968, Literary Services and Productions Ltd., *passim*
16. Pers. comm. R. Cooke; L.P. Coyle, *The World Encyclopedia of Food*, Pinter, (1982), 546

17. SRO Bridgwater Papers, box 431

18. *ibid*, box 327

19. *Universal British Directory*, 1790

20. SRO Bridgwater Papers, box 432

21. *Salopian Journal*, 9th December 1835

22. LSL DP/416 QE/7/1. The tracing of the Whitchurch section is held by WAAG

23. *Whitchurch Herald*, 18th March 1875

24. Letter from Noel Newbrook, grandson of John Newbrook, *penes* WAAG

25. Pers. comm. George Ashley

26. Pers. comm. Joan Barton

27. Deeds, *penes* A.J. Minshall Ltd. See note 12

28. as note 24

29. S. Watts, Whitchurch Probate Inventories, 1535-1650, LSL, qL 55.5 np. Vol I

38 Watergate

1. M.Moran, The Old Shop, Somerwood, *T.S.A.S.*, Vol. LXIV (1985), 69-75

2. A restored example, 'Llanfadyn', may be seen at the National Museum of Wales, St. Fagan's, near Cardiff

3. Similar infilling has been noticed in a number of Whitchurch houses.

4. N.J. Baker, 'Further Work on Pride Hill, Shrewsbury', *T.S.A.H.S.*, Vol. 68, (1993), 43-52

5. This section is compiled by Joan Barton and Richard Hughes

6. Info. from the present owner, Mrs C. Themaris

7. Census returns

8. W.A.A.G. Collection

9. Census returns

10. *Kelly's Directories*

11. Info. from Jack Wilkinson, now (1993) aged 88

21 - 23 High Street ('Walker's')

1. There are witness marks for another on the front of 'Reynald's Mansion' in High Street, Much Wenlock.

2. The painting is by Eva Layton and hangs in the Caldicott Library, Whitchurch.

3. This section is compiled by J.M. Barton.

4. L.S.L. qH 55.5, *Sylvia Watts, Whitchurch Probate Inventories, 1535 - 1650*, Vol 1, n.p.

5. *Ibid*

6. S.R.O. Box 428, no. 276, Bridgwater Papers; facsimile in R.B. James, *Old Inns of Whitchurch*, W.A.A.G., (1984), 22

7. S.R.O., The Bridgwater Papers, Copyhold surrenders and Admissions, 1633 - 1815. R.B. James' transcriptions of these are held by W.A.A.G.

8. S.R.O. 4791, Salop Fire Office Records; D.B. & K. Barnard, 'Firemarks', *W.A.A.G. Newsletter no. 4* (1978), 10-11; The Salop Fire Office plate is on no. 21 (Policy no. 5701) and the Sun Insurance plate is on no. 23 (Policy no. 455405)

9. *Salopian Journal*, March 17th 1819, n.p.

10. *Shropshire Directories*

11. Parish Registers
12. Census Returns, 1861, 1871
13. *ibid*
14. *Shropshire Directories*
15. R.B. James, *Shops and Shopkeepers*, Part 1, W.A.A.G.(1988), 17

34 - 42 High Street
1. SRO 212/Box 418 has a plan and elevation of the property, with house-place, parlour, brewhouse, shops etc. labelled
2. R. Hughes, *A Pavement Safari*, W.A.A.G. (1993), 23,24; *Whitchurch Remembered*, W.A.A.G., Shropshire Libraries,(1980), 14

35 & 37 High Street
1. R.B. James, *Old Inns of Whitchurch*, W.A.A.G. (1984), 17; info. from Mr Howells

60 High Street
1. We are grateful to Nick Joyce for info. on the Friar Street painting. The conservators were the Perry Lithgow partnership and Stephen Calloway and Michael Snodin of the V.& A. gave advice. See N. Joyce, 'Sophisticated Stencils', *Old House Journal*, Feb. 1992, 58-62
2. Sampling and analysis was carried out by D. Miles
3. This section is compiled by J. Barton
4. *Pigot's Directories*, 1823, 1828/9
5. R.B. James, *Shops and Shopkeepers of Whitchurch*, Part I (1988), 2, 12-14
6. *ibid*
7. *ibid*, 14; *Kelly's Directory* 1909; Photograph in WAAG collection
8. Info. from Rod and Janet Forster

High Street Garage & 2 Bargates
1. *Whitchurch Remembered*, Shropshire Libraries pub., (1979), 3
2. C.A. Hewett, *The Development of Carpentry 1200-1700*, David and Charles, (1969), 196
3. *eg.* at 38 Watergate, Whitchurch. (see report)
4. *egs.* at Padmore in Onibury parish (dem. see *Archaeol.J.*, 142, (1958), 340-360); Riggs Hall, Shrewsbury (see *T.S.A.S.* LX1, (1983), 52; Coats Farm in Rushbury parish, Lower Farm in Munslow parish, 15, King Street, Ludlow and 1, High Street, Newport.

17 Green End
1. N. Pevsner, *The Buildings of England (Shropshire)*, Penguin, (1958), 315
2. This section is compiled by Joan Barton
3. *Kelly's Directories* (Shropshire), 1822-28. Richard Corser's will of 5th Jan. 1825 is among family papers held by his great grandson, Denis Corser of Newport. In it there is reference to the purchase of the house. We are grateful to Mr Corser for access to the collection.

4. R. Corser, Memorandum Book 1827-33, *penes* D. Corser

5. LSL. BB87, C. Cunliffe Brookes, *Fontes Rivorum or Springs of the Brookes*, (1931), 9

6. Governors' Minute Books, Sir John Talbot's School; *Piggott's Directories* (Shropshire) 1828-1836

7. R. Corser, *op. cit.*

8. Whitchurch Parish Registers; Richard Corser's will, *supra*, 2

9. R. Corser, *op. cit.*

10. Whitchurch Parish Registers

11. It is from Robert that Mr Denis Corser is descended. (see fn.2, *supra*)

12. Lichfield Joint Record Office B/C11 19th Jul 1843

13. *Kelly's Directory*, 1870. This followed the allocation of street numbers to all Whitchurch properties.

14. Census returns, 1851-88

15. Whitchurch Parish Registers

16. R.B. James, *Shops and Shopkeepers in Whitchurch*, Part 2, WAAG, (1991), 18

17. Classified Trades Directory (1885)

18. LSL. q C20, *Industries of Shropshire*, (1891), 94

19. Census return 1891

20. *Kelly's Directory*, 1905

21. *ibid.*,1909, 1926

22. *ibid.*, 1926

23. Info. from Mrs Norah Ayton, widow of Mr A. Ayton

18 Green End

1. H. Colvin, *A Biographical Dictionary of British Architects 1600 - 1840*, 3rd ed., Yale UP (1995), 997-8

2. *Whitchurch Remembered*, Shropshire Libraries (1980), 62

Gazetteer of other Whitchurch properties

1. See the chapter on 18 Green End for reference to Turner

2. P. Stamper, *The Old Rectory, Whitchurch: A Brief Site History*, Shropshire Archaeology Service, A report for North Shropshire District Council, (1966), 1-7

Ash Wood, Ash

1. The history of Ash Wood is documented by Richard Hughes, the present owner. Publication forthcoming.

2. A dialect word meaning 'trodden down'. G. Jackson, *Shropshire Word Book*, Shrewsbury (1879, repr. 1982), 316

3. N.W. Alcock. *Cruck Construction*, CBA Research Report, 42, (1981), 96

4. Manor Cottage, Prees and 6/8 Dodington

5. 'House' or 'house-place' in 16th, 17th and 18th century probate inventories usually means the main living room, and the use of the term is widespread. It is unusual to find it still used in the 20th century.

6. Detailed in Appendix A

7. *e.g.* at Northwood's Farm, near Audlem, Cheshire.
8. The testing and analysis was carried out by D. Miles.
9. H.B. Finch, *Whitchurch in the reign of Queen Elizabeth*, (1895), 16
10. Carried out by D. Wilson, Keele University
11. A copy of the will and inventory is held in the archive at Ash Wood. In his family history (forthcoming) the present Richard Hughes analyses the comparative values and evaluates the farming pattern in detail. I am grateful to him for making the archive available for present purposes.

Grove Farm, Ash Parva

1. D.Mason, *An Archaeological Investigation at Grove Farm, Ash Parva,* Jan. 1992, for Roscoe and Bean, Architects
2. W. Shaw Sparrow, *The English House*, (1908), opp. 304
3. Report of R.C.H.M. (England) March 1990
4. This section is compiled by Joan Barton and Madge Moran
5. L.S.L. S912/A6, A7, Tithe maps of Ash Magna and Ash Parva
6. Letter from the County Archivist to N. Shrops. Dist. Council dated 4th May 1984
7. Deeds of Grove Farm, *penes* Mr. R. Rowland; Ash Parva Annuity Trust Account Book, *penes* Mr. R. Hughes; Letter from Hannah Hughes to Warren Upton & Garside (Solicitors), 25th July 1942; *Whitchurch Herald* 1st Nov. 1901. We wish to thank Mr. R. Rowland, Mr. R. Hughes, & Messrs. Hatcher Rogerson, Solicitors (Wem) for access to the relevant documents.
8. Deeds of Grove Farm, *ibid*
9. L.S.L. S 912/A7 and Apportionment
10. see fn. 5 *supra*
11. *ibid*; deeds *penes* R. Rowland; Annuity Trust Account Book *penes* R. Hughes
12. *ibid*
13. deeds *penes* R. Rowland
14. This section is based on information from Mr. R. Hughes of Ash Wood
15. See chapter on Ash Wood

Manor Cottage, Prees

1. Census returns
2. N.W. Alcock, *Cruck Construction*, CBA Research Report, 42, (1981), 96
3. *Ibid*, 8, 96
4. J.T. Smith & E.M. Yates, 'On the dating of English Houses from External Evidence', *Field Studies*, Vol 2, No.5 (1968) Fig.8
5. J.W. Tonkin, 'The White House, Aston Munslow', *T.S.A.S.* Vol 58, part 2 (1966), 145
6. M.Moran, 'Two Early Timber-framed Hall-houses in Shropshire', *T.S.A.H.S.* Vol 68 (1993) 80,85,88
7. F.W.B. Charles, 'Scotches, Lever Sockets and Rafter Holes', *Vern. Archit.*, Vol 5, (1974), 21-4
8. Info. from Mrs J. James
9. C.A. Hewett, *The Development of Carpentry, 1200-1700*, David and Charles, (1969), 196

10. R.C.H.M. Photo 87/1996

11. *V.C.H. (Stafford)*, Vol 3, (1970) 7-15

12. *Ibid*, 22-3

13. *Ibid*, 52; *V.C.H.* (Shropshire) Vol 1V, (1989), 129-30; R.W. Eyton, *Antiquities of Shropshire*, Vol 9, (1859), 247

14. S.R.O. 731, bundle 201, map and survey of Prees township, *c.*1835; L.S.L. (Shrewsbury) C O4 Acc. 855, p.266 (Copy of Act of Parliament, 24th June 1794)

15. I am grateful to George Baugh and Dr. David Cox of the V.C.H. (Shrewsbury) for verification of this point and for their help with the ecclesiastical history, and to J.A. Patrick of Prees for his help.

16. Testing and analysis was carried out by Daniel Miles in June 1994.

17. P. Smith, *Houses of the Welsh Countryside*, H.M.S.O., (2nd.ed. 1988), 43-5; In Shropshire Padmore, Wolverton, Catherton Cottage and Shepton Fields *et al.* are in this category. See *Archaeol. J.*, Vol 142, (1985), 340-360; *T.S.A.H.S.* Vol 68 (1993), 79-92; *T.S.A.S.* Vol 65, (1987), 45-49; *V.C.H. (Shropshire)*, Vol 8, (1968), 133 respectively.

Providence Grove

1. Vernacular Architecture, Vol 27 (1996), 103,105. The dendrochronologist was Daniel Miles. We are grateful to Mrs Roberts, the present owner/occupier for permission to examine and record Providence Grove, for allowing us access to her title deeds and permission to carry out the dendrochronology.

2. This section is compiled by Joan Barton. Jean North translated the Latin document and we are grateful to Dr. David Cox of the V.C.H. for helpful comments.

3. E.B. Fryde, D.E. Greenway, S. Porter & I. Roy, *Handbook of British Chronology*, (3rd edition), Royal Hist. Soc., (1986), 16, 42

4. L.S.L., qIp64, B. Bryan, *A History of Prees*, (1986), 16, 42

5. L.S.L., qJ64, D. McBride, *A History of Hawkstone* (1993), 6

6. *Ibid*

Oldfields Farm, Moreton Say

1. I wish to thank all the members of the Bennett family who kindly allowed me to examine and record their home, Henry Hand, Eric Mercer, Ian West and Fred and Irene Powell who helped with the recording and gave valuable advice. The presentation drawings are by Henry Hand. I also wish to thank Daniel Miles for his dendrochronological expertise. Although the results were inconclusive as regards the hall, the samples will remain in the archive and may prove effective in the future.

2. T. Rowley, *The Shropshire Landscape*, Hodder & Stoughton, (1972) 139

3. *eg.* 'Padmore in Onibury parish' (*Archaeol. J.*, Vol 142); 'Cleeton Court in Cleeton St. Mary' (*T.S.A.H.S.* Vol. 65); 'Wolverton in Eaton-under-Heywood' (*ibid*, Vol 68, (1993), 79-92); and Eudon George in Chetton.

4. P. Smith, *Houses of the Welsh Countryside*, R.C.A.H.M., 2nd ed. (1988), 98,99. At Ty-mawr, (Castell Caereinion, Mont.) there is a dais truss similar, though not identical to that at Oldfields, *(ibid)*, fig 67,b.)

Alkington Hall

1. Sampling and analysis was carried out by D. Miles. I should also like to thank the Fearnall family for their help, hospitality and patience, and Ian West for his help with the interpretation.
2. N. Pevsner, *Buildings of England (Shropshire)*, Penguin, (1967), 58
3. W. Watkins-Pitchford, *The Shropshire Hearth-Tax Roll of 1672*, Shrop. Arch. & Parish Reg. Soc., (1949), 73
4. N. Pevsner, *op. cit.*, 290
5. H. Avray Tipping, English Homes, Period III, Vol I, *Country Life*, (1929) 139-146
6. E. Mercer in booklet of Soc. of Archit. Historians' Annual Conference at Newport, Shropshire, (1988), 57
7. D. Lloyd, P. Howell, M. Richards, *The Feathers*, L.R.P., 5 (1986), 58-9
8. E. Mercer, *English Art 1553-1625*, OUP., (1962), 93-4. At St. John's the diaper work proved to be painted on.
9. *eg.* W. Gedde, *A booke of sundry draughts...* (1615-16) This is copied in H. Shaw, *The Glasier's Book* (1848); R. Freeman, *English Emblem Books*, Chatto & Windus (1948), *passim*
10. This section is compiled by J. Barton and M. Moran
11. *Oxford Dictionary of Place-Names*, Clarendon Press (1947), 6
12. *Domesday Book (Shropshire)*, Phillimore, (1986), 14,14,8
13. *Ibid*
14. Hamon le Strange, *Le Strange Records*, Longmans, (1916), 288
15. *Domesday Book, op. cit.*, 14,14,7
16. L.S.L., M/S 2790, G. Morris, *Shropshire Genealogies*, 352-5
17. L.S.L., M/F 43, E. Clarke, *A History of Whitchurch Grammar School, 1550-1950*, unpub. M.A. thesis, 332. (A copy of the thesis is also held in the Caldecott Library, Whitchurch; *V.C.H. (Shropshire)*, Vol 2, (1973), 159-61; 24th Rep. Com. Char. H.C. 231, (1831), xi, 336-40; J.M. Barton, *Whitchurch Schools 1550-1950*, WAAG (1989), 4-52
18. L.S.L., qH 55.5, S. Watts, *Whitchurch Probate Inventories 1535-1650*, Vol 1, n.p.
19. L.S.L., M/S 2790, *op.cit.*
20. E. Clarke, 'The Talented Cottons of Alkington', *Shrops. Mag.* (April 1952), 14-20
21. L.S.L. qH 55.5, S. Watts, *Whitchurch Inventories 1535 -1650*, Vol 2, n.p.
22. H. Forrest, 'Alkington Hall', *T.S.A.S.* 4th Ser, Vol XI (1927-8), 93,4; Mrs Stackhouse-Acton, *The Castles and old Mansions of Shropshire*, (1868),38
23. N. Pevsner, *op. cit.*, 220; pl. 36a
24. J. Wright,(ed.) *English Dialect Dictionary*, Frowde, (1902) Vol 3, 54
25. J. Newman, 'An Early Drawing by Inigo Jones and a Monument in Shropshire', *Burlington Magazine*, CXV, (1973), 360-7. (copy in L.S.L., JV71.9 vf)
26. E. Clarke, per fn. 20, *supra*, 15, 20
27. G. Morris, *op. cit.*
28. Info. from Miss Ann Fearnall
29. See fn. 17, *supra*
30. E. Clarke, per fn.17, *supra*, 369; S. Watts, *op.cit.*
31. Sir James Murray, *A New English Dictionary on Historical Principles*, Vol V111, part 2,

Oxford, (1914), 149

32. E. Clarke, *ibid*, 371

33. T.C. Mendenhall, *The Shrewsbury Drapers and the Welsh Wool Trade in the XVI and XVII Centuries*, OUP (1953),4

34. G. Morris, *op.cit.*, 352

35. E. Clarke, per fn 17, *supra*, 363, 368. William Alkington of Alkington was named as a feofee of the Grammar School in 1550. His will is dated 17th April 1555 (Lichfield Consistory Court)

Park Farm, Alkington

1. For an account of Alkington Hall see pp.195

2. *Vernacular Architecture*, Vol 27 (1996), 104, 106. The dendrochronologist was Daniel Miles and the project was part-funded by Eric Windsor. We are grateful to Mr & Mrs Windsor for their kindness and hospitality during class visits and for their help, interest and co-operation.

3. This section is compiled by Joan Barton. WAAG hold an archive on Park Farm. Extracts only are included in this report. Much of the information is taken from the deeds kindly made available to us by Mr. Windsor.

4. SRO The Poor Law Assessment 1825

5. SRO 3091/215 Tithe Apportionment for Alkington

6. *ibid*

7. *ibid*

8. Census Returns

9. Abstract of Title, Park Farm, courtesy of Eric Windsor

10. *ibid*

The Ditches Hall, Wem

1. I am grateful to Michael Holmes for help with the heraldry.

2. Info. from Mrs Williams, the present occupier, to whom I am grateful for access and permission to record.

3. Most of his research was done at the Local Studies Library in Shrewsbury, but he does not always note the sources. However, see Samuel Garbett's *History of Wem* (1757)

4. *Shropshire Magazine* Nov. 1951

5. *The King's England, Shropshire*, 1948, p.225

Ridgwardine

1. E. Eckwall, *English Place-Names*, Oxford, 4th ed. (1960), 387; H.D.G. Foxall, *Shropshire Field-Names*, S.A.S., (1980), 12

2. A. Brian, 'A Regional Survey of Brick Bonding in England and Wales', *Vern. Arch.*, Vol 3, (1972), 15

3. We are grateful to D. Pannett for help with the geology

4. The Barkhill Account Book is held by R. Hughes in the Ashwood archive.

5. P. Smith, *Houses of the Welsh Countryside*, HMSO, 2nd ed., (1988), 161-3, 208-9

6. Pers. comm., Daniel Miles, dendrochronologist

7. S.R.R.C., C 67 S. Bagshaw, *Gazetteer of Shropshire*, (1851), 277

8. W. Watkins-Pitchford, *The Shropshire Hearth-Tax Roll of 1672*, S.A.S., (1949), 54

9. This section is compiled by J. Barton

10. J. Morris (ed.), *Domesday Book* (Shropshire), Phillimore, (1986), 4,19,8

11. *ibid*, 4, 23, 9

12. *ibid*, 4,1 9, 8 (notes)

13. *ibid*, Ch 4, 23 (notes)

14. U. Rees, *The Cartulary of Shrewsbury Abbey*, Nat. Lib. of Wales (1975), Vol 1, 86, no. 94c

15. *ibid*, 88, nos. 96, 97

16. *ibid*, Vol 2, 231, no.271

17. *ibid*, 357, no, 391b

18. C.R.O., DCH/C/465, Cholmondeley deeds, 1560; N. & S.V. Rowley, *Market Drayton: A Study in Social History*, (1966), 3

19. S.R.R.C., MIC 150, J. Morris, *Shropshire Genealogy*, Vol 1, 281; C.R.O. DWN/1/72 (Wm. Church's mortgage on Betton and Ridgwardine)

20. J. Morris, *ibid*, 282; S.R.R.C. M/F P 97/60 (1743-1752), Drayton-in-Hales Par. Reg.

21. S.R.R.C., C 46.2, J.B. Blakeway, *The Sheriffs of Shropshire*, (1831), 240

22. Deeds of Ridgwardine Manor, *penes* Drs. R.B & C.J. Johanson. Most of what follows comes from this source.

23. J. Jackson, *Shropshire Word Book*, (1879, rep. 1982), 464

Gazetteer of other properties

1. N. Pevsner, *Shropshire*, Penguin (1958), 61

2. *e.g.* at Old House Farm, Loppington and Newton Farm, Stoke St. Milborough. See C. Ryan & M. Moran, The Old House Farm, Loppington, *T.S.A.S.* Vol LXIII (1985), 15

Index

Providence Grove *xvi*, 179-186
Puleston, Judge & Lady 30-1

quince tree 85

RCHM *ix*, 167-8
Radford, Alexander William 238
   Arthur 238
Ranelagh, earl of 186
Raven Inn (see 17 - 23 Watergate)
   Well 85
rat-trap brickwork *xviii*, 84
Read, John Henry 109
Rectory, Whitchurch *xvii*
recusancy 156
Red Brook 1
Rhodes, John 19
   Thomas 21
Richard I 3
Richard, John 218
Richard's Drapers & Haberdashery 86
Richards, Harry 256
Richardson, Robert 19
   William 21
Rider, Robert 69
Ridgwardine Manor *xvi*, 225-38
Rigby, William
Ring of Bells, the 104
Rivington 62
Roberts, Alfred John 185
Robinson, Thomas 9
Roe, Thomas 218
Rogerson, Dr Eveleyn 69
   Felicity 69
   Dr Gerard 69
   Martin 69
Roles, J. 100
Roman period *xv*, 1
roof construction (*see also crown-post; cruck
  construction*) *xv*
Rosemary Lane 54
Rowland, Mr 136
   Roger 163, 168, 170
   Roger Spencer 170
Rowley, Humphrey 21
Royal Seal 70
rush-taper marks 92, 115, 231-2

St. Alkmund 1
St. Alkmund's Church 3, 210, 253
St. Catherine's Church 39
St. Mary's Cottage, St Mary's Street *xvii*, 123-6
9 St. Mary's Street 127
17 St. Mary's Street 127-8
Sadler, Thomas 100
Salisbury Road 53
Salop Fire Office 136
Sandford Estate 245-6
   Hall, Prees 245-6
   Richard 169
saye 211
'Scotch', a 175
'Secretary hand' 184
Sedgeford 1
Severn, river 215
shanty town 241
Shenton family 222
Shirley House, Prees 243
Shirley's Plaice 107
Shirreff, Major Charles 68
shoe-making 3
shops 23
Shrewsbury *xvi*, *xviii*, 3, 206
   Abbey 237
    abbot of 237
   Street 179, 185
1 Shrewsbury Street, Prees 242
2 Shrewsbury Street, Prees 242
Shropshire Gazetteer 5
   Union Canal 254
Sir John Talbot's School 210, 252-3, 254
Slack, Sarah 223
Slum clearance 11
Smith, Francis *xix*, 5
   Hencock 177
   Jane 208
   John & Son 6
   Peter 236
   William *xix*, 5
   W.H. & Co 6, 52, 54, 58, 104, 145, 146, 254
smokehood 177
solar *xviii*, 98, 115-6, 117, 119, 121, 122, 167,
  175, 190, 194
Soulton Hall, Nr. Wem 206, 247-8
speculative system building 80
Spencer, Daniel 69